WRESTLING WITH THE ANGELS

A History of Jewish Los Angeles

ISBN 978-0-9788951-0-5
Printed in United States of America

Blazer Communications,
15060 Ventura Boulevard, Suite 210
Sherman Oaks, CA 91403
Ph: 818/786-4000   Fax: 818/380-9232
Email: blazergrp@aol.com

WRESTLING WITH THE ANGELS

A History of Jewish Los Angeles

Phil Blazer
Shelley Portnoy

Blazer Communications
Sherman Oaks, California

DEDICATION

My father served overseas during World War II like thousands of Jewish American vets, defending this country's values and ideals to guarantee our freedom and independence. Dave Blazer, returning from India to his home state of Minnesota in 1946, along with my mother, Bernice, gathered their family and prepared to move and start a "new life" in the land of opportunity and sunshine—Los Angeles, California.

And just as they did, thousands of Jewish Americans did the same, with the indomitable spirit and courage that brought the Jewish pioneers to Los Angeles nearly a century before them. These pioneers were explorers, inventors, creators, producers, and builders. They led us to the Los Angeles and Jewish community as we know it today—shining like a great star. Thank you Mom and Dad, for giving me the opportunity to follow in yours and their footsteps and to be a pioneer as well. — Phil Blazer

At the foundation of all history there is always the family—the generations that live on to tell the stories, the victories and trials of the past, and the experiences that create and inspire the stories of the future. This book is dedicated to all the parents and all the children everywhere...

Especially for my honored and loving parents, Lillian and Jack Rothstein, And for my cherished children, my beautiful daughters, Alisse and Danielle.

May their spirit and their goodness and their zest for life live on in a world of peace and freedom and human dignity—and may this legacy be carried on through the many generations to come. — Shelley Portnoy

NOTES FROM THE AUTHORS

This is the first of a two-volume set chronicling the history of Jewish Los Angeles. This first volume covers the history of Jewish life in Greater Los Angeles from 1850 to the present. The second volume, *Pioneers of Jewish Los Angeles:1850-2007*, will highlight biographical sketches and short stories about the women and men who built Los Angeles and its Jewish institutions. We invite you to submit your personal and family stories and photographs for inclusion in Volume II to Blazer Communications.

Some explanatory notes about this first volume, *Wrestling With the Angels: A History of Jewish Los Angeles*. The title *Wrestling With the Angels* is a biblical reference from the story of Jacob wrestling with the Angel, Genesis, Chapter 32. The symbolic and mystic overtones of this parable resonate throughout Jewish history [see more about this in the Preface, page iv]. The metaphor of Jacob wrestling with the Angel lends itself to the history of the Jewish people, much as the Jews in Los Angeles struggled and confronted the elements and challenges encountered in building and developing this great city. Even the name "Los Angeles" translates loosely to "City of the Angels" from the original Spanish name given to the pueblo by the Spanish Governor Felipe de Neve in 1777, "de la Reina de Los Angeles sobre el Rio del la Porciuncula."

Note that there are articles included at the end of each of the first nine chapters; these articles supplement the historical text and are intended to add color and first-hand experiences describing the early days, as well as in-depth personality profiles of some of those mentioned in the book. All of the articles printed at the conclusion of the chapters have been included as initially written. In some cases the articles have been modified in length for space considerations (as indicated by asterisks in the text) but the original language has been left intact.

The authors are also co-producing a two-hour documentary for television on *Wrestling with the Angels: A History of Jewish Los Angeles*. Over 165 television interviews have been completed in the last several years with survivors, historians, academicians, film and entertainment representatives, Jewish community leaders, media representatives, and numerous other people who have any history with, or information about, the history of Jewish Los Angeles. Many of these interviews have aired on the weekly television program, *Jewish Life with Phil Blazer*, which is televised every Sunday morning in Los Angeles, as well as in many other markets throughout the country. The interviews will be part of the material used for the television documentary. A list of those who have been interviewed and will be participating in this project may be found on page 316 of this volume.

The authors would like to extend special thanks to Gladys Sturman, Publisher and Editor-in-Chief, and David W. Epstein, Editor, of Western States Jewish History, for their contributions from the *Western Jewish Quarterly*. We also acknowledge and honor several among the many dedicated historians of Jewish Los Angeles that have provided a wealth of information and first-hand knowledge of the history included in this book:

Rabbi William M. Kramer	Rabbi Max Vorspan
Dr. Norton B. Stern	Dr. Lloyd P. Gartner
Reva Clar	Harris Newmark

We extend our appreciation to our staff at Blazer Communications for their assistance in the completion of this book: Jill Amar, Karen Begim, Carol Belitz, Adam Blazer, Hanan Druker, Craig Durst, Bobby Klubeck, Olga Kramarova, Sue Liberman, Jodie Myers, Guia Pineda, George Robins, Hal Sloane.

We wish to thank all of our sponsors, and those of you who have helped to make this project a reality based on your emotional, financial, and moral support (see list of Sponsors, page v). And finally, we would also like to thank the many citizens, immigrants, and pioneers that comprise the population of Los Angeles, especially those in the Jewish community, for their support and encouragement in the creation and completion of this book. All of you have built a city to be proud of and we gratefully appreciate all of your contributions.

Next Volume —

Pioneers of Jewish Los Angeles:1850-2007

Participate In Our Next Book Publication

Do you have a family member or friend who was a pioneer in Jewish Los Angeles? Are you a leader in any of the organizations that "pioneered" new ideas and creativity in the building and development of the Jewish community in Los Angles? If you or someone you know has a short story, anecdote, photograph, amusing reminiscence, or intriguing relationship or connection to the growth and success of Jewish Los Angeles, we invite you to submit the information along with any relevant photographs, for inclusion in the next volume in this series, *Pioneers of Jewish Los Angeles:1850-2007* (working title).

With this first volume, *Wrestling With the Angels: A History of Jewish Los Angeles*, we have presented a comprehensive description of the history of Jewish Los Angeles against a backdrop of the broader general history of the city, from its beginnings under Spanish rule in the late 1700s. We introduce the arrival of the first "eight bachelors" who came in 1850, the beginning of the Jewish population, and continue through the years to present-day Los Angeles, culminating with a representative cross-section of the Jewish organizations that provide leadership and infrastructure for Jewish issues and cultural advancement today. Many of the Los Angeles pioneer founding families have been mentioned briefly in this first book; they are intended to represent scores of other ground-breaking personalities, whose contributions, while equally significant, could not be included because of space considerations.

For the next volume, we invite you to give us information on any pioneers that you know or possess written history about, people that you believe to be a part of the rich tapestry of this city. We also welcome any photographs from your family archives or other sources that will provide a distinctive perspective on Los Angeles from 1850 to the present. You may submit biographies of members of your family (living or deceased), or friends and acquaintances, as long as they have lived in Greater Los Angeles. Any relevant photographs would be welcomed, but are not required.

This innovative project offers the citizens of Los Angeles a way to be proactive in providing evidence and recording historical data to ensure the accurate documentation of the city's story. Inclusion in *Pioneers of Jewish Los Angeles:1850-2007* will be at the discretion of the authors and will be based on a number of factors including uniqueness, representative elements, and historic interest.

Volume II will be a vitally important cornerstone in honoring and memorializing our Jewish ancestors and leaders, today and for generations to come. It is also a rare opportunity to reserve a place in history for yourself or someone you know, and to relate details of Los Angeles from a personal and first-hand perspective. Please submit your information to Blazer Communications, at the address indicated below, or telephone and discuss your ideas with one of our researchers.

Blazer Communications, 15060 Ventura Boulevard, Sherman Oaks, CA 91403
Telephone: 818/786-4000 • Fax: 818/380-9232 • Email: blazergrp@aol.com

SPONSORS

Aron Abecassis

Barbara and Raymond Alpert

Joyce and Stanley Black

Debbie and Robert Block

Robin and Elliott Broidy

Toni and Bruce Corwin

Susanne and Jan Czuker

Ruth and Leo David

Familian Foundation

Gilbert Foundation

Beverly and Herb Gelfand

Ileen and Stanley Gold

Paul Goldenberg

Doretta and Jona Goldrich

Elaine and Bram Goldsmith

Roslyn and Abner Goldstine

Samuel Goldwyn, Jr. Foundation

David Gursky

Fern and Marvin Jubas

Manny Kaplan

Joyce Eisenberg-Keefer and Mel Keefer

Trudy and Louis Kestenbaum

Laurie and Lyn Konheim

Libby and Marvin Markowitz

Jonathan Mitchell

Todd Morgan

Rocky and Lon Morton

Gitta and Jack Nagel

Soraya and Younes Nazarian

Melanie and Robert Rechnitz

Linda and Dan Rosenson

Corrine and Lenny Sands

Fela and David Shapell

Annette and Leonard Shapiro

Fred Simmons

Sondra and Marvin Smalley

Rita Spiegel

Linda and Jack Suzar

Marcie Polier Swartz and David Swartz

Charlene and Steve Ustin

Anna and Max Webb

Barbi and Larry Weinberg

Edna Weiss

David Wiener

Susan and David Wilstein

Karen and Gary Winnick

Judy and Marvin Zeidler

Ruth Ziegler

Daphna and Richard Ziman

SPONSOR ORGANIZATIONS

Cedars-Sinai Medical Center, City of Hope, Hillside Memorial Park and Mortuary, The Jewish Community Foundation, Jewish Federation of Greater Los Angeles, Jewish Home for the Aging, Los Angeles Jewish News, Magbit Foundation, Mt. Sinai Memorial Parks and Mortuaries, Ralphs Markets, Security Pacific Bank, The Skirball Cultural Center, Vista Del Mar Child and Family Services, Wells Fargo Foundation

WRESTLING WITH THE ANGELS

On his journey back to Canaan, Jacob seeks reconciliation with his brother Esau, with whom he has been estranged for many years. Yet, before he meets Esau, an Angel comes to Jacob at night and wrestles with him until dawn. Jacob asks for a blessing from the Angel as a conclusion to the wrestling match. The Angel blesses Jacob with a new name—Israel. The Angel spoke to Jacob saying, "You have wrestled with God and with men and have prevailed."

Perhaps the most mysterious incident in the Torah's account of Jacob's life is the nightlong battle described in the closing verses of the 32nd Chapter of Genesis. "And Ya'akov (Jacob) was left alone with a man who wrestled with him until the break of dawn." The Sages identify the mysterious figure as the "guardian angel" of Jacob's brother, Esau. This wrestling match has great symbolic and mystical overtones—a paradigm, in one sense, of the historical battle between the Jewish people and their enemies.

"No more shall you be called Jacob, but Israel," declared the Angel, "for you have wrestled with God and with men, and have prevailed." Like his grandfather Abraham before him, Jacob received a new name from God, symbolizing a transformation. Jacob (Ya'akov) bravely defended himself until dawn, at which point the Angel bestowed on him a new name—Israel (Yisrael). The name is derived from the Hebrew word *sar*, meaning noble and eminent. Among the understandings of the name Israel are: one who wrestles with God; one who is straightforward (direct, honest) with God; "fighter for God" is another possible translation. We perceive Jacob's courage, tenacity, strength, and heroism in the face of a powerful opposing force.

Spiritually and physically touched by the angel, Jacob emerges as the archetypal Jewish ancestor. Even flawed and bewildered, he continues on to face and wrestle with God and man. Jacob, perhaps more than any other figure, symbolizes the resolute and valiant character of the Jewish people. That is why Jacob's descendants will forever be called the Children of Israel—whether they are the pioneer builders of Tel Aviv, Los Angeles, or Gondar, Ethiopia. Jacob became a heroic individual with a king-like stature, a distinguished and dignified leader. He wrestled with an angel and went on to start a nation. Jacob became the father of the 12 holy tribes from which the Jewish people came forth.

Since then, wrestling with God (nature, the Divine) has been at the core of Jewish identity. The wrestling can take different forms, from striving to understand the Holocaust to disagreeing over the meaning of a sacred text. Wrestling with angels is impressive, as is standing firm and symbolically remaining morally pure. This quality of confrontation and engagement with God, versus pure submission, represents a distinguishing characteristic of Judaism. It describes the cosmic integration between two nations and two worlds: spiritual and material.

This effort has been said to be conducted on two planes—"with the Divine and with men." In the struggle with men over more than 4000 years, the Jewish people have wrestled with the Egyptians, the Canaanites, the Babylonians, the Persians, the Romans, the Spanish Inquisition, Nazi Germany, and Islamic terrorism. These forces, among others, have done their utmost in attempting to destroy the Jewish people and their culture and spirit, but the Jews have prevailed and continue to triumph in the long and difficult struggle.

Jacob wrestling with the Angel is a compelling metaphor for the obstacles confronting the Jewish pioneers that arrived in the early days in the "City of Angels." These ground-breaking immigrants and transplanted travelers from the East and Midwest "wrestled" with the elements, the lawlessness, the lack of business and moral ethics, the challenges stemming from the integration of many cultures, languages, and customs, and the Herculean task of building a city out of a dusty desert. From a biblical allegory to one of "taming the Angels" a monumental and fascinating story can be told—the history of Jewish Los Angeles.

CONTENTS

> *We have built a life here in Los Angeles. America and Los Angeles have given us that opportunity, and we are ever so grateful....* Meyer Gottlieb

FOREWORD

Meyer Gottlieb's life story is representative of many the Jewish pioneers who have settled in Los Angeles since 1850. He is an immigrant, a survivor, and a Jewish community leader. As president of Samuel Goldwyn Films, he is also a 30-year veteran in the Hollywood film community.

I believe that our past memories and experiences should be used to improve the future. That is the way that I live my life, and hopefully, that is the way I have raised my children, and my grandchildren as well. I think that is the important message to take from the lessons of the past. We must remember that we have responsibilities and obligations. When you are a survivor and have personally experienced all kinds of tragedies, you must never forget!

I was born after the outbreak of the Second World War in a little village known as Klesov, in Poland, which is now part of the Ukraine. Germany had already invaded Poland, and they were horrible times.

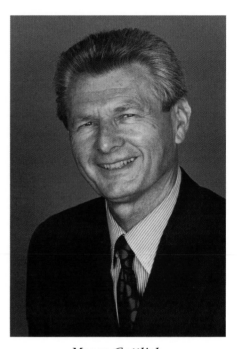

Meyer Gottlieb

My father was in the Polish military in the equestrian corps. He was an officer and when called up to defend his country, he was sent to the German front. The Poles were defeated, they withdrew and my father came home and alerted all of my family members about the dangers of the German invasion. As with many in the sad historic and classic story, the older people remembered the Kaiser in World War I, and said that the young people should leave the country because they would not bother the old people, and in a short period of time everything would be back to normal. Tragically, we know what actually happened.

My mother, my father, my two uncles, my brother and I were hiding in the forest when Russia entered the fray and invaded from the other side. The Russians invaded and took on the Germans. My family survived for a considerable period of time by withdrawing with the Russian military into Siberia. They put us in a work camp in Siberia where we stayed throughout the war, without any choice in the matter, from about 1940 to 1945.

During this time, my mother gave birth to another child who died because of the terrible wartime conditions. He lived for only a week. I must have been about three years old, and that is the only thing I remember of Russia—my father taking this little infant, wrapping him in a *tallis*, and burying him in a potato field. I have that memory. I do not know his name, although I'm sure they named my little brother; but I do have this image in my mind of cold, dark times, a *tallis*, a shovel going into earth, and a child being buried with prayers and tears. This is a part of my very dark and personal nightmare that I remember. As with most Holocaust survivors, I never want to talk about these personal stories.

My father was killed in the war. After serving in the Polish army, he was drafted again and then rejected by the Russian military, first for being a Pole, then for being a Jew. But as the war progressed poorly for Russia, they ended up taking everybody, and sadly took my father. He died on the front fighting the Germans within months of the end of the war in 1945.

Once the war ended, Stalin wanted to get rid of all the Jews. He rounded us up, put us on trains, lorries, trucks, cars, and expelled tens of thousands of Jews through Czechoslovakia and dumped us in the U.S. occupied sector of Germany. I was five years old. At first there was total disarray in Germany, but ultimately, DP (Displaced Persons) camps were created. We resided in three different DP camps. When I see news footage of what is happening today in Africa and other countries where genocide is taking place, it brings back the same horrible memories. Food distribution consisted of men sitting in the back of trucks throwing food out; food that we did not recognize as food, but we ate because we were hungry. I have a very vivid memory of running after a truck to get some food, and being so weak from hunger that I passed out.

In the camps, little boys my age (I would have been 7 or 8) were being instructed by the *Haganah* in military training. We practiced fighting with sticks, climbing on ropes and ladders, we were trained to hide and find, and to be organized. All this was being done to prepare us for immigration to Israel.

This next event was *beshert* [destined]. The Red Cross published lists of survivors and distributed them across the United States. As it turned out, a great aunt of my mother's lived in Los Angeles. She saw our names on the list just weeks before we were supposed to leave for Israel. She contacted the Red Cross and arranged for us to come to America instead of going to Israel; we were going to America to be with family.

How did we get to America? It was not a very luxurious trip; we traveled on a troop carrier known as the USS Pershing. We slept in bunks, just as the soldiers and sailors. It was a very difficult journey and many were seasick. I was a little kid, so I was running around having a good time. I would run up and talk to the captain. Since I was speaking Yiddish I doubt that he understood a word that I said! To me it was an adventure. As a child, it was actually the most fun that I could remember.

In 1949, we arrived in Boston, not Ellis Island. We got off the ship and were greeted very briefly, and then put on a train directly to Los Angeles. The journey was probably not more than two weeks, from Germany to arriving in Union Station in Los Angeles. Today it seems like an eternity. To the best of my knowledge, the only reason we were able to come to Los Angeles was because of the sponsorship by my mother's family. Essentially, my great aunt said that she would take care of us financially, and her sponsorship allowed us to enter Los Angeles. This guaranteed that we would not be a burden on the government.

My memories are very limited. I was in awe of Los Angeles, compared to where I came from—seeing the energy, the modern buildings, the transportation, the automobiles, trains and television. I was seeing an entirely different world. I do not know if "shocked" is the right term. I do not speak about my history very much, even with my own family, but when my children have asked me how I felt when I came to Los Angeles, I tell them that I felt like I was reborn in Los Angeles. It was like a new birth, a new beginning.

Even when I tried to engage my mother to talk about the Holocaust, she would just say things like, "That's something you shouldn't know about; that's something we shouldn't live through again; it's something for us to forget; let's thank God that we're past that time." Now mind you, I lost almost all of my family, my father, all my grandparents, seven of my twelve aunts and uncles were killed by the Nazis, along with dozens of cousins. The pain was so great my mother could not bring herself to talk about it.

When we came to Los Angeles there were those Jews who said to us, "Oh we read about all these terrible things, about the Holocaust, about the gas chambers, how horrific! But you don't look so bad." They expected us to look worse. And then there were those Jews who totally empathized and understood the suffering that we had endured, and were noticeably grateful that we survived. We experienced all of these things and more.

We were obviously very poor, and my mother, God bless her, was a seamstress earning fifty dollars a week. She was raising a family and paying all the bills, which was quite amazing. She was a very strong, loving, and caring woman. We lived in an integrated neighborhood in the West Adams area, which consisted of Latinos, African Americans, and Jews. Our landlord was a Latino with a good heart. He allowed my mother to pay our rent late on many occasions. There were immigrant organizations my mother was in contact with, which she referred to as the *greens* (new immigrants). In the neighborhood, we created our own extended families. You had parts of families that came together to create a whole Jewish family. We celebrated and mourned together. When there were good occasions we would celebrate, and when there were sad occasions we would commiserate together.

Entering the public school environment in Los Angeles when I was nine years old was dramatically different than it would be today. I did not speak a word of English. I was a stranger in every respect. Then I had to assimilate into a classroom of boys and girls that were entirely unlike me. There were no bilingual programs. There were no issues that dealt with how to integrate foreign students. The teacher introduced me as an immigrant and survivor. She asked me to sit in the back of the class, all by motions and pointing. My primary language was Yiddish. There were some Jewish kids in the class. She selected the smartest kid in the class, a little boy who happened to be Jewish, to spend some time with me. He devoted half an hour a day with me, trying to teach me to read and to speak English.

I have wonderful memories of integration into the school and made friends quickly. When you are a child and you are immersed in a foreign language, and you want to integrate with the kids and play, you interact. Literally, within weeks I was speaking English and within months I was reading, and I felt like one of the kids. And that is the way the process started. Compared to my life experiences, this was not bad. Today we go out of our way to make sure that our children transfer easily from one school to another. For me, it was a transfer from one world to another.

I went to Hamilton High School, graduated, attended UCLA and received a Master's Degree in 1964. I thought I wanted to be an accountant and began working for Price-Waterhouse. I think I may have been the first, second, third, or certainly among the first handful of Jews employed by them. So I was at the forefront of that frontier as well. As it turned out, most of my clients were in the entertainment industry, so I became a bit of an expert in that area.

After spending ten years at Price-Waterhouse I decided that I wanted to make a career change. A friend of mine told me, "There is this man, Samuel Goldwyn, Jr., who is a film producer and he needs a business partner." It was 1976 when Sam and I met, and we talked for a couple of hours. He said, "Well I like you," and I said, "Well I like you, I think we can get along." He said, "Do you want to try it?" I said, "Sure, let's try it, and see if we can make it work." We shook hands, and that was about three decades ago. We are still partners and have created several companies, and fortunately we have been very successful.

The origin of Hollywood and the founders of the film entertainment industry were, in large part, of Jewish origin. We have to remember that they were raised in a time when they were driven by assimilation. So the concept of being a Jew was a concept that was recognized but not acted on. I think today we have a different perspective. Today, I believe there is a renewal of pride, recognition, and acknowledgment in Jewish life. I think there is a greater recognition of responsibility and actively working together to improve the lives of everyone. There is an openness, a new freedom of expression. Maybe it's the "flavor of the month," but Jewishness is "in" at the moment, for Jews and for non-Jews. We can see it in film

Meyer Gottlieb (left) with his older brother Aron at a Displaced Persons Camp in Germany, 1947. Meyer's mother, a seamstress, made the boys' clothes from U.S. Army issued blankets given to them by the soldiers

and entertainment programs. We see Jewishness being sprinkled in television shows and feature films. There are Jewish characters, Jewish meanings, Jewish thoughts being openly presented as part of the entertainment fabric. It's more from the perspective of a celebration of life, a celebration of culture than it is of being amusing. I think we are in a good period and a good era, and I hope it will continue and flourish.

In America, I have experienced good luck and good fortune. Going from the darkest days of your life into the sunshine is a journey one remembers from both the dark side and the light side. We thank God that we did survive and ended up coming to a place where we could thrive and build a life. That is essentially what my family has done. We have built a life here in Los Angeles. America and Los Angeles have given us that opportunity, and we are ever so grateful.

INTRODUCTION

Raymond Chandler, recognized as perhaps the quintessential Los Angeles fiction writer, described the City of Angels as "rich and vigorous and full of pride, a city lost and beaten and full of emptiness." How could he simultaneously be so unequivocally buoyant and gloomy about the same place? Perhaps it is because Chandler believed that the city was like its inhabitants—constantly reaching for the light, but occasionally sidetracked by the darkness. Some might call a city that celebrates the glossy and superficial star-struck—yet this is a city that is in touch with its soul while constantly seeking the spiritual light.

Los Angeles is not only a city—it is a state of mind. Or perhaps many states of mind—a virtual cornucopia overflowing with impressions. Thirteen million people call Los Angeles home, and if you ask them what defines the city, you might get thirteen million different answers. Is it Tinseltown, as some refer to it? Or a beach town? Is it a place to ski the mountains, surf the waves, or roller blade on Venice Beach? Is it one big theme park of fame and fantasy or a melting pot of ethnic diversity? Stroll on Pico Boulevard, where Orthodox Jews hold on to century-old customs. Witness different traditions as they collide at the intersection of Melrose Avenue and Fairfax where Orthodox Jews in skullcaps share the walkways with New Age rockers sporting spiked rainbow-colored hair and leather and chain fashion ensembles.

Los Angeles is really a sprawling combination of eighty-eight unincorporated cities—including Beverly Hills, West Hollywood, Santa Monica, and Malibu, the beaches on the West side and the suburbs in the valleys—many areas that combine to cover four hundred and sixty-eight square miles. It is one of the biggest cities in the world. There are millions of people who moved here from somewhere else—other parts of the globe and other parts of America; as many as 65 percent of the population are not native to Los Angeles. Something compelling drew them here....

The city is a powerful magnet. For over a century and a half of its official history, it has offered the promise of dreams fulfilled. A paradise where warm weather and the fragrant aroma of orange blossoms and jasmine wildly stimulate the senses. A beckoning oasis where children grow up believing that they can become president—just as one of its movie stars did in 1980. It is a wondrous place in which to stake a claim on your share of the American Dream.

Flying over the Southland, one is struck by its spectacular and varied geography: the San Fernando Valley, the canyons, the Santa Monica Mountains, the skyline of the downtown metropolis, and the grandeur of the Pacific Ocean. We are in awe of the size and scope and sheer beauty of the region.

To be sure, for most of America, the name Los Angeles conjures up a number of eclectic images—some elicit the magical surprises that can make proverbial fairy tales come true, while other images elicit a more pragmatic picture:

- A sprawling megalopolis that is home to Hollywood—a city synonymous with the glamour of celebrities and the exotic excesses of show business;
- Beverly Hills, enclave of the rich and famous, flaunting its celebrated Rodeo Drive where shopping is a favorite recreation and dressing in elegant fashion has become a status symbol;
- The colorful panache: a panorama of sparkling nightclubs, sleek fast cars, and shockingly beautiful women;
- A pop cultural stew with a robust mix of flavors that stirs and sifts together surfers, bikers, blondes, and Mickey Mouse;

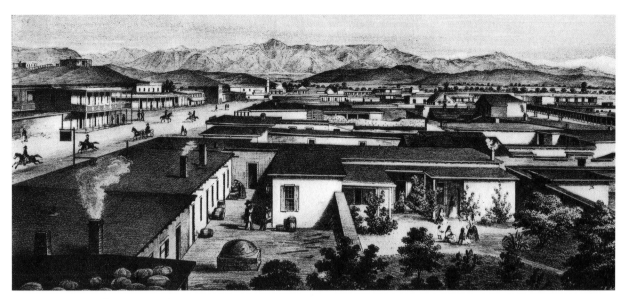

Early sketch of Los Angeles

- Thousands of miles of freeways and roadways with perpetual and seemingly endless traffic jams, and always the ubiquitous smog that accompanies the traffic;
- A sparkling deep purple-blue ocean that abuts breathtaking mountains, creating a bounty of natural beauty that stuns the senses.

For those who look beneath the glittery surface, there is a Los Angeles that is demonstrably and visibly one of the greatest cities in the world. There is a balance and symmetry to the city's unabashedly flamboyant, sybaritic character.

Disney gave us that paradigm of pop culture Mickey Mouse, the universally recognized playful host of Disneyland, a technologically dazzling environment that beckons and tantalizes children and adults alike. In stark dichotomy to the Disney playground is the Walt Disney Concert Hall, displayed as a stunning masterpiece of modern architecture, brilliantly designed by world-renowned Angeleno Frank Gehry. It is the centerpiece of a cosmopolitan downtown complex that features an opera house, two dynamic stages, and a state-of-the-art sports complex.

Los Angeles is also home to dozens of other theaters and museums, many featuring works of the great classical masters as well as contemporary artists. At the pinnacle is the Getty Center, a city unto itself, a world-class art center dedicated to enthusiastic art lovers as well as aspiring artists. The Los Angeles County Museum and the Museum of Tolerance are among the favorite destinations of millions of tourists that vacation in the city, as well as popular leisure time destinations for the city's residents.

Los Angeles' universities are world famous and are among the top academic institutions globally, attracting renowned scholars and educating the best and the brightest in science, the arts, business, and athletics—many destined to make their mark on the world. The booming downtown financial center houses one of the most recognized newspapers in the world, the Pulitzer Prize winning *Los Angeles Times*.

Peeling back the layers to explore the city's diverse cultures, one discovers stark contrasts among the different groups of people in Los Angeles and yet somehow they all fuse into a dynamic and vibrant tapestry. There have been such divisive events in history as the explosive Rodney King verdict of 1992 and the subsequent riots which exposed a city that was struggling and being torn apart. Historians note that only two years later, the aftermath of the 1994 earthquake and subsequent rebuilding of large parts of the city, reawakened hope as it stirred neighbors and strangers alike to come together in their hour of need and restore and reinvigorate the city. And, as history reflects, in the rebuilding there emerged a strengthening and a renewal—showcasing a community that unites and celebrates its differences.

On almost any given night you can stroll along Santa Monica's Third Street Promenade, observe the crowd, and view in microcosm the true character and flavor of Los Angeles. Amidst the boutiques and popular fashion chain stores and restaurants, there is a teeming, multicultural and multiethnic community. People from virtually every corner of the planet can be found here, representing every possible ethnicity—Nordic types, Mediterranean types, Hispanics, African Americans, Native Americans, Asians, Muslims, and Jews. Every one of them brings a rich history and a slice of culture that contributes to the city's fabric of life and vitality.

The name of the city and many of its streets are derived from its Spanish influence, an influence that dates back to the city's founding. Los Angeles has the distinction of having one of the longest streets in the country, Sepulveda Boulevard, reminiscent of the history that stems from the city's Spanish roots. Sepulveda, along with Pico and Figueroa, are major arteries on today's street maps of Los Angeles. This Spanish influence evolved into a Mexican flavor, as Hispanic culture left its powerful imprint on the city's architecture, its food, its music, and its media.

There are other spheres of ethnic influence that become obvious to even the casual observer. The African American experience was infused into the music. The rap and hip-hop genre that energized and fueled the multi-billion dollar recording industry was born out of poverty and anger on the streets of Watts and Compton. When buying gasoline, carpeting or oriental rugs, it is likely you are doing business with Middle Eastern immigrants that readily gravitated to these ventures through familial, social, and cultural ties. There is Chinatown, Japantown, and Koreatown, where various exponents of Asian culture remind us that in the modern world the Pacific Ocean is a small pond in the vast complex geopolitical landscape. Chinatown thrives with its Asian flavor, geographically dating back to one of the very first sections of frontier Los Angeles, *Calle de los Negros*.

As for the Jewish influence on Los Angeles, its scope is pervasive and powerful. The Hollywood movie machine was largely created and developed by a handful of Jews who emigrated here from Germany, Russia, and Poland early in the 20th Century. From these simple and primitive beginnings evolved an industry that dominates the world in entertainment and glamour and panache. Los Angeles is a provocative city of dreams and illusions, of big business and mega entertainment conglomerates, and its Jewish citizens were instrumental in the development and structure of the city.

The sheer number of Jews is also significant: with half a million Jewish people in Los Angeles, only New York and Tel Aviv have a bigger Jewish population. In the City of Angels you never have to travel very far to find a good Jewish deli, its aromas and popular food reminiscent of a tradition that nourishes the body while it simultaneously nurtures the soul. And looking beneath the surface, it is evident that the Jewish tradition goes far beyond feature films, banking and commerce, and chicken soup. The story of the creation of the motion picture industry has too long overshadowed a more far-reaching one. The story of the many ways in which Jews have impacted the very creation and sustenance of Los Angeles is a fulsome tale—one of hopes, dreams, determination, passions, and perseverance. In so many ways their significant efforts and contributions provided the cultural, economic, political, educational, and social foundations upon which the city, as we know it today, was built.

The Jews of Los Angeles crossed oceans and deserts to make something of themselves and the Promised Land they discovered. This is their story...*the history of Jewish Los Angeles.*

CHAPTER ONE

Los Angeles Before the Arrival of the Jewish Pioneers: 1781-1849

In 1847, William Rich Hutton, while on a trip to California stopped in Los Angeles and sketched the town, providing the first look at this sleepy pueblo

The first settlers that came to live in the land known as the City of Angels were farmers of mixed blood—these early inhabitants established a rudimentary foundation for ethnic tolerance that would later benefit Jews and other immigrants.

Long before there was Cantor's Deli or Universal Studios or Malibu surfers, there was a tiny, dusty village. The Spaniards founded Los Angeles on September 4, 1781, and the city has been expanding and flourishing since then. Spain at the time was trying to separate itself and gain power over the competing European nations. Russian, British, and French efforts to carve out new lands and obtain trading advantages compelled Spain to establish a presence in Alta (upper) California. They sent Franciscan missionaries to safeguard trading rights and Christianize the Native American population.

The Indians greeted the would-be conquerors with gifts of welcome—in return they found their land despoiled, their women molested, the men forced into labor and beaten and punished if they refused to speak Spanish. The Indian culture suffered and was ultimately destroyed by the white man's diseases and undiluted cruelty. Historian Carey McWilliams commented that the "survival of the Indians was in inverse ratio to the contact with the [Spanish] missions." Rather than learn from the Indians, the rapacious foreigners debased, abused, and finally obliterated their culture. Los Angeles was a settlement controlled by Spain and colonized by Mexico. There was minimal contact with the outside world, except for two trading ships a year.

The first civilian settlements were founded when the governor of California, Felipe de Neve, and his soldiers rode north from Baja (the southern part of the province of California), which was then considered the capital of California. In 1777 they reached their destination of Monterey in Alta California (the northern region) and Neve named it the new capital of the province. One of the first settlements was situated along what is today the Los Angeles River. Teodoro de Croix, the Spanish Inspector General, agreed to the grand name proposed by Governor Neve for this new pueblo: "de la Reina de Los Angeles sobre el Rio del la Porciuncula"—a big name, a glorious name, as if even then they could envision how vast the

Mexicans, Native Americans, and white settlers came before the first Jewish pioneers who arrived in the early 1850s

city of Los Angeles would become someday.

The official date documenting the birth of Los Angeles—September 4, 1781—was the day on which it is believed that Neve completed the blueprint plan for the pueblo. Neve's plan encompassed a geographic region of about twenty-seven square miles.

The first settlers that came to live in the land known as the City of Angels were farmers of mixed blood—these early inhabitants established a rudimentary foundation for ethnic tolerance that would later benefit Jews and other immigrants. These first settlers were a mixture of pure Spaniards, Indians, mestizoes, and mulattoes—many with African roots. Their first primitive homes were little more than huts made of tree branches and reeds with a clay-like mud added as the roof.

In small numbers, American "Yankees" began to come into Los Angeles and socialized and intermarried with the Mexican-Spanish families, thereby becoming landed aristocrats. Through this natural occurrence of intermarriage even the most prominent of families were of mixed blood, and considered quite respectable, including the Pico family, one of the most politically influential of the early family mergers. This acceptance of racial diversity paved the way for California's early African American pioneers who were among those welcomed into the racially mixed society in the early years of the settlement.

Spanish rule was terminated in 1821 as a result of the Mexican Revolution, and in March 1825, California officially became a territory of the Republic of Mexico. The Mexican period in California, lasting until 1848, was known principally as the era of the *ranchos*. Under the previous Spanish rule, all lands in California were claimed by the king of Spain, who granted them to the Catholic Church for their missions and to select individuals. When California came under control of the Mexican government the missions were secularized and the governors gained the power to grant state lands, the *ranchos*; their owners were called *rancheros*. During the secularization of the missions the period was rife with political intrigue and power struggles that erupted over conflicts in land ownership and efforts to grow the region.

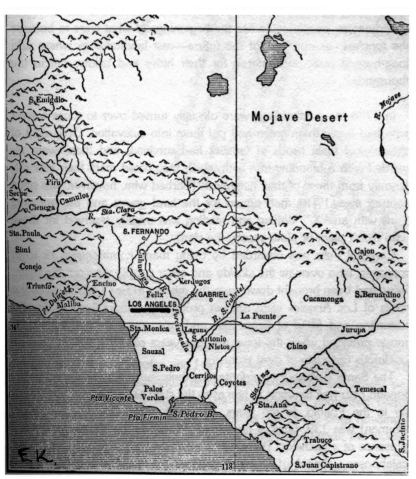

Map of the Los Angeles district around 1810

18

Native American woman selling her goods on a downtown Los Angeles street to raise money for the Spanish mission

Calle de los Negros (now the northern end of Los Angeles Street, east of the Plaza) dates from the 1830s. It was often referred to as a center of criminal activity in the first decades of the American era. By the early 1870s, the street was largely comprised of Chinese residences and businesses

This early print of a saloon and gambling house shows Mexican rancheros on the left, Chinese on the right, and ruined gambler cursing the playing cards on the floor

Kit Carson was chief-of-scouts of the American forces that captured Los Angeles from Mexico

In 1841, the first organized immigration party came to Los Angeles County. Its members were largely from Pennsylvania and included among the forty members, three that would later be well-known citizens —William Workman, D.W. Alexander and Benjamin David Wilson. From 1844 to 1849, Wilson was numbered among the very few merchants of Los Angeles.

Wilson was elected in April 1850 as the first clerk of Los Angeles County, but only with the understanding that he was to leave most of the work to Dr. William Jones. When the city was incorporated, Wilson was elected its first mayor (see article on page 24). In 1853, he became the government's Indian Agent for Southern California.

Wilson became a strong leader in both county and municipal governments. He was among the first to protest against California being admitted to the Union as a "slave state." In 1855 and 1869-70, he served as state senator of Los Angeles. In all of these public positions Wilson, according to his biographer, "proved to be a

Sketch of Los Angeles from the official report of the railroad survey made by U.S. Secretary of War Jefferson Davis, 1853

strong and trustworthy character."

James Polk was president of the United States in 1844, elected on a platform of expansionist policy. In 1845, the United States annexed Texas (which had been separated from Mexico in 1836) and in early 1846, the United States went to war with Mexico for possession of California. In August 1846, the American flag was raised in Los Angeles virtually without a shot being fired. The Mexican-American War was concluded officially a year and a half later on February 2, 1848 with the signing of the Treaty of Guadalupe Hidalgo. As a result of the war, the United States acquired rights to California, Texas, and the Southwest. The real gem in the newly acquired land was California when, as the treaty was signed, gold was discovered at John Sutter's mill near Sacramento.

Gordon DeMarco, author, writes that "during the period between the peace Treaty of Cahuenga in 1847 and statehood in 1850, California experienced five military governors; a gold rush that saw dreamers, drifters, honest working men, con artists, and thieves flow into the state like a flash flood down a desert wash; and a state constitutional convention where the Californios (early Hispanic settlers), although heavily outnumbered, had a voting delegation that gave every indication of feeling reasonably satisfied with the outcome." Because of its sordid reputation, the pueblo that became Los Angeles was originally known as "Hell Town." Adding to the pueblo's unsavory reputation as a rough and tumble law-

Peter Burnett, the first American governor of California; after leaving that post in 1851, he was appointed a justice of the State Supreme Court and later served as the president of the Pacific Bank in San Francisco

The earliest known photograph of the Plaza of Los Angeles taken in the 1860s

less town, was the frenetic search for gold which elicited a critical series of challenges for the young territory.

There were only 800 English-speaking Americans in a population of 13,000 Spanish-speaking citizens in California in 1846. Four short years later those 13,000 Californios were inundated by 100,000 "Yankees." The economic centers of the state became Sacramento and San Francisco, probably because of their proximity to where the gold fields were discovered and flourished. The Los Angeles County census of 1850 enumerates and describes the people who were living there at the time: "Many were domesticated Indians—the mission Indians who came out of the pueblo; of the rest, 699 people claimed birth in 28 foreign countries, and there were at least 8 Jews, 15 blacks and 2 Chinese." Their occupations were listed as laborers, farmers, ranchers and overseers, and merchants.

It was at this burgeoning period of history that we find one of the most valuable sources describing what these early days of statehood were like, in the memoirs of one of the first Jewish pioneers, Harris Newmark, *Sixty Years in Southern California, 1853-1913*. Harris Newmark stated clearly that the Jews of early Los Angeles were a "hearty lot." An analysis of the environment of the times when the early Jews arrived in Los Angeles gives some insight into the adventure that would establish the next chapter of Los Angeles history. These first Jews—eight Jewish bachelors—paved the way for the emergence of Jewish culture in Southern California, and were the first of the Jewish citizens that would become essential to the building of the city.

Los Angeles' First Elected Mayor Recalls the Very Early Days

by Benjamin David Wilson

The following narrative of Benjamin David Wilson was dictated by him to Hubert Howe Bancroft on December 6, 1877. Bancroft was gathering data for a history of California. The text is a condensed version of Wilson's original narrative, and his language is unedited.

I, Benjamin David Wilson of Nashville, Tennessee was born December 1, 1811. My father was born in a fort in the Territory of Tennessee in 1772, in what is now Wilson County. He died when I was eight years old, having lost by bad speculation, his fortune, which left his family poor.

We were assisted to some education by our grandfather. When I was about fifteen years of age, I went into business for myself, at Yazoo City above Vicksburg, where I kept a little trading house to do business with Choctaro and Chickasaw Indians. My health entirely broke down and I was told by physicians I could not live in that country; must either leave or die.

Los Angeles' first elected mayor, Benjamin David Wilson

A party of about twenty of us was formed in September 1841; we left from the most western part of New Mexico, headed for California. We met with no accidents on the journey, drove sheep with us, which served us as food and arrived in Los Angeles early in November of the same year. Most of the foreigners of our party came here (Los Angeles) with the intention of settling. I had no such idea; my plan was to go to China and from there return home.

But I did not carry out my original intention, and instead I purchased a ranch in 1843 and stocked it with cattle. That place is now Riverside. There was no place in the world where I could enjoy more true happiness and true friendship than among the native Californians. There were no courts, no juries, no lawyers, nor any need for them. People were honest and hospitable and their word was as good as their bond. So I settled upon the ranch and a *ranchero*'s life for some years.

✳ ✳ ✳

I was married in 1844 to Ramona Yorba, a daughter of one of the owners of the Santa Ana Ranch. In the fall of 1844 my ranchman reported that a large bear had killed one of our best milk cows. I went out with one other and we split up to go look for the grizzly. I took a servant with me, both of us well armed and as the bear made his appearance we both fired at him. I was the one who had the run-in with the bear. I bled so much from my wounds that I lost my sight and speech, though I still retained the power of my senses (I later made a full recovery). The bear in question remained on the ranch still killing cattle.

In 1845, the Mojave and other Indians were raiding the ranches in this part of the country. I took command of an expedition to go in pursuit of the Indians. I organized the expedition in San Bernardino, and sent the pack train and soldiers (less twenty-two which I retained with me) through the Cajon Pass. Myself and the twenty-two went up the San Bernardino River and when we arrived at the Lake the whole Lake and swamp seemed alive with bear. The twenty-two young Californians went out in pairs and each pair lassoed bear, and brought the result to the camp, so that we had at one and the same time, eleven bears. This prompted me to give the Lake the name it now bears (Big Bear Lake).

❋ ❋ ❋

We continued our course down the Mojave River and met the balance of the command. I saw four Indians coming towards us, but they didn't see us. They were right opposite on the plain and I rode towards them. I spoke to them and they answered in a very friendly manner. My object was not to kill them, but to take them as prisoners that they might give me information on the points I desired. It was evident that they had taken me for a traveler. Immediately discovering the true state of things, one Indian whipped out from his quiver an arrow, strung it on his bow and left nothing for me to do but to shoot in self defense. We both discharged our weapons at the same time. His shot took effect in my right shoulder and mine in his heart.

By this time my command arrived. The other three Indians were making off over the plains. I ordered my men to capture them alive, but the Indians resisted stoutly, refused to surrender, wounded several of our horses and two or three men, and had to be killed. In the meantime, I discovered I was shot with a poisoned arrow. I had to immediately take care of my wound. With me was a Comanche Indian, a trusty man who had accompanied me to California. The only remedy we knew of was sucking the poison with the mouth out of the wound. (I have frequently seen Indians preparing the poison and it is nothing more than putrid

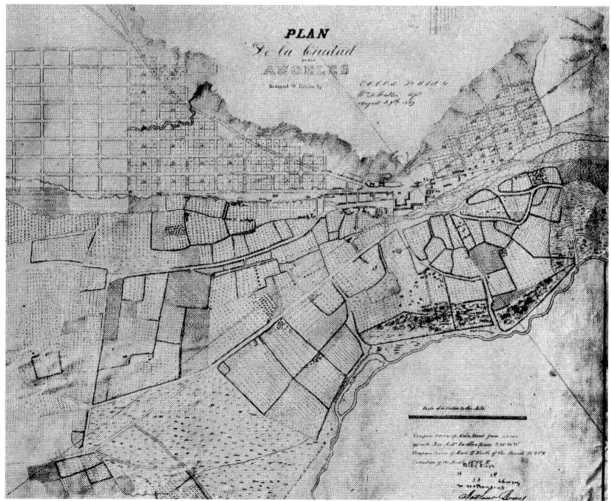

First survey map of Los Angeles made in 1849 by General E. Ord

Military headquarters at Wilmington, in the harbor area, during the Civil War. Notice the camel (center), to the left of Union soldiers, imported by Jefferson Davis from Arabia in the 1850s

meat or liver and blood, which they dried into thin sticks and carried in leather sheaths.) By the time I got to the river, my arm and shoulder were immensely swollen; at once my faithful Comanche, Lorenzo Trujillo, applied himself to sucking the wound and in the course of three to four days it had entirely disappeared.

✳ ✳ ✳

In 1845, I acted in the campaign between the Micheltorena and California parties. General Micheltorena's officers and men were all well known to the people of Los Angeles. They had made themselves obnoxious by their thefts and other outrages of a most hideous nature. It was announced that a revolution had broken out in the North against Micheltorena and his rabble and that they were on their way here in pursuit of the California revolutionists; all classes joined the movement to get rid of what was considered a great scourge.

I was on my ranch at Jarupa in early 1845 and acting as the *Alcalde* [mayor] of the district. I first refused to accept the duties. Not being a citizen of Mexico, I was not obliged, but at the request of friends and for the defense of my own interests, I consented. I was acting as such when an order came to me from the Prefect of the District to summon every man capable of bearing arms in my district and gather every man I could find on my way to Los Angeles. I obeyed and arrived with some 20 or 30 men. Upon my arrival in the town almost every man I knew was armed and determined to do everything in his power to prevent Micheltorena and his scum from entering Los Angeles.

We arrived in the Cahuenga Valley and Pio Pico heard that Micheltorena had camped the night before at Encino. We took our positions and awaited the enemy's arrival. This was about noon. Both parties began firing their cannons at each other. I don't think anyone was hurt or killed. We learned that the Americans and other foreigners in the Micheltorena party were commanded by some of our old personal friends. Feeling convinced that they had engaged themselves on that side under misapprehension or ill advice and that nothing was wanting but

Pio Pico, the last Mexican Governor of California

an understanding between them and us to make them withdraw from Micheltorena and join our party, we soon obtained the desired information of their whereabouts.

I was the one to approach them under a white flag as I had a personal acquaintance with their leaders. We got to the point we started for and raised our white flag, at which moment we were fired upon by cannon loaded with grape shot; no one was hurt and we had gained our point. The Americans on the other side had seen our flag. We dropped down into a ravine and waited for the coming of someone from that side. That was that episode.

✳ ✳ ✳

We returned to Los Angeles City where I was engaged in merchandising. Nothing worthy of mention happened till 1849, when a convention was called by General Riley to form a Constitution of California. At that time, this part of the country was much depopulated by the rush to the gold places that had been discovered in the spring of 1849. We held a public meeting and selected the best men we could find—Abel Stearns, Manuel Dominguez, Stephen C. Foster, etc. We had no directions to give our representatives, except that we wished not to be a state yet, but if we had to be a state, we (although most of us were Southern men) were very positive that we wanted no slavery. We had enough of a variety of races and the character of the country was not favorable to any but free labor.

The following year California having been voted in the Constitution as a state, we held a convention of the Southern county in Santa Barbara, at which I was a member. The purpose was of sending a protest to Congress, that in the case California was admitted as a State of the Union, the Southern portion would be allowed to form a Territorial Government, and allowed to remain as a Territory of the United States. Our efforts proved unavailing. After the state was organized, I was elected the first Clerk of the County of Los Angeles, making the condition with my friends that I should not serve personally, but would appoint Dr. Wilson Jones, as my deputy to run the office. When the town of Los Angeles was incorporated as a city the people elected me its first mayor. I only served a few months, and then resigned.

In 1855 I was elected state senator, and served out my term; again served in 1869-70. Since then I have spent my time as a horticulturist in Los Angeles County at Lake Vineyard. My family consists of a wife, and three daughters — one by my first wife and two by my second wife — all living, and four grandchildren. Hope to pass the remainder of my days in peace with God and man, as well as myself.

Benjamin D. Wilson
December 6, 1877

Rancho Life is a Foundation of the Early Years

by Gordon DeMarco

In his book, *The Cattle on a Thousand Hills*, Robert Glass Cleland compared the *rancho* in economic and social terms with the medieval English manor. The Indians functioned as the peasants while the *dons* (lords) pursued the courtly life. As California was ideally suited for cattle ranching and the hide and tallow trade, for which the cattle were ranched, and since these were solid, lucrative businesses, the courtly life of the *ranchero* took on the appearance of romantic royalty.

The extravagant festivities—the weddings, the fandangos, the religious festivals—were frequent occurrences at the *ranchos* of the Bandinis, the Lugos, the Stearns, the Del Valles, and others. Even more characteristic of *rancho* lifestyle was the resplendent attire sported by the *rancheros*. One of them, Jose Arnaz, described a fashionable fiesta outfit:

> Shoes of deerskin embroidered with gold or silver threads; breeches of cloth, velvet or satin reaching to the knee, and open on both sides, bordered with gold braid and silver buttons; vest of velvet, silk or cloth, and over it a jacket of blue, black, or green cloth embroidered in gold and silver thread. Add to this outfit a gay sash of red satin…and a wide sombrero with a cord of silver or gold encircling the crown, worn jauntily tipped on one side.

Life on the *rancho*, like the manor or the southern plantation, was self-sufficient, pastoral, ostentatious, over-indulgent, and certainly picturesque and romantic in its social life. It was also, like the manor and the plantation, a way of life that was locked in the past and continually fighting a holding action against the future of human and economic progress. The *ran-*

Ranch hands mount up for a day of cattle herding

THE OLD
SPANISH AND MEXICAN
RANCHOS
of LOS ANGELES COUNTY

Mojave Desert

Prepared by
TITLE INSURANCE
AND TRUST COMPANY
TITLE INSURANCE BUILDING
433 SO. SPRING STREET · LOS ANGELES

Circa, 1860

cho, like its manor predecessor and plantation contemporary, was doomed to extinction.

Richard Henry Dana, author of the classic *Two Years Before the Mast* offered an observation of the Californio *ranchero* that addressed both the relaxed, traditional backward-looking lifestyle and the coming inevitable collision with the aggressive Yankee vision of the future. In the 1830s when, as a sailor, he came in contact with the Californios, he saw the *rancheros* as "thriftless, proud, and extravagant, and very much given to gaming." He observed them to be more interested in fandangos than industry. "Yankees," he wrote, "can't afford the time to be Catholics…. In the hands of an enterprising people [Americans] what a country this might be!"

These words were written more than ten years before the enterprising visionaries of the United States decided it had to have California.

CHAPTER TWO

Birth of the Jewish Community in Los Angeles: 1850-1859

Harris Newmark, the leader of Jewish life in Los Angeles, with his granddaughter, circa 1900

The Jewish people and their culture were crucial to the development of Los Angeles in many areas...

Much speculation has been offered about what brought the Jews to Los Angeles—what tempted them to confront the hardships of the journey from Europe and the East Coast and try their luck in this lawless town? In addition to the more obvious benefits such as the weather, the perfect conditions and climate for agriculture, an abundance of land for both living and farming, and the gold rush, there were also more fundamental and life enhancing issues. Many were seeking freedom from religious and political persecution abroad, others came in search of economic opportunities for creating new wealth, and some came for the lifestyle benefits that emanated from a social mobility and acceptance not easily available in the more sophisticated cities in the East.

The Jewish people and their culture were crucial to the development of Los Angeles in many areas: economics, politics, social interaction, religious tolerance, philanthropy and charitable organizations, banking and innovation in business. The thread of Jewish influence can be clearly seen by examining the development of Los Angeles from the earliest days in the middle of the 19th Century.

What did this dusty little desert settlement look like when the Yankees and immigrants began arriving in Los Angeles in 1850? Imagine a small frontier town where Main Street is the only street, with occasional rough dusty paths haphazardly finding the way to tents and crudely made hovels of commerce. Graded streets and sidewalks were unknown at the time.

Joseph Newmark (uncle of Harris Newmark) along with his wife, child and mother-in-law. This photograph is a classic in the early history of Jewish Los Angeles

42		*Census of the City an*		
1	**2**	**3**	**4**	**5**
		Bernada	25	f
		Jacob Frankford	40	m
92	92	Morris Michael	19	m
		A Jacoba	25	m
93	93	Augustin Wasserman	24	m
		Felix Pachman	28	m
94	94	Timothy Foster	41	m
		John F Simmons	30	m
		David Douglass	30	m
		Julia	45	f
95	95	Phillip Sichel	28	m
		Joseph Plumer	24	m
		Goodman	24	m

The first eight Jewish residents of Los Angeles, who were listed in the 1850 census of that city, were recorded in January 1851. All eight were men and all lived and operated stores in the same building known as Bell's Row, a two-story structure located at the southeast corner of Aliso and Los Angeles Streets. The eight were Jacob Frankfort, Morris Michaels, Arnold Jacoby, Augustine Wasserman, Felix Bachman, Phillip Sichel, Joseph Plumer and Morris L. Goodman. The carelessness of the census-taker is marked by the misspellings and omissions in many of the names

Deep mud filled the streets after the heavy winter rains, which in summer were thick with dust. A constant spray of sand blew from endless vacant lots leaving piled heaps of sand in front of the meager buildings. To make walking possible, planks and boxes lined the squalid streets so one could navigate the sand hills and other obstacles.

People in the town could virtually do as they pleased—there were few restrictions, and customs and habits of the day were free and easy. Rubbish was routinely tossed into the street—old worn out clothes, broken furniture, even dead animals and other trash were commonly left on streets until some poor citizen down on his luck would salvage something from the piles of cast away debris.

There was a lack of civilization and genteel behavior; relatively few women were seen, and most people rode on horseback in order to navigate the muddy streets. The town had no style or signs of progress; tents of all sizes and colors were abundant, intermixed with small adobe mud huts. There was a preponderance of saloons and gambling houses; these also flourished without restrictions of any sort, without even a limit on how many people could safely crowd into each establishment. These places attracted criminals and con men, setting the stage for a wild and raucous environment.

One very popular district in Los Angeles at the time was *Calle de los Negros*, commonly known as "Nigger Alley." Both sides of the Alley had saloons and gambling houses and both sexes patronized these establishments commonly dealing the popular card games of the day—Monte and Faro. The employees who kept the "bank" and dealt with the money all had pistols and settled disputes on the spot—"authorities" were rarely contacted.

Jewish pioneer Harris Newmark describes it this way:

> Human life at this period was about the cheapest thing in Los Angeles and killings were frequent. Nigger Alley was as tough a neighborhood, in fact, as could be found anywhere, and a large proportion of the twenty or thirty murders a month was (sic) committed there. About as plentiful a thing also as there was in the pueblo was liquor. This was served generously in these resorts, not only with

respect to quantity, but as well regarding variety. In addition to the prodigality of feasting, there was no lack of music of the native sort—the harp and the guitar predominating. These scenes were picturesque and highly interesting. Nigger Alley, for a while the headquarters for gamblers, enjoyed through that circumstance a certain questionable status; but in the course of years it came to be more and more occupied by the Chinese, and given over to their opium dens, shops and laundries.

Crossing to the part of town that catered to the more "refined" citizens, one would find higher grade liquor and billiard parlors. Here ranch owners, cowboys, and merchants all found some form of gambling, the "long and the short purse being equally accommodated."

Horace Bell, another of the colorful early pioneers in Los Angeles, wrote in some detail about the Wild West days in Los Angeles: "There were more desperadoes than in any place on the Pacific Coast…the murder rate in 1853 in this town of less than four thousand was over one per day!" How did Los Angeles become this "Hell Town" in the early 1850s? Mostly men drifted into the town, spillover from the gold mines—drifters, thieves, con men—many given to cruelty and violence. Poor and illiterate Mexicans also passed through Los Angeles on the way to the gold fields; many stayed until they could earn or acquire enough money to take them further north. Little wonder that the intimidating *banditos* and the lack of morality imposed a scandalous reputation on the pueblo commonly referred to as Hell Town.

At the other extreme, there was also great wealth in Los Angeles, due in large part to the gold boom. Money was being made not just from the mines, but also from the *rancheros'* huge herds of cattle, a business that quickly gave birth to the rapidly growing beef industry. The *rancheros* grew rich on the *ranchos* and lived as if the boom would last forever, spending money extravagantly and indulgently. With that kind of money being flaunted in a town with the combustible racial mixture and social inequality that was then Los Angeles, it is easy to understand why the human beings that were dislocated and disenfranchised roamed the streets looking for trouble.

Adding to the volatile mixture of social and economic disparity was the lack of any structured government or law enforcement. In desperation local citizens formed vigilante groups to try to combat the lawlessness. Crime was rampant and the American population blamed the Indians and the Spanish-speaking, especially the Mexicans and Latin Americans, although the criminals came in all colors and nationalities.

Into this Hell Town entered the first Jews to arrive in Los Angeles—eight bachelors counted by the 1850 census. These first eight Jewish men were from Germany and Poland. One of them, Morris L. Goodman, was elected to Los Angeles' very first city council in 1850, and another, Arnold Abraham Jacoby was elected in 1853. The other six

Rabbi Abraham Wolf Edelman and members of his family in front of their South Flower Street home

Solomon Lazard's store sketched by artist in the 1850s

were: Morris Michaels, Phillip Sichel, Augustine Wasserman, Felix Bachman, Joseph Plumer and Jacob Frankfort. These Jewish pioneers and those that followed them had a strong commitment to establish their presence in this new land, having endured the long and difficult journey to get there.

It was not easy to travel to the west coast of California in the 1850s—the journey was hazardous, long, tedious, unpredictable, and quite expensive. In recounting the demands of the journey it is significant to understand the hardships that travelers endured in order to ultimately reach this remote desert town. Historian William Deveril explains about the various modes of transportation needed and the exertion of the trip: "People traveling to Southern California could get here a number of different ways. Probably the most common way, coming from the East, would be to take a clipper ship all the way around the tip of South America, and then fight your way up north along the South American coastline. Pretty difficult travel. Another

Solomon Lazard's store moved to Main Street near Temple Street, 1866

way, equally difficult, would be to dock on one end of the Isthmus of Panama and then walk across the Isthmus of Panama, (in the pre-canal days of course), and get picked up by a ship on the other side and brought up this way. It was a journey of several months, although during the gold rush period there were a number of clipper companies that plied this trade and brought miners and adventurers, tourists and settlers that way around South America."

In his memoirs, Harris Newmark's description of his journey from Europe in 1853 gives a detailed and personal account of the struggles of the pioneers and the hardships encountered on the strenuous trip. Newmark begins his journal entry

S. Lazard & Co.,
WHOLESALE AND RETAIL DEALER IN
Fancy and Staple
D R Y   G O O D S,
CLOTHING,
    BOOTS AND SHOES,
        HATS,
            BLANKETS,
                CARPETS, Etc.,
MAIN STREET,
OPPOSITE THE BELLA UNION HOTEL,
                    Los Angeles.
Jan. 4, 1869.

Los Angeles Daily News, *1869*

upon boarding the ship in Europe, where immediately, he wrote, passengers met with rough seas and many suffered from seasickness for much of the trip. At this time, the steamer service between Liverpool, England, and New York sailed semi-monthly. Most of the passengers had little money and traveled in steerage, forced to provide their own necessities. Newmark, traveling in the first class salon, reported that fresh food was served in the dining room the first week; afterward, meat spoiled, and food became stale and rancid, including the water that was stored in barrels on the ship.

After forty-nine days in these deteriorating and squalid conditions, Newmark's ship reached New York where all on board were required to remain until the health officer checked them out. Boats alongside the ship provided fresh food and staples while the newly arrived immigrants had their first views of New York from the deck of the ship. Newmark left the ship and booked passage on another vessel, traveling via Nicaragua to California, waiting in New York for a few weeks until the ship sailed. He was warned not to drink the ship's water unless it was first mixed with brandy. Fortifying himself for the trip (including the brandy), he left New York, traveled through warmer climates, changed modes of transportation: from the ship to flat-bottomed boats, moving onto dry land for a time, walking and climbing through rough terrain, then returning to the boats with all those on board "miserably packed together." This was not a journey for the timid and these early pioneers strenuously earned the right to enter this new golden land.

Newmark writes, "It would be impossible to describe the hardships experienced on these crowded little steamboats…. The only drinking water came from the river, and it was then that my brandy served its purpose: with the addition of the liquor, I made the drink both palatable and safe. Men, women and children were parched and packed like so many herring. The heat was intense; the mosquitoes seemed omnivorous. This part of the trip was replete with misery for many." Newmark narrates that he was delighted to see orange, lemon, and coconut trees as he sailed. The travelers once again changed to larger boats, reached land and rode mules

The pioneers arrived at the Los Angeles Harbor prior to the arrival of the railroad. Dead Man's Island (upper right) no longer exists

about twelve miles to reach San Juan del Sur in Central America, a Spanish-American village with one main street, oppressive heat, and offers of high priced hammocks which served as beds. The following day they were transported by natives through the surf to small boats then back onto a large steamer to begin the last lap of the journey; finally they entered the Golden Gate, having reached San Francisco after an exhausting and demanding three months of travel. Now the weary travelers began the final push—traveling from San Francisco to reach the southern part of the state—and ultimately to Los Angeles.

At this time no stagecoach line existed between San Francisco and the southern part of the territory so the travelers were compelled to continue the journey by steamer bound for Los Angeles, arriving in the port at San Pedro where they scrambled to seek land transportation for the final part of the journey to Los Angeles. Coaches were provided for those fortunate few who had the foresight or knowledge to write ahead to one of the only two established coach companies. Lively betting took place on which of the two coaches from the competing companies would be the first to arrive in the City of Angels. The race consisted of a two and a half hour trip taken at breakneck speed over bad roads, in a coach pulled by four to six horses, for an expensive ticket that cost five dollars. The trip terminated at the town's only hotel, the Belle Union, a one-story adobe house. This treacherous and risky adventure to Los Angeles, undertaken by the most determined traveler, could be completed in about four months, according to Newmark, quoting from his own experience.

After this exhausting four month excursion, over land and sea, by steam ship, flat-bottomed boats, walking, riding mules and horses, small boats, and stage coaches, newcomers arrived from every part of the world and confronted the primitive conditions and the elements. The eclectic melting pot consisting of immigrants, Native Americans, Mexicans, and East Coast and Midwest adventurers, all merged into the ethnic diversity that was to define Los Angeles from its beginnings and into the future.

William Deveril gives his thoughts and impressions of what those first days were like in the new frontier town: "Early Los Angeles in the mid-19th Century was a very diverse place, so it would not be uncommon at all to hear English, Spanish, Dutch, French, German. There were a lot of folks here during the early period that came from all parts of the globe. People came for a variety of reasons. Many of those who were drawn to Northern California because of the gold rush, drifted south by sea or land to Los Angeles in search of adventure or the next opportunity. A number of folks came north from Mexico…many coming because of the newness of the place."

Deveril continues, "There was a fair amount of community and camaraderie. There were polyglot communities that tended to amalgamate Europeans with one another, Europeans and European Americans. Many came from European capitals, and the provincialism of America was something that struck them. People that came from New York, Philadelphia, Boston…tended to think of the west as the far flown isolated frontier, oftentimes referring to life on the east coast as 'back in the states.' The folks that got the short end of the stick were the native Californians, the Native Americans, the Gabrielinos, for instance, the [San Gabriel] mission Indians and the people of Mexican descent. Among the Europeans and European Americans there was camaraderie; it was an intellectual community with access to venture capital, and they exhibited an obvious spirit of working together as Los Angeles started to get its feet under it and look towards the future."

Rabbi and history professor, William M. Kramer commenting about the times speculated, "Jews have wandered this earth for some four thousand years. The search for the 'promised land' is both literal and figurative. It was the promise of the good life that brought the early pioneers to Los Angeles. And when they found it, they weren't shy. They wanted to have

On Downey's Old Block where the stores of Harris and Jacoby, Maurice Kremer, and Solomon Lazard were located, 1875

Pioneer merchant Solomon Lazard was a member of the City of Los Angeles Council for many years beginning in 1854

a say in how this city would grow. What made Los Angeles so attractive was its contrast with the cities most American Jews called home. In place of the grit and grime of East Coast and Midwest cities, Los Angeles, even in its earliest days, offered year-round sunshine, a more casual life-style—and a chance to make a fresh start. The opportunity to achieve the American Dream was on every corner."

The American Dream—what did it mean to these foreigners who came from other countries speaking little or no English? What prompted socially established Jewish Americans from New York and the Midwest to take the hazardous and often heart-breaking journey across the country to this dusty lawless territory? Noted Jewish historian and UCLA Professor of History, David Myers conjectures about what drove these Jewish pioneers to the new state of California:

Los Angeles presented more economic opportunity, more freedom to imagine oneself anew. In a sense, shorn from one's own homeland, shorn from the tradition of anti-Semitism that so many European suffered from and sought liberation from, Los Angeles was yet another unconquered horizon that beckoned alluringly. It did so with the promise of clean air and large tracts of land and wide, open space, which the urban experience in New York did not afford. We recall the accounts of Jewish immigrants cramped into tenements on the lower East side, as such a formative experience for many of them, and as such a powerful impression for us. Los Angeles in that regard was just the opposite. It was a venue in which you could find open spaces and establish oneself with the prospect of new economic opportunity. I think there was something of that spirit that drove the Jewish immigrants here.

In discussing the early history and his views on why the Jewish pioneers chose Los Angeles as their destination, Kramer postulates: "Sephardic Jews have historically liked to live adjacent to a port...for a Jew from Greece it wasn't life unless he could see water. Another reason [for the move to Southern California] was the gold strike in the San Fernando Valley, small but tempting. And some Jews came here because they liked the cattle business; these were, for the most part, the Bavarian Jews who had been in the cattle business in the old country. Some Jews came from the East because they had bad marriages, bad businesses, bankruptcies, or simply because they wanted to get away from the snow and sleet."

Kramer describes what the Jews found in Los Angeles:

This was the Golden Land. In your backyard you could grow oranges. Next to your garbage can, a tomato plant sprouted up because one of the cans fell over. If you were a smart Jew you could buy a little land yesterday, sell it tomorrow, drop dead in the process but leave a huge estate.

Professor Myers also speaks about the temptations of Southern California:

What better setting than Southern California and the sun? But the first substantial group of Jews to make their way to Los Angeles were coming in order to discover completely unconquered terrains of economic opportunity. These people were not from impoverished backgrounds. They were people in search of economic horizons and they established themselves rather quickly. They had a good deal of commercial experience, they had marketable skills and they inserted themselves into the economic life of the community as well as the social and political life of Los Angeles.

Karen Wilson, historian of Jewish Los Angeles, stated that the Jews came to Los Angeles "where there were not a lot of other Jews and yet they created Jewish community and maintained Jewish identity even as they Americanized and even as they built what became the most important American city in the 20th Century, in terms of the growth and a model of urban life. I am very interested in these people who chose to come to a place where there were very few Jews, and who were willing to build a community and develop the city of Los Angeles. [It is puzzling

Mr. and Mrs. Maurice Kremer were one of the first Jewish pioneer families. Photograph taken at their golden wedding anniversary in 1906

inasmuch] as with the history of most of Los Angeles, it is very hard to explain why there is a city here. There is nothing natural here to create a city—we are miles from a port or a harbor—at the time the agricultural industry did not really exist—there was no obvious reason to have a city here, no obvious reason for Jews to come, and yet they did."

Wilson speculates about what brought the Jewish pioneers to Southern California:

> My best theory is that they were adventurous, and they were visionary people. I think they brought a kind of cosmopolitan world-view, actually. In many cases, they were young as well. Some of the men, such as Harris Newmark and the Hellman brothers came when they were in their teens, very young and very confident in their abilities to make their way in the world—this probably presented the most wide-open opportunities for them…. Then there would be a chain migration; one or two family members would be here and then more would follow…. Los Angeles in the 1850s was predominantly male, Jewish women started arriving in 1851—Ernestine Greenbaum seems to have been the first Jewish woman, arriving here with her husband. Women were very important, not only in establishing family life in the city, but also for their role in business and the establishment of the charitable organizations as well as the synagogue. The women of B'nai B'rith are credited with finally forcing the men to build a synagogue in 1872.

In Southern California new people were the norm and not the exception. This was a place that was constituting itself anew. Beginning with its early Native American and Mexican origins, the arrival of all types of newcomers from Europe and other parts of the United States brought both Jews and non-Jews. With that spirited innovation that they brought, Jews, even with their aura of uniqueness, were not considered that much different from the others who arrived in the town of Los Angeles. They were welcomed to participate in ways that were not available to them in the more highly structured society in the East, where the rigid established social stratifications prevented Jews from obtaining the access they found in Los Angeles.

Jews Establish Commerce and Law and Order in Early Los Angeles

The first Jews that ventured to Southern California were mostly merchants who sold staples and luxury items to those getting rich in the gold fields and cattle ranches. The merchants' advertising served as the basis of revenue for the first newspaper in the territory, the *Los Angeles Star*. Thus the Jews were influential from the very first in the commercial enterprise that helped establish the success of the newspaper and improve communication. The *Star* was founded in May 1851; printed half in English and half in Spanish it was known to its Spanish readers as *La Estrella de Los Angeles*. The newspaper reported mostly local news which was of primary importance to the residents. The citizens were relatively isolated since there was still no telegraphic communication and the news brought by mail was often delayed for weeks or months. It was not unusual for national and international news from the outside world to be unknown until a month or two after the event had occurred. When California was admitted to the Union in 1850, the news did not reach the West Coast until six weeks after the Congressional action.

Jewish influence also impacted and initiated the beginnings of law and order into the lawless community. In 1853, the first "military company" was formed to establish law in this wild town. A Jewish pioneer, Solomon Lazard, one of the first elected to the city council, had established a career as a successful and respected merchant. When the city's military company was instituted, Lazard was an early volunteer and commissioned as a first lieutenant. A few years later Lazard was appointed inspector of elections, an exceedingly more dangerous than honorary position. Historian Max Vorspan, author of *History of the Jews of Los Angeles*, explains: "Considering how votes were bought and sold, how Indians were corralled and served intoxicants until the polls opened and then delivered in carts to vote, only a man of courage and integrity could serve." Vorspan goes on to conjecture about some of the reasons why Jews were accepted and welcomed into leadership roles in politics:

Hilliard Lowenstein arrived in Los Angeles from Loebau, Prussia in the early 1850s. He was a business partner of Samuel Meyer. He returned to Europe to wed his partner's sister Rosa Meyer (right). Photographs taken around 1875

They [the Jews] were among the respected elements of society, merchants and men of affairs well known and respected by the Mexican population. For business reasons many Jews learned Spanish, which further attracted the Spanish speaking voter. Furthermore, the Jews' not insignificant numbers could mean a certain number of votes when, as during the Civil War period, three hundred votes could elect a city councilman and seven hundred to eight hundred could bring into office a supervisor of Los Angeles County. Finally, the ancient rabbinic principle, 'where there is no man one must strive to be a man,' had its application on the Western frontier. The community was rough, lawless, untutored in government. The Jews were peaceable, intelligent, literate. They were needed in city government.

Jewish citizens moved freely in the hectic unsettled society of the period. Due to their religious individuality, which they were determined to protect, each one remained a fully accepted but sharply defined and identifiable person. Active in politics, they were predominantly Democrats and very involved in local issues. In 1850, the first city council elected Morris Goodman as councilman, one of the first eight Jews in the town. The Jewish economic interests led them naturally into the political life of the community and the social

Assimiliated Dutch Jews, I. Lankersbim (left) and I. N. Van Nuys were the first owners of land in the San Fernando Valley. They purchased the land in the late 1860s and early 1870s for an average price of $1.50 per acre

life of the clubs and lodges that were beginning to form. Among the first of these societies was the Hebrew Benevolent Society.

First Religious Services and the Hebrew Benevolent Society

While rudimentary religious services were held by Jews in their homes as early as 1851, the services were not formalized until the arrival of Harris Newmark's uncle, Joseph Newmark and his family in 1854. It is noted in the early literature that they brought with the family a servant who was among the first of the Chinese people to live in Los Angeles. Harris Newmark remarked: "Joseph Newmark brought with him to Los Angeles a Chinese servant, to whom he paid one hundred dollars a month…. It was but five or six years before, that the first Chinese to emigrate from the Celestial Kingdom to California—two men and one lone woman—had come to San Francisco from Hong Kong. A year later, there were half a hundred Chinamen in the territory, while at the end of still another year, during the gold excitement, nearly a thousand Chinese entered the Golden Gate." The emergence of the Chinese as an organized community was to have considerable effect upon the construction of the railroads in the next decade.

Joseph Newmark acted as rabbi to the small but thriving Jewish community until the arrival of Rabbi Abraham W. Edelman in 1862 and the establishment of the Congregation B'nai B'rith. Rabbi Newmark and the young and enthusiastic Jewish community in the 1850s had an urgent need—they lacked a Jewish cemetery. At a meeting held at the home of Joseph Newmark on June 24, 1854, they formed a *Gemilat Chesed*, which translated into English as Hebrew Benevolent Society.

Three Sephardic Jews played a key role in the organization and establishment of the new Hebrew Benevolent Society. Renowned artist and photographer, Solomon Nunes Carvalho, traveled west with John Charles Fremont's Fifth Expedition acting as official photographer for the military excursion. Carvalho was very experienced in Jewish life and arrived in California

This adobe housed the first City Hall and jail and was located on Spring Street opposite today's City Hall. Several Jewish pioneers were members of the early city councils

bringing "that love for organized Jewish community life which had been aroused in several of the oldest Jewish communities in North America and transmitted it to the pioneers in a town which eventually was to contain the third largest Jewish community in the United States," explains Kramer.

Carvalho's ancestry was impressive; he could trace his family back to Spanish-Portuguese Jewry in London in the 1700s. Carvalho was a dedicated student of the Bible and Jewish scripture and he quoted the Torah and Psalms with ease. As a result of his background, he brought a wealth of experience and energy in helping to organize the small Jewish group in Southern California, which had only thirty members. It is thought that Carvalho modeled the Los Angeles organization on similar groups he had worked with in Charleston, Baltimore, and Philadelphia.

Two close acquaintances of Carvalho, also Sephardic Jews, the Labatt brothers, Samuel K. and Joseph I., were instrumental in assisting Carvalho. Samuel K. Labatt was the first president chosen to lead the Hebrew Benevolent Society, elected with Carvalho in attendance. In a resolution passed by the Society, it was "resolved unanimously that the thanks of this meeting be tendered to Mr. S. N. Carvalho for his valuable services in organizing this society, and that he be elected an honorary member."

In their document of incorporation, the founding members stated that the Hebrew Benevolent Society was formed for the purpose of "procuring a piece of land for the burying ground for the deceased of their own faith, and also to appropriate a portion of their time and means to the holy cause of benevolence under the name and style 'Hebrew Benevolent Society of Los Angeles.'" As mentioned, Samuel K. Labatt was president and Solomon Lazard was elected as one of the board of trustees. A short announcement of the new society was published on July 8, 1854. What is notable and intrinsic to the Jewish tradition of community is that even in the remote West, the founding members considered themselves part of the established American Jewish community and took action to maintain their connection with American and European Jewry.

Harris Newmark describes his impressions of the Hebrew Benevolent Society: "Its principle objects were to care for the sick, to pay proper respect, according to Jewish ritual, to the dead, and to look after the Jewish Cemetery which was laid out about that time; so that the Society at once became a real spiritual force and continued so for several years…. Mr. [Joseph] Newmark had been ordained and was permitted to officiate; and one of the immediate results of his influence was the establishment of worship on Jewish holidays. The first service was held in the rear room of an adobe owned by John Temple. Joseph Newmark also inspired the purchase of land for the Jewish Cemetery…. Its [HBS] aim was to give relief…to every worthy person that appeared, whoever he was or whatever his creed."

Newmark chronicles the purchase of the sacred land: "In 1854 the first steps were taken to establish a Jewish cemetery here, and it was not very long before the first Jewish child to die in Los Angeles, named Mahler, was buried there. This cemetery, on land once owned by Jose Andres Sepulveda, was beautifully located in a recess or little pocket among the hills in the northwest section of the city, where the environment of nature was in perfect harmony with the Jewish ideal— 'Home of Peace.'" Today this section of Los Angeles is known as Chavez Ravine.

The Jewish population of this new western community fought to maintain

Los Angeles Daily News, *1869*

Los Angeles Daily News, *1869*

their religious and moral traditions established throughout their 4000-year history, and thus became the first group to establish a charitable organization in Los Angeles, as a state historical marker proclaims at the site today. The Hebrew Benevolent Society has the honored distinction of being the predecessor of all benevolent societies and charitable institutions in the city.

The Hebrew Benevolent Society grew slowly in the first few years, although a majority of the Jewish people in Los Angeles, San Bernardino, and neighboring communities were members, paying dues of $5.00 for the year. The financial report for 1859 reflects that "the society began the year with $87.20, and added new members which grew the treasury to $475.50. The committee for charity spent $233.50, which left them with $384.20 [sic]." This rudimentary financial record documents the beginnings of Jewish philanthropy in the tiny pueblo that would become a dominant city in the landscape of California. As the first charitable organization, the Hebrew Benevolent Society opened the door for all organizations that were to follow in the developing and civilizing of the community.

Jewish Community Encourages Civilized Behavior in Society

Life in the 1850s was rough and uncomplicated and the need for social intermingling was met by the emergence of fraternal orders and social clubs, societies that began with the precedent of the Hebrew Benevolent Society. The women in the Jewish community expanded the scope of the Hebrew Benevolent Society by establishing the Ladies Hebrew Benevolent Society in 1870, the first women's philanthropic organization in Los Angeles. Rosa Newmark, wife of the patriarch Joseph Newmark, encouraged the women to "add feminine tenderness to the acts of charity and of comforting mourners." In addition to charity and good deeds, the Ladies Hebrew Benevolent Society also performed the rites of bereavement, prepared the female dead for burial, and provided comfort to mourners.

The Jewish community, as it grew, brought civilized behavior and societal manners into the wild frontier, despite the lack of conveniences. Newmark, explaining the simple life style, writes that there were few extravagances in the furnishings of the pioneer homes—the ordinary comforts were not available. Most of the people lived in adobe homes with whitewashed walls, (frame houses began to be built much later). Adobe was a simple construct—readily obtainable mud mixed with straw, which was then dried for months in the sun—these materials were easily accessible and the sun-baked adobe also kept the homes cool. The practical elements of the adobe homes are described by Newmark, "The composition was of such a nature that, unless protected by roofs [sic] and verandas, the mud would slowly wash away. The walls, also requiring months in which to dry, were generally three or four feet thick; the houses in the summer season were cool and comfortable, while in winter they were warm and cheerful. They were usually rec-

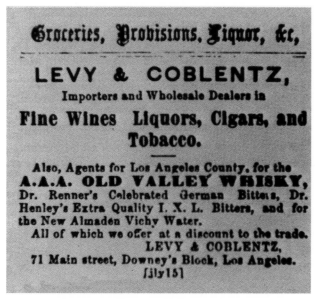

Los Angeles Daily News, *1870*

tangular in shape, and were invariably provided with patios and verandas. Conventionality prescribed no limit as to the number of rooms, but there were few, if any, 'frills' for the mere sake of style."

Plain food was plentiful—wild game, chickens, turkeys and fresh vegetables. The selling of vegetables was the harbinger of the large agriculture industry that would become an integral part of the Los Angeles economy. The business of vegetable markets began with a simple process that was called "truck-gardening." An enterprising future farmer rented a piece of land, grew vegetables, and peddled them from a wheelbarrow for fairly high prices. A prosperous truck-gardener soon was able to save enough money to buy land and a horse and wagon. The early entrepreneurs in this business were mainly Chinese vegetable men who soon began to monopolize the fresh produce market. Many of them peddled vegetables from wagons. From these very primitive beginnings emerged the farm industry, so important to the future economy of Southern California.

Phineas Banning (standing) established stagecoach lines in and out of Los Angeles with two of his investors including Harris Newmark (not pictured)

Water and its uses were critical to this region from the very early days of the pueblo, and people recognized the importance and scarcity of water. Thus emerged one of the most impor-

The "general store" became an integral part of daily commerce in towns throughout the West

The water wheel located adjacent to the Zanja Madre *(mother ditch) at South Alameda Street*

The Los Angeles River brought water to the residents of the city, but there was a need to channel the precious resource through tunnels and ditches

tant of the early public officials— the *Zanjero*, the administrator responsible for maintaining the irrigation ditches that were channeling water from the Porcunculo River (now the Los Angeles River). The *Zanjero*, or Water Commissioner, was officially in charge of the water rights beginning in 1854. He was paid more than the mayor and the institution of the *Zanjero* lasted into the early 1900s. The *Zanjero* issued permits that authorized the use of water for irrigation purposes. The *Zanjero*'s job included keeping animals and laundry out of the waterways and assuring that the water went into the proper channels according to previously agree-upon quotas.

Water use for domestic purposes was more expensive than for irrigation, and most of the water was supplied by a carrier who charged fifty cents a week for one bucket a day; no deliveries were made on Sundays. Newmark describes the duties and responsibilities of "Bill the Waterman," a tall American, about thirty years old, who wore long rubber boots that reached nearly to his waist, presenting the general appearance of a "laboring man. His somewhat rickety vehicle slowly conveyed the man and his barrel of about sixty gallon capacity from house to house. He was a wise dispenser, and quite alert to each household's needs." The quality of the water was sometimes questionable as Newmark confides:

> Bill obtained his supply
> from the Los Angeles
> River, where at best it

Photograph of the students representing the first public school in the San Fernando Valley. Public education was first introduced by Los Angeles City Councilman Morris L. Goodman in 1850

was none too clean, in part owing to the frequent passage of the river by man and beast. Animals of all kinds, including cattle, horses, sheep, pigs, mules and donkeys, crossed and recrossed the stream continually, so that the mud was incessantly stirred up, and the polluted product proved unpalatable and even, undoubtedly, unhealthful. To make matters worse, the river and the *zanjas* were the favorite bathing places, all the urchins of the hamlet disporting themselves there daily, while most of the adults also frequently immersed themselves. Both the yet unbridged stream and the *zanjas*, therefore, were repeatedly contaminated, although common sense should have protected the former…as to the latter [*zanjas*] there were ordinances drawn up by the Common Council of 1850 which prohibited the throwing of filth into fresh water designed for common use, and also forbade the washing of clothes on the *zanja* banks. This latter regulation was disobeyed by the native women, who continued to gather there, dip their soiled garments in the water, place them on stones and beat them with sticks, a method then popular for the extraction of dirt.

The Jewish community in Los Angeles was adventurous, respectful of the polyglot of ethnic differences; they were charitable and proud of their heritage, which they reflected by continuing and safeguarding the traditions of their beliefs. Wilson explains it this way:

The Jewish people were not shy about their heritage. There was a visitor in the 1860s that described Los Angeles as a city of about 3500 to 4000 people with examples of old Spanish, Indian, American and German Jews, so clearly, they [the Jews] were visible even to a casual observer and they were not shy about their Judaism. In fact, one of the really interesting things about the history of Jewish Los Angeles is that they not only helped build the Jewish community here, but also simultaneously helped build the city of Los Angeles. They called upon their non-Jewish neighbors to help build the Jewish community. For example, there was a French Catholic baker, who in 1859 under the supervision of Josephine Mark baked the first matzo in Los Angeles so that they could have it for the Passover Seder. And the Jews helped their Christian neighbors in similar ways. Rosa Newmark, Joseph's wife, organized the first fundraising benefit for St. Vincent's College when the Catholic residents decided to create a college. She organized the fair that raised the first money to get that college off the ground. That was an example of both their [the Jews] commitment to Los Angeles and their commitment to their neighbors and education.

The early Jewish pioneers showed a willingness to adapt to a rough primitive environment as well as to aspire to a sense of upward mobility. The "Israelites" as non-Jews called them, found a remarkable atmosphere of acceptance in Southern California, and they were grateful for the lack of persecution that had hounded them for centuries. They became Americans, living side by side with Protestants and Catholics. They entered politics, ran for office, joined the local societies and were socially active. In frontier Los Angeles the Jews were given the gift of freedom, that peculiarly American brand of freedom. They were allowed to thrive as they never had in the East or in European cities. The Jewish pioneers flourished in this land of opportunity and pursued new businesses, new careers, married and grew their families, and worshipped and maintained their Judaism in an atmosphere of freedom and tolerance. In Los Angeles they had found a home.

Morris L. Goodman: Los Angeles' First American-Born City Councilman

by Rabbi William M. Kramer

The American flag was hoisted high in a city that had been Mexican, when on July 3, 1850, the City Council of Los Angeles was established. Morris L. Goodman raised his right hand and said:

> I solemnly swear to support the Constitution of the United States and of the State of California, and that I will faithfully perform the duties of member of the Common Council of the City of Los Angeles, according to my best knowledge and ability.

Goodman was the only one of the seven-member Council elected on July 1 and sworn in July 3, who had not been a Mexican citizen previous to the American conquest and California statehood. Manuel Requena, Cristoval Aguilar and Julian Chavez were Mexican citizens by birth, while David W. Alexander, Alexander Bell and John Temple had acquired Mexican nationality.

As the famed pioneer California historian J.M. Guinn wrote:

> All of these except Goodman had been citizens of Mexico. Goodman chose to be an American, when seven years before taking office in Los Angeles, he took his oath as an American citizen in the Court of Common Pleas, Cincinnati, Ohio. He had been born in Bavaria in 1819 and was twenty-four years old when he was naturalized in 1843.

News of the gold rush brought Goodman to Los Angeles during 1849. Here he became a merchant, which required him to learn Spanish, for as Guinn put it, if one "wished to do business with the native Californians [he] had to acquire a speaking knowledge of the Spanish language." The language facility thus acquired by Goodman was an essential in his political career, for "the Council proceedings for four years after the organizing of that body were [conducted and] recorded in the Spanish language. Some of its members understood no other language."

Within six months of its formation, the Los Angeles City Council had only two of its original seven members left. Indeed, before sixty days had passed, two had resigned. Goodman remained in office five and one-half months, and during that time played a memorable role at the beginning of American Los Angeles.

An examination of the minutes of the City Council revealed [a part of] his contribution. On July 3, 1850, the first meeting of the Council, when no regular meeting place existed and there was no office space for the Mayor and the Recorder, it was Goodman who moved that

Fire department squad rushes up the First Street hill to put out a fire. Morris L. Goodman, a Jewish pioneer, elected to the first City Council of Los Angeles, was responsible for overseeing community services, including fire department and establishment of the first public school in the city

Maurice H. Newmark, a friend of Goodman

a committee be appointed "to secure a suitable locality."

On July 27, 1850, the City Fathers first confronted the issue of "the education of our youth." Goodman was made a committee of one to act as a school board to determine teacher qualifications and curriculum.

Four days later the Council adopted Goodman's recommendations that a teacher be hired at fifty dollars per month to teach English, French and Spanish. The teacher would be allowed to accept tuition fees, but in consideration of the city's subsidy, "the Council shall have the privilege of sending to that school six orphan boys or others whose parents are poor, and who shall be taught free of charge."

At the August 13 Council meeting, Goodman unsuccessfully sponsored a resolution, which would have permitted local merchants who lived in their stores to sell merchandise including liquor after the established closing hours.

❅ ❅ ❅

On September 13, John Temple and Morris Goodman gave a report of the Finance Committee, and recommended payment for food furnished to the prisoners in the city jail. On October 2, Goodman reported that business and gambling licenses had brought in $1,536.82 to the city treasury, having been collected by the City Marshall.

At the same meeting he also proposed that the City Recorder be authorized to pay the local Indian accolades or chiefs "the sum of twelve and one-half cents out of every fine collected from Indians whom the said accolades may bring before the Recorder for trial."

At the meeting of October 9, Goodman moved that the Council "authorize the Mayor to establish a City Police Department, consisting of a Captain and two roundsmen; the Captain to receive $100 per month and the roundsmen seventy-five dollars per month." The motion was defeated.

At the October 30 Council meeting, Goodman was one of the two men to whom proposals were referred "offering to construct a bridge across the canal which crosses the street leading to the plaza." They reported on November 6 that the bridge should be built, "and the notices in both languages be accordingly posted...calling for bids."

At the council meeting of December 18, 1850, the resignation of Morris Goodman was read and accepted.

❅ ❅ ❅

Goodman was elected a county supervisor in 1860. He was a leader in the County Democratic Committee, a sometime U.S. deputy marshal and a member of the 1852 Los Angeles Vigilantes.

In 1873, Goodman, for business reasons, moved to the city of Anaheim, then part of Los Angeles County, where he, once again, was active in political affairs. He was one of the sixteen men who called a meeting to discuss the possibility of dividing Los Angeles County. The meeting was held on April 12, 1873. Sixteen years later, in 1889, Orange County was created out of part of Los Angeles County.

A pioneer of both Los Angeles and Orange Counties, he [Goodman] deserves to be remembered. A major leader of fraternal groups, he was buried with Masonic rites in the Anaheim cemetery.

Solomon Nunes Carvalho:
Founder of the Los Angeles Jewish Community

by Rabbi William M. Kramer

As indicated in the first volume of this work it had been thought that there were no Jews of Spanish or Portuguese origin in pioneer California. They were forgotten. This field, which dealt with the historical recovery of these early West Coast settlers, was opened up by the work of Norton B. Stern and this writer in 1975.

✳ ✳ ✳

It was Solomon Nunes Carvalho, a visiting Sephardic Jewish leader from the East Coast, who assisted the Jews of Los Angeles in establishing their first organization in July 1854. Called the Hebrew Benevolent Society of Los Angeles, it had as its first president, Samuel K. Labatt, one of the sons of Abraham C. Labatt, the Sephardic Grandee of San Francisco. Samuel Labatt had been an officer of the New Orleans Hebrew Benevolent Society. At that time he and his brother Joseph Labatt operated a general merchandise store in Los Angeles. Joseph was active in the Los Angeles City Guards, a local militia. Samuel was a pioneer of Jewish anti-defamation work in Los Angeles, in association with his brother Henry of San Francisco.

Carvalho came west with John Charles Fremont's Fifth Expedition. He joined Fremont as a result of their meeting for the first time in August 1853, when the explorer was organizing what was to be his final expedition of discovery. Carvalho had served Fremont both as an artist and as a photographer. The new Los Angeles arrival was already distinguished for his drawings, paintings and as a Daguerreotypist.

John C. Fremont, leader of the Fifth Expedition, circa 1850

51

As Bertram Wallace Korn observed on Carvalho's travel to the West:

> Dr. Leon Watters, the historian of early Utah Jewry, has firmly established the fact that there were no practicing Jews in Salt Lake City at the time of Carvalho's recuperative residence there [he did however dine with Brigham Young and was a guest at a ball tendered by the governor so there were Mormon contacts but not Jewish ones]; the photographer, therefore, had no opportunity to return to Jewish life immediately. But once he arrived in Los Angeles, he brought a wealth of energy and experience to bear upon the problems of its small and struggling Jewish community. There were perhaps thirty Jews in Los Angeles at the time of Carvalho's arrival, June 1854; they had no synagogue, no cemetery, no charitable organization. Probably on the model of the organizations he had known in Charleston, Baltimore, and Philadelphia, Carvalho helped them to organize the first Jewish society in Southern California… the Hebrew Benevolent Society of Los Angeles….

As historian Andrew F. Rolle wrote, following his cross-country journey which included not only Salt Lake City but also "a watering hole called Las Vegas," Carvalho went on to another "remote Mormon settlement, San Bernardino."

Now he was in languid Southern California, a softer land of vines, olives, figs, and oranges. In June of 1854, when he finally arrived in sleepy Los Angeles, Carvalho had been gone from the East Coast for nine months. Although there was no real Jewish community in the tiny pueblo, he did find some thirty Jews living there. As they had no synagogue, he helped to organize the first Hebrew Benevolent Society. To raise funds for indigent or stranded persons he also raffled off three of his paintings at the Bella Union Hotel. One of these portraits was of California's last Mexican governor, Pio Pico.

Solomon N. Carvalho, an American-born Sephardic Jew, was the artist and photographer of Fremont's Fifth Expedition to the West in 1853 and 1854. Arriving in Los Angeles in June of 1854, Carvalho assisted in the establishment of the Hebrew Benevolent Society on July 2, 1854

The writer remembers but cannot document, seeing paintings by Carvalho in the 1980s, on exhibit and for sale, at the store and gallery of Jake Zeitlin on La Cienega Boulevard in Los Angeles. An exhibit of his work titled: "Solomon Nunes Carvalho-Painter, Photographer and Prophet in 19th Century America," was also presented at the Finegood Gallery, Bernard Milken Jewish Community Center in West Hills, from March 10 to May 26, 1991. West Hills is located in the western part of the San Fernando Valley of Los Angeles. A letter signed by Carolyn Lieber, Ruth

Rauch and Stephen J. Sass described the painter as "this country's first successful Jewish artist." The program observed the 500th anniversary of the Spanish Inquisition.

✱ ✱ ✱

In Los Angeles Carvalho decided to settle down for a while, although it is clear that it was his intention to return back East. To support himself he would use the skills that got him his appointment by John Charles Fremont. He was already recognized for these skills back East: "Solomon Carvalho brought, not only his brush and paints and palette, and his talent and training as a portrait painter to these communities in the Far West which welcomed him as a person and as an artist...."

As Rolle mentioned, Carvalho raffled off three of his paintings at the Bella Union Hotel for charity. That event was the subject of a news item: "We call the attention of our readers to a Raffle of three original beautiful paintings by Carvalho, the celebrated artist. There are only eighty chances and three prizes, therefore one ticket may draw either. The tickets are for sale at the Bella Union Hotel, and the pictures may be seen at the Daguerrean Gallery over the New Tienda [Tienda] de China."

For those unacquainted with the term "Daguerrean," the Library of Congress observed that Carvalho took all of his pictures using the Daguerreotype process, which was a direct positive process with no negative. Because of this when Carvalho returned from the West, he arranged to have Matthew Brady make negatives. The Library of Congress in 1974 had only two examples of Carvalho's work, one of which was a self-portrait and the other a portrait of his children.

✱ ✱ ✱

The "Tienda" was on the first floor of the two-floor building whose upper story served as the studio of Carvalho. And since it was at a time when merchants who were single men or married men whose wives had not come West, roomed in their stores, it is likely that it was also the residence of the artist. The "Tienda" was operated by the Sephardic Labatt brothers, Samuel K. and Joseph I., and it may be assumed that it was in mutual conversation that the three Sephardim determined to organize the Jewish community. Samuel was elected the first president and Carvalho was with him at the first meeting of the new organization. An area newspaper referred to the building:

A sketch of the first commercial orange grove planted by William Wolfskill

Looking north along Fort Street, now Broadway, 1869

The Tienda de China, on Main Street, is finished on the outside and presents a fine appearance, being an ornament to that part of the city. The upper part of this building has been occupied several weeks for offices, and Messrs. Carvalho and Johnson's Daguerrean [sic] rooms.

The editor of the *Los Angeles Star* visited Carvalho's studio/gallery and reported:

Carvalho the Artist—We have been much gratified by a visit to the studio of Mr. Carvalho. We noticed his arrival here a fortnight ago, since which he has been induced to remain and paint several portraits. The picture of Don Pio Pico, ex-Governor, is the most perfect specimen of the art of portrait painting we ever saw. We also saw unfinished portraits of the celebrated Utah Chiefs, Wakar, Grosapine, Squash Head, Petetnet; also portraits of Chiefs of the Pauvan, San Pete, Pah Utahs, Piede and Digger Indians drawn from life by Mr. Carvalho during his journey from Salt Lake — also a large number of views illustrating the whole country…. Those who want a superior portrait, would do well to take advantage of this opportunity. Mr. Carvalho has also ordered the apparatus for taking Daguerreotype likenesses, which will enable him to satisfy the tastes of the most fastidious.

In later years he did an oil painting of Abraham Lincoln which was acquired by Los Angeles historian Justin C. Turner and given to Brandeis University. Turner was an advisor to *Western States Jewish Historical Quarterly*, and he provided a copy of the Lincoln portrait which was printed in its July 1970 issue.

❊ ❊ ❊

In addition to being a painter for Fremont, Carvalho was the expedition's photographer and an article on this other skill of his also appeared in the press:

Enamel for Daguerreotypes. A valuable discovery with Daguerreotypes has been made by Mr. S.N. Carvalho, an artist of Charleston S.C. It has been hitherto necessary to enclose Daguerreotypes in cases and cover them with glass, as the least friction destroyed the work of sun and shade. Mr. Carvalho has discovered a perfectly transparent enamel, insoluble by all ordinary agents, a thin coating of which being spread upon a plate, it may be carried about without other protection or sent by post to any part of the world. The enamel produces no perceptible effect upon the picture.

❊ ❊ ❊

Carvalho's arrival in Los Angeles in June 1854, triggered a major event in the founding of the organized Jewish community of the city. The Jewish community wasn't very old.

When the Federal Census of 1850 was taken in Los Angeles, a community of eight Jews was recorded. All of them were bachelors who lived in their stores on the ground floor of the city's leading commercial building, a two-story structure located at the southeast corner of Aliso and Los Angeles Streets. The number had increased from eight to about thirty at the time that Carvalho visited the small town.

The month after he came to Los Angeles with two other Sephardim he was instrumental in establishing what is now known as the Jewish Family Service of the Jewish Federation of Los Angeles from which the latter organization derived. He was recognized as a founder of this antecedent organization, known as the Hebrew Benevolent Society, which had its first formal meeting on July 2, 1854. It was described in the press:

> The Israelites of the city formed themselves into a society under the name of the Hebrew Benevolent Society. At a meeting the following gentlemen were elected officers of the Society: S.K. Labatt, president; Jacob Elias, secretary and treasurer; S. Lazard and H. Goldberg, trustees.

> The five purposes of the society were to act as a burial society, a social-fraternal club, a Jewish philanthropic agency, a general charity composed only of Jews, and as High Holy Day or "at need" synagogue.

As Thomas Cohen said, "This organization was the first such group in Los Angeles and marked the beginning of community effort and cooperation. Our present vast and complex Jewish community structure of greater Los Angeles stems from this small beginning."

❋ ❋ ❋

As is true in each new Jewish community the first need is for a cemetery. Worship services could be conducted in any home or rented hall, but sanctified burial space was the natural priority. It certainly was in Los Angeles where street killings were proportionately as common then as now, and drive-by shootings were invented on horseback. Also, infant deaths

One of the homes of Governor Pio Pico located in the community of Whittier

Selling hot tamales

and deaths resulting from infectious diseases, which took the lives of children and adults without warning, were commonplace.

At the first Jewish community meeting on July 2, 1854 it had been determined to incorporate and incorporation took place four days later on July 6, for the purpose, among others, of owning and holding certain real estate to be devoted to burial purposes for deceased members of the Jewish faith. The very next day, at the City Council session, the minutes record the fact that the Mayor said that the Council might designate a "…piece of public land for a graveyard for those belonging to the Hebrew Church."

❋ ❋ ❋

Carvalho came to California experienced in Jewish life, friend of some of its leaders and acquainted with its institutions on the Atlantic seaboard, and therefore, as Korn said in 1954, in addition to his professional skills "he also brought that love for organized Jewish community life which had been aroused in several of the oldest Jewish communities in North America and transmitted it to the pioneers in a town which eventually was to contain the third largest Jewish community in the United States."

As various sources reveal, Carvalho's Sephardic Jewish background was impressive. It was said that on his mother's side he was descended from Moses Cohen D'Azevedo who had been the *haham* [spiritual leader] of Spanish-Portuguese Jewry in London in much of the 18th Century. Similarly, serving as the *hazzan* [cantor] of the Portuguese Jewish community of the Barbados Island was his uncle Emanuel Carvalho. The *hazzan* later moved to various places including New York and Charleston, and then to Philadelphia, where he is credited with having published the first Hebrew grammar book written by a Jew and published in the United States.

Korn also pointed out that Carvalho had studied Bible as a child and continued his learning of Scripture until as an older adult, he wrote a volume on *Mosaic Cosmology*. His written and spoken language had a scriptural quality, he quoted the Torah and Psalms with ease. He was also the son of a man who had created the congregations known as the Reformed Society of Israelites in Charleston. Carvalho's first writings appeared in the *Occident*, where he defended Rabbi Julius Eckman who was under attack in the Charlestown Jewish community and who later became the first ordained rabbi to serve California.

Solomon N. Carvalho accompanied Colonel John C. Fremont on his cross-country expedition of 1853, as an artist. Upon his arrival in June 1854, he helped in the organization of the Hebrew Benevolent Society.

Recognition of Carvalho's role in founding the organized Jewish community of Los Angeles came about in a resolution adopted by that group and printed in a national Jewish publication:

> Resolved unanimously, that the thanks of this meeting be tendered to Mr. S.N. Carvalho for his valuable services in organizing this society, and that he be elected an honorary member; also that these proceedings be published in the *Occident.*

First Jewish Community Site Located in Chavez Ravine

by Thomas Cohen

California State Historical Landmark Number 822 was dedicated amid colorful ceremonies on the morning of September 29, 1968, in the Chavez Ravine, Los Angeles. This first Jewish community site was formerly the sacred burial grounds established by the Hebrew Benevolent Society of Los Angeles in 1855. The dedication was the culmination of research begun by Dr. Norton Stern in the fall of 1966, who was soon joined in this task by the writer of these lines. This joint research, by Stern and Cohen, was partially motivated by the fact that although the existence of this old cemetery was well-known, its exact location was not. An accurate and documented location was needed to proceed.

None of the known reference sources on Los Angeles Jewish history indicated the precise location of the cemetery other than that of the corner of Lilac Terrace and Lookout Drive. This corner, a mile from the city hall, is just south of the Dodger Stadium in the Chavez Ravine. Subsequently it was realized that the land previously occupied by the cemetery is now being used by the Naval Reserve Armory.

To relocate the site of this first Jewish community property required a study of the history of the Hebrew Benevolent Society of Los Angeles and a title-search through various official city and county archives. This was undertaken.

On July 2, 1854, a group of Jewish men met in Los Angeles to organize a benevolent society. The contemporary newspaper account states that:

> The Israelites of this city formed themselves into a society under the name of Hebrew Benevolent Society. At a meeting held on the 2d inst. [installed] the following gentlemen were elected officers of the Society: S.K. Labatt, president; Chas. Shachno, vice-president; Jacob Elias, secretary and treasurer; S. Lazard and H. Goldberg, trustees.

> This organization was the first such group in Los Angeles and marked the beginning of community effort and cooperation. Our present vast and complex Jewish community structure of greater Los Angeles stemmed from this small beginning one hundred and fifteen years ago.

The organization's purpose is stated in the preamble to its Constitution and By-Laws:

Whereas: the Israelites of this city, being desirous of procuring a piece of ground suitable for the purpose of a burying ground for the deceased of their own faith, and also to appropriate a portion of their time and means to the holy cause of benevolence—unite themselves for these purposes, under the name and style of 'The Hebrew Benevolent Society' of Los Angeles.

On July 6, 1854, the society incorporated, "…for the purpose, among others, of owning and holding certain real estate to be devoted to burial purposes for deceased members of the Jewish faith." The very next day, at the City Council session, the minutes record the fact that the Mayor said that the Council might designate a "…piece of public land for a graveyard for those belonging to the Hebrew Church." The Council indicated that this matter should come up properly by petition with an accompanying map. Jacob Elias, secretary and treasurer of the society, engaged Mr. George Hansen, a surveyor, to make a map of survey of a plot of land suitable for a cemetery. The survey was made on July 12, 1854. At the July 14 City Council session, the society submitted a petition asking for land for a burial ground.

Later a request was forwarded to his Honor the Mayor and the City Council:

Gentlemen: A petition was handed to your honorable body…requesting the donation of pi(e)ce of ground to be used as a burial ground and other benevolent purposes, for the benefit of the Hebrew Benevolent Society of this place. Desiring to know your intention with regard to it, we beg leave to call your attention to the same. By order of the Board of Trustees, Los Angeles, September 20, 1854. Jacob Elias, Secty.

The city approved the request and title was ordered made out on September 22, 1854. Title was granted to the Hebrew Benevolent Society on April 9, 1855:

Between the corporation known as the 'Mayor, Recorder and Common Council of the City of Los Angeles'…and…of the Hebrew Benevolent Society of Los Angeles…in consideration of the sum of one dollar…do grant, convey and quit claim…that certain tract of land…North 84 degrees West two hundred yards thence North 42 degrees East seventy-five yards, thence South 48 degrees East two hundred yards, thence South 42 degrees West seventy-five yards…as a burying ground for the Israelites forever.

The recordation took place on April 17, 1855. After taking possession, enclosing the property was necessary. The grounds of the cemetery were on the gentle slopes of a hill with no adjoining neighbors. An advertisement for the construction of a cemetery wall and gates was placed in the *Los Angeles Star*.

On June 17, 1869, the Common Council of the city approved the granting of additional land to the Hebrew Benevolent Society for their cemetery. At the same time the society granted a portion of the existing to the city for a street. This was approved by the Mayor and Trustees of the society on June 25, 1869. The recordation of June 26, 1869, included the following: "…for the better regulation and uniformity of the streets…and for better accommodations…in its cemetery…." The proposed street was to be located along the new eastern boundary of the cemetery.

From 1855 to 1869, the cemetery was not located with any adjoining land tracts and this mutual exchange would correct this. The location of the cemetery would be in line with the eastern boundary of the 35-acre lot No. 6 of Block 45. Some adjustments were made on the

The original Jewish cemetery, established in 1854 (see arrow), located in Chavez Ravine, 1900

A California Registered Historical Landmark of the first Jewish site in Los Angeles (its cemetery); the marker is located in Chavez Ravine adjacent to Dodger Stadium and behind the Fire Department Training Center. The plaque reads: "The Hebrew Benevolent Society of Los Angeles (1854) **first charitable organization in the city... [author's bold].***" This property represented the first organized community effort by the pioneer Jewish settlers*

Los Angeles' first tennis club before the fashionable "lightly-attired" player

boundaries at this time.

The poor condition of the road leading to the cemetery brought a petition from the society to the Mayor and Common Council dated March 13, 1873, stating "That the main and only entrance to said cemetery is on the promised street…(and) that said street be immediately opened…as agreed." The petition also noted that the cemetery was now enclosed with a substantial picket fence, that it was laid out in blocks and avenues, that these avenues would be planted with trees and ornamented and that all this will be at considerable expense to the society. The petition called attention to the mutual deeds and covenants of June 25, 1869.

Sometime later, Mr. Maurice Kremer, then president of the society, sent a letter to the city concerning the street, "…so that vehicles can go to our cemetery with safety." This was done because no satisfactory response was received concerning the petition of March 13, 1873.

In 1875, Samuel Meyer, president of the society, noted in a letter to the city of Los Angeles that the bridge ordered built by the Board of Public Works over the arroyo was not built. And the street proposed in 1869 was never built, because of the hilly terrain.

✳ ✳ ✳

In January, 1870, Mrs. Joseph (Rosa) Newmark organized the Ladies' Hebrew Benevolent Society. The officers were: Mrs. W. Kalisher, president; Mrs. Harris Newmark, vice-president; Mrs. John Jones, treasurer; Mrs. B. Katz, secretary; and Mrs. A. Baer, collector. It was this society's "function to prepare the dead for interment, and to keep proper vigil over the remains until the time of burial."

Care and upkeep of the cemetery was the responsibility of the Hebrew Benevolent Society until 1891. In January of that year, the Home of Peace Society was founded by Jewish women of Los Angeles, led by Mrs. Maurice Kremer. This group was established for the purpose of beautifying the cemetery and maintaining it properly and they took charge of the grounds.

We know that by the late 1890s, the board of Congregation B'nai B'rith included a cemetery committee. Herman W. Hellman, president, wrote to the board of directors and members on October 28, 1900, as follows: "The purchase of a new cemetery ground is called to the attention of the members and hope the new board will take this important matter into consideration." In January, 1902, Congregation B'nai B'rith proposed:

> …to establish a Jewish cemetery in which Jews belonging to any congregation in Los Angeles can be buried at uniform prices; that this congregation will donate to the Hebrew Benevolent Society a piece or part of our cemetery in which to bury the indigent Jewish dead.

On January 28 the board recommended the purchase of thirty acres of land at $150 per acre. A special meeting was called on January 30, which adopted the recommendations. One of these was that special consideration would be given to members of the Hebrew Benevolent Society, who were in good standing and members before January 1, 1902.

A map of survey was drawn in May 1902, of the B'nai B'rith Cemetery on Whittier Boulevard to the east of Los Angeles. This cemetery contains about thirty acres of level ground while the old one had about 4.2 acres, which was not level. The dedication of the new cemetery was held on May 18, 1902.

On June 30, 1902, the Hebrew Benevolent Society filed a petition with the City Council asking that the city relinquish its reversionary interest in their cemetery property so that part of the land could be sold. The petition reads in part:

> No attempt has ever been made to realize profit from the use of the lands conveyed to it by the city; on the contrary, amounts received from parties using the same have been barely sufficient to defray the expense of care and maintenance. At the same time, the society has assumed the burden of burying such a number of objects of its beneficence as that at the present time upwards of one-half of the bodies in the cemetery are the remains of those, who, but for the work of your petitioner, would have been the objects of public charity.

Sketch of the store of the Hellman family, supporters of the Hebrew Benevolent Society

During the period of its existence your petitioner, in common with the Hebrew Ladies Benevolent Society, an auxiliary organization, has expended over one hundred thousand dollars for charitable uses, and takes pride in saying that through its efforts and expenditures, and the efforts and expenditures of the Hebrew Ladies Benevolent Society, the municipality has not been called upon at any time, to the knowledge of the officers and of your petitioner, to render aid or assistance of any kind to any member of the Jewish faith, and the Jewish poor have not in any manner been a burden upon the city.

The growth of our city, the increase of population, and the development of the oil industry on the lands adjacent to the cemetery site, have tended to render the same unfit to be devoted to that purpose. It has become almost inaccessible, completely surrounded by oil wells, derricks and tanks, and brick yards and kilns, the smoke from which has so discolored the shrubbery and monuments that they have become black and unsightly.

The foregoing considerations have rendered it absolutely necessary that the members of the faith should procure a new site for the burial of their dead, which has been accomplished through the efforts of the Congregation B'nai B'rith, by the acquisition of land for that purpose without the limits of the city, to which site it is the desire of your petitioner that the remains buried in its present cemetery should be removed. Your petitioner, being without the necessary means with which to defray the expense of removing the bodies of the indigent dead buried at its present cemetery, has devised the plan of selling the real estate at present owned by it and devoting the means realized therefrom to that purpose. To do this it will be necessary that the City of Los Angeles relinquish its reversionary interest in the cemetery property, and your petitioner respectfully requests such relinquishments at the hands of your honorable body.

The early days of downtown Pasadena and its Colorado Boulevard

Traveling on horseback to Boyle Heights and East Los Angeles during the pioneer days

As the land will be entirely unsaleable until the removal of all bodies is accomplished, no harm can come to the city from granting this request. The removal of the cemetery to a point without the limits of the city is exceedingly desirable to the municipality, and this can only be accomplished by enabling your petitioner to raise the funds therefore by a sale of property.

The petition was signed by J. Schlesinger, president, and Victor Harris, secretary. The Land Commission on July 7, 1902, recommended to the City Council that the city relinquish its reversionary interests to the Hebrew cemetery property. This was approved by the City Council on September 15, 1902, by a 6-to-0 vote. The city ordinance relinquishing the reversionary interest included a quit-claim deed to the property. This deed was recorded on October 27, 1902.

※ ※ ※

The first burial in the old cemetery had been in 1858, and by 1902 there had been over 360 burials. Markers and monuments of various kinds were used to locate the graves. Generally slabs of white marble, one to two inches thick, were utilized. Old photographs reveal that some wooden markers were used. More elaborate monuments were made of granite and other stone. Many of these markers and monuments can be seen at the Home of Peace Memorial Park today

The task of removal began on November 8, 1902. The remains of many of the well-known pioneer figures of the Los Angeles Jewish community were moved from 1902 to 1905 to the B'nai B'rith Cemetery.

Mr. S.S. Federman, president of the Hebrew Benevolent Society, prepared a petition for leave to sell real estate on October 19, 1905. The petition, filed with the Superior Court of Los Angeles County, states that the Hebrew Benevolent Society of Los Angeles,

> …was organized and exists solely for benevolent purposes and not for profit…(that) no burials have taken place for the past two years…(and) that a portion of the premises hereinabove described has never been used or utilized for burial purposes, and that such a portion of said premises the same is not required and is not in use for burial purposes, nor will same be required or used for such purposes, and it is for the best interest of this corporation that such land be sold…(and that this land is) desired by the City of Los Angeles for the purpose of erecting and maintaining thereon a detention hospital, and that there is, at the present time, an opportunity to sell the same at a fair and reasonable price, to wit,

the sum of two thousand dollars; that if such opportunity is not availed of the same cannot be hereafter sold at any fair evaluation, because of the erection and maintenance by the city on premises adjacent thereto of its said detention hospital and Pest House for the care and isolation of persons suffering from contagious diseases.

The petition was ordered granted October 27, 1905, and the judgment on November 6, 1905. The City of Los Angeles lost no time in using this land, formerly a part of the Hebrew Cemetery. Plans were prepared for an eight-inch vitrified sewer line which would run through the length of the property from the Pest House on the northwest to Bernard Street on the east. This sewer line would serve about ten buildings on the city property.

After 1902, several cemeteries were established for the purpose of providing burial according to the Orthodox ritual. The Beth Israel Cemetery is owned by Congregation Beth Israel, which was founded in 1892. They bought their cemetery in 1906 and their first burials were in January, 1907. It adjoins the Home of Peace Memorial Park. On one occasion the Ladies Hebrew Benevolent Society paid the bill for two burials at the Beth Israel Cemetery, then indicated that no more such bills would be accepted. This may have

Maurice and Matilda Kremer (not pictured) of Los Angeles had twelve children. Maurice married Matilda Newmark in Los Angeles on April 9, 1856, with her father, Joseph Newmark officiating. Kremer held a number of civic offices in Los Angeles including city clerk, tax collector, and member of the school board. Four of the Kremer children are shown in this 1887 photograph. Clockwise from the left are Agnes, Fred, Eda, and Abraham Kremer, the youngest, born in 1877 at the family home at Fourth and Broadway (Fort Street), which is now downtown Los Angeles

An old adobe saloon during the Wild West days

shown their preference for the B'nai B'rith Cemetery as they had close associations with Congregation B'nai B'rith. Some remains were moved from the old Hebrew cemetery to the Beth Israel Cemetery since there are at least nine graves with monuments inscribed before 1902.

✳ ✳ ✳

The *Chevra Chesed Shel Emeth* was organized on February 7, 1909, for the purpose of providing "proper burial of Orthodox Jews" and for buying a burial ground. Their Mount Zion Cemetery adjoins the Home of Peace Memorial Park. Congregation Agudas Achim Anshei Sefarad organized on August 23, 1909, for conducting "religious services according to Orthodox Jewish ritual, (and) to buy…real property (for) cemetery purposes." This organization changed its name to Congregation Agudas Achim in 1921. The Agudas Achim Cemetery also adjoins the Home of Peace Memorial Park. The congregation merged with Rodef Sholom-Etz Chaim Congregation in recent years and is now known as Judea Congregation.

The majority of remains from the old cemetery in Chavez Ravine were moved to the B'nai B'rith Cemetery in May, June and July, 1910. They were all located in the Benevolent section of the new cemetery, as approved by the Board of Directors of the Congregation B'nai B'rith. By the end of 1910 all removals were completed.

✳ ✳ ✳

On January 19, 1916, the first joint meeting between the Ladies Hebrew Benevolent Society and the Hebrew Benevolent Society was held. In attendance were Mrs. Herman W. Frank, president, Mrs. P. Lazarus, Mrs. V. Katze, Dr. S. Hecht, Mr. I. Norton, Mr. P. Stein and Mr. A. Shapiro. The purpose of the joint meetings, which were held for two years, was to combine both organizations into one.

In 1918, the amalgamated organizations created the Jewish Aid Society of Los Angeles. The incorporators on May 29, 1918 were: Alexander Meyer, Rev. S. Hecht, M.N. Newmark,

Los Encino, 1928. Originally this property was granted by Pio Pico to the Mission Indians, but was later taken from them by Vicente de la Osa, a land speculator in the 1850s. The old adobe on the property was known as Osa Adobe; property was later used as a roadhouse for travelers. Eugene and his brother Philippe Garnier purchased Rancho Encino with the intention of using the land to breed fine Merino sheep for wool. The Garnier farmhouse was built of limestone quarried on Rancho Encino by Eugene Garnier around 1870. The house featured sleeping rooms, a kitchen and a dining room. The Rancho included the adjacent old de la Osa Adobe and its property as well

Dr. D.W. Edelman, Philip Stein, A. Shapiro, Mrs. H. W. Frank, Mrs. I. Eisner, Mrs. V. Katze, Mrs. Carl Stein, Mrs. Alexander Brownstein, and Mrs. H.H. Lissner. Miss Dora Berres was the first professional social worker brought into the Jewish community. She served as the executive secretary of the Jewish Aid Society of Los Angeles from 1918 to 1923. Other executives of this and succeeding organizations were Herman Blumenthal, Mrs. Lenore Livine, Mrs. Emma Shencup, Miss Freda Mohr (from 1932 to November 1966), and presently Theodore R. Isenstadt. The first president of the Jewish Aid Society of Los Angeles was Mr. Alexander Meyer, who held this office until 1934.

On April 12, 1928, the Hebrew Benevolent Society gave a grant deed to the Jewish Aid Society conveying title to the remaining cemetery property. This was done, though the Hebrew Benevolent Society had been defunct for ten years. It was considered unfinished business by the surviving trustees. Recordation was requested by the Title Insurance and Trust Company on April 27, 1928.

Emphasis of the times was on social and personal problems. Relief and aid were not the solution to these problems, so the name of the organization was changed in August, 1929. The new name was the Jewish Social Service Bureau.

For a short period in the 1930s the remaining cemetery property was leased out as a rub-

The four-horse "tally-ho" was a primary means of travel to the vast outskirts of greater Los Angeles

bish dump. In 1938, the federal government proposed a Naval Armory adjacent to the vacant cemetery land. This adjacent land included the portion purchased by the City of Los Angeles in 1905 from the Hebrew Benevolent Society. Arrangements were made and the city conveyed its land, by grant deed to the federal government. On November 30, 1942, a "Lis Pendens" action was taken by the federal government concerning the remaining vacant cemetery land. On April 29, 1943, the Jewish Social Service Bureau, with the approval of the Jewish Welfare Federation Board, sold the remaining cemetery property to the federal government for $4,200. Final judgment was on August 23, 1943. This ended Jewish ownership of the cemetery property except for the sub-surface oil, mineral and gas rights which are retained by the Jewish Family Service. These oil rights still bring a small amount of royalties annually.

✳ ✳ ✳

The Jewish Social Service Bureau changed its name on August 15, 1946, to the Jewish Family Service of Los Angeles. It had been certified by the Family Service Association of America and in fact, became the first agency in the State of California to gain certification and full membership in the FSA.

On September 8, 1967, Dr. Norton Stern and this writer submitted a detailed three-page memorandum to the Jewish Federation Council of Greater Los Angeles, through Mr. Julius Bisno, associate executive director. This paper outlined the historical facts and enumerated the data collected, suggesting that the Jewish Federation Council would be the proper party to make application for a State Historical Marker for this first site of the Los Angeles Jewish

Sketch of the old town of Los Angeles

community. In October the executive committee, and on November 14, 1967, the board of directors indicated their approval of the project. On November 1, a request was sent to the Board of Public Works, City of Los Angeles, asking permission to place the monument, if granted, on city land along Lilac Terrace in Chavez Ravine. This city land use was approved by the board on November 20, 1967.

In mid-December the application for a California Registered Historical Landmark was made out by Dr. Norton Stern and this writer, signed by Victor M. Carter, president of the Jewish Federation Council and sent to the California Historical Landmarks Advisory Committee at Sacramento. This committee met at El Molino Viejo in San Marino on January 24, 1968, and unanimously approved the historical landmark. Julius Bisno and Dr. Stern appeared for the applicants.

The application had pointed out that three "firsts" were involved: 1) This was the first property owned and administered by the Los Angeles Jewish Community; 2) The Hebrew Benevolent Society of Los Angeles was the first charitable organization in the city; and 3) It was the first sacred Jewish burial place in Southern California.

It was on the issue of the second point, that in February, the State Park Historian asked for additional information. To conclusively prove that the Hebrew Benevolent Society was the first charitable group to be established in Los Angeles, and to clear the way for the wording which was to appear on the plaque to be placed on the site, Dr. Norton Stern undertook a special research project on this point. The results were submitted by letter to Julius Bisno on March 28, 1968, and submitted by him to the State Park Historian in Sacramento by telephone. Following this, plans were laid for preparation of the site and the date of dedication was set.

The historical research was greatly enhanced by photographs of the Hebrew Benevolent Society cemetery as it had been. Dr. Edwin H. Carpenter, western bibliographer for the

Huntington Library, provided a photograph [see page 59] of the site taken from the Fort Moore hill in 1885. He also provided the lead to Mr. Everett G. Hager of San Pedro, who had four photographs taken within the cemetery about 1901. Mr. William Mason, of the history department of the Los Angeles County Museum, supplied an 1890 photograph of the cemetery. Maps were provided by the city and country departments and by the County Museum.

Mr. Morton M. Silverman of Malinow and Silverman, accepted the responsibility of preparing the site for the dedication. This was cleared, a foundation pit dug and a concrete base for the heavy granite monument was prepared. The Lodge brothers, Max and Sidney, of the Lodge Monument Company, donated the monument and affixed the bronze plaque fabricated by the state to it.

Planning and arrangements for the dedication ceremonies were under the supervision of Julius Bisno. Victor M. Carter, president of the Jewish Federation Council, officiated and addressed the gathering, followed by Dr. George Piness, president of the Wilshire Boulevard Temple, with concluding remarks by Los Angeles County Supervisor Ernest E. Debs. Numerous community leaders including city, county and state dignitaries were present at the dedication, held on Sunday morning, September 19, 1968. About three hundred people attended, among whom were many descendants of pioneer Jewish families and students of Los Angeles Jewish religious schools. When Victor M. Carter unveiled the handsome bronze plaque, the following inscription was read by all:

**The Hebrew Benevolent Society of Los Angeles
(1854), first charitable organization in the city,
acquired this site by deed on April 9, 1855
from the city council for a sacred burial ground.
This property represented the first organized
community effort by the pioneer Jewish settlers.**

**California Registered Historical Landmark No. 822
plaque placed by the State Department of Parks and
Recreation in cooperation with the Jewish Federation
Council of Greater Los Angeles.
September 29, 1968**

Letter from Mother to Daughter

The day after the marriage of her youngest daughter, Mrs. Joseph Newmark of Los Angeles wrote this letter to her second oldest daughter, Mrs. Harris (Sarah) Newmark, then living in New York City. The letter describes the preparations for the wedding, the clothing worn by the principals and members of the family, the home of the newly united couple, the furnishings of that home, names of the guests at the wedding and the gifts given and sent to the bride and groom. In addition, a number of other matters are referred to, such as the novelty of ice cream in Los Angeles, the excitement attendant upon receiving a telegram, the food served at the wedding dinner, etc. It contains a wealth of social history from more than one hundred years ago and is virtually unique as a contemporary document from the City of the Angels.

Los Angeles, November 21, 1867

My Dearly Loved Sarah:

According to promise I am now seated to give you a full description of loved Harriet's wedding, house and trousseau. I will send this by overland, as I think you will get it before the steamer letters.

I will commence with her trousseau. Her wedding dress was a white satin under-dress with net over made much shorter, looped up with orange blossoms, the waist trimmed with lace appliqué, double row around the bosom, with a row of orange blossoms in the center; veil tucked up to the waist, very long; wreath of orange blossoms, the latest style, not to go around the head, but to hang down each side nearly to the waist; white satin boots.

Dear Eugene brought her bridal dress from San Francisco, that is to say, the material. Mrs. Cohen made it very tastefully and fitted her, and it fitted beautifully. She looked so sweet and unassuming. Everybody said she was the prettiest bride they ever saw. I can assure you, dear Eugene is not a little proud of her. He was dressed very nicely, all in white, black swallow-tailed coat and white necktie, and embroidered bosom shirt. He looked very well.

Rosa Levy married Joseph Newmark in New York in 1835. She arrived in Los Angeles with her family in 1854. The Newmarks had six children, four girls and two boys. Rosa is known to have initiated the founding of Los Angeles' first women's charitable organization, the Ladies' Hebrew Benevolent Society (1870), and she was a fundraiser for Los Angeles' institution of higher learning, now known as Loyola University

Many persons told me and your loved father we should be very happy having daughters all married well, and certainly I am very thankful to our heavenly Father that He has been so gracious to us. If only my blessed Edward's knee was well, and my loved Carrie's eyes, and if only we all lived in one city, but I suppose that would be asking too much and we must be as satisfied as we possibly can.

She has a beautiful light lavender corded silk dress trimmed with white satin and crystal beads, which dear Eugene also brought her from San Francisco, and appliqué set, and a handsome black sacque and white satin hat trimmed with pearls, which is what she will wear, please God, the day he calls.

I can assure you I feel very happy as she has a very nice young man for a husband. She could not have done better had she been very accomplished.

She has, of course, several other dresses, which I believe I wrote you about in one of my journals. She has a set of undergarments made with her Valenciennes lace insertion and trucks, one with frills, four with embroidered Spanish work and several others. I can assure you she has very nice clothes, and thanks to Almighty God, they are both as happy as possible, and Heaven grant they may always remain so.

The home is beautifully furnished, good enough for any city. I will give you a description of it as minutely as possible. It has a very large hall, oil clothed, with hand stand and hall lamp. Parlor, dining room and kitchen, are on one side, bedroom, spare room, bathroom and a servant's room on the other side. I will commence with the parlor furniture: horsehair sofa and chairs, black and walnut marble-top table, étagère with closet, rosewood cabinet piano, lace curtains with scarlet draperies and plenty of ornaments which were presents. Brussels carpets in parlor and dining room to match, as they have folding doors between. A beautiful sideboard, marble-top with two shelves with looking glass, walnut center table, and a beautiful work table (cost thirty dollars) and chairs.

Supporters of the Ladies Hebrew Benevolent Society (Jewish Family Service), 1882

Kitchen: a beautiful cooking stove with a broiler like loved Carrie's, but the stove is superior and has everything necessary for use. Their bedroom furniture, of course, includes a high-backed bedstead, bureau, washstand, nightstand, wardrobe and chairs. The curtains are the same in the parlor, Brussels carpet, and also the same in the spare room with the cottage furniture, bathroom oil-clothed, servant's room has carpet and necessary furniture. In their bedroom is a handsome toilet set of buff, gold and white.

The weather was beautiful on the wedding day. The ceremony was in the parlor, which was decorated with flowers. The dinner was in the dining room, and in the evening, dear Eugene gave a very nice party at the Bella Union Hotel. What do you think of us having ice cream? This is something new for Los Angeles, and everybody says it was the nicest party ever given in Los Angeles.

Now I will tell you what we all wore. Loved Matilda, a Bismarck silk dress, which dear Eugene brought her from San Francisco, trimmed with white satin and crystal beads. Loved Carrie, her wedding dress made high and trimmed with satin and pearl beads. The blessed children, Rachel and Emily, white alpaca trimmed with scarlet silk. Darling Jeannette wore a very handsome white dress with Valenciennes lace and insertion, which was sent from Paris as a present. I think I have given you the full particulars as far as possible. I wore my lavender silk that I wore at loved Carrie's.

We sent you a wedding cake by express. It will not leave San Francisco until the steamer of the 30th. You will please give all the loved family some and also send a piece to Louis. It is nothing extra, but the best we could get there. Loved Harriet and Eugene's names are on it in icing, but I cannot say if it will be there when you get it. At any rate, I thought you would like to have some of the wedding cake.

I don't know if I wrote you who the bridesmaids and groomsmen were. They were Constant Meyer and Matilda Edelman, Loeb and Augusta Mallard, Herman Hellman and Josephine Mallard, I.W. Hellman and blessed Emily. He went to San Francisco just before the wedding, for business, and brought my sweet Emily a pair of gilt leather boots and white kid gloves. Loved Rachel was a bridesmaid with Alphonse Lazard. My sweet Emily said she wished Emily Newmark and Estelle were here to be bridesmaids. You may be sure there were many more wished the same. We missed you all very much, my loved ones, you may be sure. What would I not have given for you to be present.

I felt more reconciled when we received your dispatch, my loved Meyer, Sarah and Harris, as it really appeared we were much closer, knowing you sent it that very day, and we received it while taking dinner. You can imagine the excitement it caused. I heard the bell ring and thought that it likely that it was a dispatch and sure enough it was. Dear Eugene read it aloud and everyone was pleased to hear it.

Governor Downey and Mrs. Downey were present. Also the French Consul, Dr. Griffin, and Mrs. Sichel. Mr. Sichel had to leave by the steamer the day before, on business. Mrs. Ogier was also present, and two Mr. and Mrs. Hellmans, and Mr. and Mrs. S. Meyer and, of course, Mr. and Mrs. Edelman.

We had a very nice dinner and had a colored man to cook the poultry. Loved Carrie made the pies; loved Matilda the chicken salad and jellies. I can assure you the chief burden rested on her. You know how handy she is with fixing. Mrs. Ogier came over on Thursday evening to help. We missed you all very much, my loved Sarah; you were always very busy. I expect you kept up the wedding day and I hope you were all very merry. On the other side I will give you a list of the presents.

Give my love to all the dear family. I will answer their letters soon. Your loved father, Matilda, Kremer, Carrie, Sol, Edward, Harriet, Eugene, Myer, my loved Ma and all the loved family. Adieu. God bless you all, is the prayer of your devoted mother,

Rosa Newmark

Kiss the blessed children and also darling Nellie.

CHAPTER THREE

Jewish Presence in Business and Politics Established in Los Angeles: 1860-1879

Rabbi Abraham Wolf Edelman, who arrived in June of 1862, was affectionately known as the "Jewish padre" of the pueblo of Los Angeles

Publicity in the East lauded California's mild climate and fertile soil. Boosterism was having a very positive effect on the pioneer immigration...

The same spirit of unrest that defined the catalyst for the Civil War that was being fought in much of the country was also present in the uneasy political and ethnic issues that began to surface in remote Southern California. In a rather surprising reflection of the prevailing politics in the 1850s, the national election of 1856 revealed that the majority of voters in Los Angeles were pro-slavery. The Democratic pro-slavery candidate outpolled the Republican by nearly two to one. In Los Angeles many transplants from the South were looking to extend slavery into Mexico and Central America. Mexico was slandered repeatedly in the California newspapers, and rumblings of anti-Black and anti-Chinese sentiment were evident and pervasive. The Know Nothing Party surfaced on a platform that was anti-Oriental and anti-Hispanic. Although the Know Nothing Party did not survive, its underlying concepts and racial discrimination continued to gain momentum.

Compounding the other political issues that were prevalent in Los Angeles during this era of rapid growth there also existed a significant inequity between the revenues collected by the southern part of the state as compared to the northern section. Although the city of Los Angeles was the center of state politics in Southern California in the 1850s, it had a disproportionately smaller number of representatives (as compared to Northern California). As a result, Southern California was virtually powerless to correct an imbalance in the tax system, where the sparsely populated South paid double the amount of taxes as the economically dom-

The elegant Pico House, the town's prestigious hotel, 1869

inant North. Civic leaders were determined to discover a way to correct the financial imbalance; their goal was to substantially increase the population, which would generate additional revenues received from taxes. They understood that in order to accomplish this goal, it would be necessary to clean up the tawdry reputation of the pueblo and launch an image campaign that would praise the wonders of this golden town.

Train station serving local Southern California communities, 1860s

In the years during and following the Civil War hostilities, the pueblo made tremendous strides to break out of and eradicate the Hell Town atmosphere characterized by crime and gambling. The pioneers began to build the city in earnest—a city that they hoped would attract civilized members of society, hardworking and industrious citizens that would increase the tax roles. In the spirit of growth and civic pride many innovations in the institutional infrastructure were developed. In the 1850s Los Angeles saw its first public school, post office, the first newspaper, Protestant church and Jewish synagogue.

Other milestones that enhanced and expanded the growing city began to dominate the landscape. The first oranges were shipped by William Wolfskill in 1856, and 1858 saw the Arcadia Block Building erected by Abel Stearns, the beginning of the first "grand" business buildings in Los Angeles. That same year Andrew Boyle purchased land on a hill called *Paredon Blanco* (White Cliffs) that would later become Boyle Heights. In adjacent Orange County, the town of Anaheim was established and settled by German Jews in 1857 near the Santa Ana River.

Los Angeles was now a town in transition, working determinedly to rid itself of its Hell

Horse drawn fire wagon, 1869

Town reputation and build a new and prosperous city. Los Angeles and its "golden" character fit everyone's dreams; it inspired innovation in thinking and a new term was coined, "boosterism." Boosterism became an active ingredient in the marketing of Southern California in a conscious and intentional effort to display the advantages of this region. Boosterism was an early form of self-promotion and the California southland initiated a campaign that could be described as a combination of regional chauvinism and the "hard sell." It was a promotional endeavor intended to bolster tourism and entice immigration, industry, and prosperity. The *Los Angeles Star* observed in 1859 "the adobe is giving way to the brick wall." Although many of the twenty-five leading *rancheros* still held most of the land, the era of the Californio was rapidly approaching an end. Los Angeles was becoming an American town.

Civil War Divides the Country and Los Angeles

The voting results from Los Angeles in the election of 1860 gave the pro-South Democratic nominee a resounding victory over Republican Abraham Lincoln. The Democrats also elected Governor John Downey and other candidates on the ticket, indicating that the Democrats virtually controlled Los Angeles.

Geographically isolated from the most populated sections of the country, most Californians did not take a political side in the Great War Between the States. A small segment of the population was actively pro-Union and this group grew in influence and eventually represented the dominant political stance of the region. Despite this influence, however, in the early days of the Civil War, Los Angeles was considered a "Confederate stronghold." As the Union became stronger in the conflict, the Democratic Party's influence weakened, and Lincoln's Republican policy and ideals strengthened. A big Republican victory in the 1864 election brought Californios into office replacing "gringo" Democrats in Los Angeles.

In the midst of this political upheaval, Mother Nature raised her impetuous head and a serious crisis of flood and drought devastated the region. DeMarco reports "Los Angeles has been plagued by a drought-and-flood cycle many times in its history, but nothing was quite so devastating as the calamities that began in the fall and winter of 1861-1862 with fifty inches of land-stripping, livestock-killing floods." The floods were followed by a two-year drought that effectively caused the economic demise of the *rancheros*. In Los Angeles County, seventy percent of the livestock perished and carcasses of dead animals littered the open range. *Ranchos* went on the auction block, and by the end of the decade the *rancheros* had virtually disappeared. The Californios began to be called "Mexicans" as they lost their land and money—they were no longer a class set apart.

The long and devastating Civil War finally ended in 1865, and simultaneously the years of flood and drought came to a halt, leaving the people of Los Angeles dazed by the years of turmoil. Economic collapse brought with it public despair and the region became "terribly poor and demoralized."

In 1869 an event occurred of such dramatic consequence that it was to reverse the economic downturn and gradually return the economy to stability. The first of the city-building actions to impact Los Angeles was the beginning of the land boom. As the *ranchos'* land came on the market, enterprising young men brokered deals and the term "subdivision" was introduced into the lexicon. Potential landowners were plentiful, arriving now in droves from the eastern states, looking for a fresh start after the painful

Photograph of Abraham Lincoln

Fourth of July parade down Main Street of Los Angeles in 1871. Proud volunteer firefighters display the city's first fire engine

times resulting from the war. They came for the opportunity to buy land and begin new lives.

The other significant event that was to dominate the landscape and jettison the growth of Los Angeles was the arrival of the railroad. Phineas Banning, who had started the first stagecoach company in the early 1850s, was one of the first Yankee entrepreneurs that challenged the rural, easy-going California tradition. Banning built a railroad between Los Angeles and the new port in San Pedro. He was part of a group hoping to persuade the Southern Pacific Railroad to build a line linking Los Angeles and San Francisco. The incredible and adventurous story of the development of the railroads will be described in more detail in the next chapter.

Meanwhile, the pioneer Jews of the 1850s and 1860s were vigorous in building the commercial and political infrastructure of Los Angeles. The earliest Jewish residents served as city council members, county supervisors, City Treasurer, Police Chief, and president of the Board of Education. They created the first social club, were among the founders of the early fraternal organizations, and served in the city's volunteer fire department.

The Hellmans and the Birth of Banking

One of the many Jewish businessmen to make his mark in the business environment of Los Angeles, specifically in banking, was Isaias W. Hellman. He was often called "the most important citizen in Southern California in the mid-19th Century."

Isaias W. Hellman and his brother, Herman, emigrated from Bavaria to Los Angeles in 1859. Isaias was a young teenager of sixteen, and went to work for his cousins Samuel and Isaias M. Hellman in their clothing and dry goods business. Six years later in 1865, Isaias had saved enough money to buy a clothing and dry goods store from Adolph Portugal; the store was located at the corner of Main and Commercial Streets.

Within a short time of establishing his business, Isaias began to transact private banking activities. His safe was located in a corner of his store, with a sign over it "I.W. Hellman, Banker." This enterprising Jewish young man offered the first banking services available to Los Angelenos. The miners and other merchants deposited their gold dust, writing checks on their deposits.

The banking procedures that Hellman developed were creative and fit into the rough and tumble atmosphere of the times. Jackson A. Graves, a long time associate of Hellman's described the process. As the miner came in with his gold dust, Hellman explained to him "'I will buy your gold dust, at current rates, and I am running a bank. Here, see this book. After I buy your gold you can deposit

Early bankers including the Hellman brothers

the money with me, take this book and check it out as you please. All checks drawn on me, while your money lasts, will be paid.' The scheme took and, strange to say, the miners spent much less money after they began to make the bank deposits, than they did before. Many of them left thousands and thousands of dollars with him, and when the mines gave out a great many of them bought land, built houses, barns, etc., and became prosperous farmers, and always had a high regard for Mr. Hellman." As the miners became farmers, they continued to avail themselves of the bank services of Hellman, remembering that he had dealt honorably and honestly with them.

Although James Hayward and [Governor] John Downey preceded Hellman in the formal opening of the first bank in the territory in 1868, it was only by a few months. On August 14, 1868, the local press announced:

> New Banking House—By reference to our advertising columns, it will be seen that the banking house of Hellman, Temple & Co., will be opened in their new building on Main Street, on the first of September next. The new banking firm is composed of Messrs. Wm. Workman, F.P.F. Temple and I.W. Hellman. Messrs. Workman and Temple are among the oldest settlers in this county, and have long been known as gentlemen of extensive wealth, and their names are a sufficient insurance of the solvency of the firm of which they are members; while Mr. Hellman, the business manager of the firm, is a young man of rare business attainments, he has the confidence of the business community among which, for

many years, he has been a successful and enterprising merchant.

Three years later in 1871, Hellman dissolved his partnerships and organized the bank as the Farmers & Merchants Bank of Los Angeles, merging his assets with John Downey, who had also bought out his partners in the other bank. The editor of the *Herald* reported in 1887 that the Farmers & Merchants Bank "is universally recognized as one of the most stable and beneficial institutions of the kind on the Pacific Coast." In documents on the history of banking in Southern California it is noted "the Farmers & Merchants Bank did more toward building the growth of Southern California than any other similar institution in the state." Jewish pioneer Isaias Hellman remained a banker for the rest of his life, a career in which he achieved remarkable success and in which he was said to have been of "inestimable service" and "a pillar of strength to multitudes of people."

Hellman's dry goods business was also prospering and, with a keen eye to the future, he began buying land, astutely realizing that real estate in Los Angeles was still inexpensive. He paid about fifty dollars for most of the lots he bought in the downtown area, while also purchasing acreage from the now defunct ranch properties including the Los Alamitos Ranch, the Repetto Ranch south of Alhambra, and the Nacimiento Ranch in Monterey County.

Distinguished and well respected among the citizenry, Hellman joined with nine other civic leaders in Los Angeles in sending this letter to all prominent citizens in the city in 1872 encouraging the expansion of the railroads into the territory:

> The undersigned, considering the present an opportune time to secure Railroad connection between this valley and the Atlantic seaboard, as well as with the commercial center of the Pacific, San Francisco, respectfully solicit your attendance at a meeting to be held at the Court House, in this city, on Saturday, the 18th at 2:30 P.M., for the purpose of consulting together in regard to the mutual interest of the whole county as far as the same may be materially affected by having the main trunk of the Trans-continental Railroad pass through our country.

Fort Moore, photographed in 1875, looking northeast from First and Hill Streets. The Fort was decommissioned in 1853 and remained part of the landscape of Los Angeles into the early 20th Century. The city's first high school is at the center right in the Mexican downtown residential neighborhood known as Sonoratown

The first building of the Kaspare Cohn Hospital (later became Cedars-Sinai Medical Center)

Listed among the other signatures were Hellman's former partner, F.P.F. Temple, Governor John Downey, and Solomon Lazard. All of their efforts met with success when the Southern Pacific Railroad completed its line to Los Angeles in 1876.

The building and expansion of the railroads was a monumental stride forward in the growth of the West, and especially Los Angeles. The railroad story encompasses many aspects of the culture of the time, involved people in various disciplines, and required extraordinary effort and cooperation from different echelons of the social strata to accomplish this miracle in transportation. One of the important threads in this tapestry is the story of the Chinese population, a story that intersected the history of the Jews and other ethnic groups in diverse Los Angeles.

Jewish and Chinese Immigrants Contribute to the Development of Los Angeles

Transplanted to the American West, Jews and Chinese shared in the pioneer experience connected by economic ties. The Chinese were filling the role of low paid immigrants, while the Jews worked in skilled labor or went into business for themselves, finding a place in the middle-class American tradition. The Chinese were more often relegated to more menial positions as household servants. They offered little economic threat to the residents of Southern California but the anti-Chinese sentiment, although more covert than in other cities, still stubbornly persisted.

When the Jews left Europe to escape persecution and immigrated to America, they quickly adapted. Possessing business experience, language facility, and urban skills, they were welcome participants in the pioneer life in the West. The Jewish immigrants from Poland and Russia may have been poor, but they were all literate.

The Chinese, in contrast, left behind a history of authoritarian rule in a country that had existed for centuries. Economic pressure to provide for their families left behind in China motivated them to perform hard labor—the only work available to them. The hard working

Chinese, known by the disparaging term "coolies," came to America and worked in the mines, agriculture, manufacturing, doing menial household tasks, operating laundries, and the backbreaking labor required in building the railroads. The Chinese were reviled and denigrated, often accused of taking jobs away from the white working class by accepting starvation wages. It was the ever-present wish by the Chinese to return to their homeland that appeared to provoke the antagonism of the caucasian Americans.

One of the more disturbing events that occurred in early Los Angeles involved both the Chinese immigrants and a prominent Jewish lawman that came to their defense. There are conflicting reports of the events that led to the Chinese Massacre of 1871. Harris Newmark's version, written at the time of the outbreak, narrates that two rival factions of the Chinese went to "war in Nigger Alley." In the course of the struggle, an American officer and his brother were shot; the shooting spread rapidly, injuring harmless

Wong Sue Ying was employed by the Jacob Baruch family of Los Angeles between 1889 and 1929. He was nicknamed "Joe Baruch"

bystanders, and an ugly mob scene soon prevailed. Townsmen quickly turned on any Chinese in the vicinity. Nineteen innocent Chinese were killed when the unruly mob sought vengeance.

History now gives us a different perspective of the incident. Contemporary research provides evidence that the story of a rivalry between Chinese Tongs (gangs) was largely a myth, a cover-up for a criminal act that was actually committed by a caucasian. Los Angeles' Sheriff Burns restored order after the melee, assisted by his deputy, Emil Harris, who fired shots in the air in order to stop the massacre. Harris, a respected and committed peace officer, went on to develop an eminent career in law enforcement, distinguished by becoming Los Angeles' first Jewish Chief of Police in 1878.

In Karen Wilson's opinion the Jews and Chinese got along "fairly well. There was the infamous Chinese Massacre in 1871 in which Emil Harris was instrumental in helping to save some of the Chinese men that were under attack…. The relationships seemed to be cordial. There was competition with the Chinese merchants and Jewish merchants, but generally the relationships seemed to be hospitable." Following the massacre, the Chinese government strongly protested the "outrage" and the United States authorities paid a large indemnity to the Chinese community.

Summarizing the relationships between the Jews and the Chinese in early Los Angeles, Rabbi Will Kramer states: "beyond the public clamor and outrages committed by the hoodlums and poor white laborers, normal relationships existed between Chinese and those Jews for whom conformity was not an economic necessity. Certainly in domestic affairs the Chinese tended to be trusted servants and food suppliers. Each race shared the roles of scapegoats for their centuries-old cultures, diverse religious practices, and non-Western languages unintelligible to outsiders. The Jewish principle of *tzedakah* (charitability in deed and meaning) and the proverbial generosity and loyalty of the Chinese, worked together in many contexts even in the worst times until the anti-Chinese furor subsided. Mutual helpfulness, warmth, and the ever-present Chinese amiability appeared in virtually every account of business or household relationships where they were maintained. The compassion expressed collectively in the Eastern Jewish press was present individually in Jews of the Far West." These two diverse traditions were to break ground and provide an important cornerstone of tolerance for the multitude of ethnic groups that followed and interacted and thrived in the developing polyglot culture of Los Angeles.

Social and Religious Life of the Jewish Community

The end of the Civil War coincided mercifully with the end of the three-year drought. Immigration resumed especially from the defeated South. Publicity in the East lauded California's mild climate and fertile soil. Boosterism was having a very positive effect on the pioneer immigration. Wagon trains with as many as a hundred wagons convoyed across the country in the late 1860s. The new settlers, most of them farmers, were instrumental in reviving business and real estate.

The social and business scene changed dramatically during this era with the focus pointed at bringing civilization into this virtually lawless territory. Success brought opportunity and encouraged civic involvement. Among many important social and economic changes several were noteworthy and evoke the flavor of the changing times. Newmark tells this charming story about the marriage of Matilda Newmark (daughter of Joseph) to Maurice Kremer in April 1856. After the bride's father performed the ceremony, ice was brought in from San Bernardino for the festivities. The ice was used to make ice cream, a new innovation and a novelty for the assembled guests. Newmark states "both luxuries [ice and ice cream] were being used in Los Angeles for the first time."

Another milestone in Southern California history was reached in 1857 when a group of German Jews purchased 1200 acres of sandy land, paying two dollars an acre, and on this land started the town of Anaheim. Felix Bachman, one of the first eight Jews in Los Angeles, had built up a large wholesale merchandise and trading business in the Southwest. Bachman was the treasurer of the German syndicate that purchased the land near the Santa Ana River. Their plan was to plant ten thousand vines on the twenty-acre plots, selling shares in the business for seven hundred and fifty dollars. The enterprise was called the Los Angeles Vineyard Society. The town's name was derived from the Spanish *Ana*, from Santa Ana (the nearby river), and the German *heim* for home. The name of the town was intended to encourage German-Jewish farmers to settle there and develop the land.

Emil Harris became the first Jewish Chief of Police of Los Angeles in 1870

Marriage between families and close friends was a fairly common occurrence at this time in Jewish history as evidenced by the marriage of Harris Newmark to his first cousin Sarah (daughter of Joseph Newmark) in March 1858. Harris writes about his wedding:

> At four o'clock, a small circle of intimates was welcomed at dinner; and in the evening there was a house party and dance, for which invitations printed on lace paper, had been sent out. Among the friends who attended, were the military officers stationed at Fort Tejon…. Men rarely went out unarmed at night, and most of our male visitors doffed their weapons—both pistols and knives—as they came in, spreading them around in the bedrooms. The ladies brought their babies with them for safekeeping, and the same rooms were placed at their disposal. Imagine, if you can, the appearance of this nursery-arsenal!

Other social and commercial events that were to have long-term effects on the culture included the arrival in 1858 of Andrew A. Boyle, for whom the eastern suburb of Los Angeles, Boyle Heights, was named. Another innovative entrepreneurial enterprise was established by Beaudry and Marchessault, a company reputed to be among the first handlers of ice in Los Angeles. They erected an icehouse in 1859 in which they stored the frozen product that was taken from mountain lakes fifty miles away. The ice, in cubes of about one hundred pounds each, was carried by thirty or forty mules and brought into Los Angeles on wagons.

The aforementioned Beaudry is the same Prudent Beaudry who provoked an unpleasant confrontation with Harris Newmark in 1865. Reporting on the incident in his memoirs, Newmark wrote that he heard that Beaudry had boasted that he would "drive every Los Angeles Jew out of business." An angered Newmark proposed to his friend Phineas Banning (who was not Jewish) who was in the freight business, that they partner in the wholesale grocery business. Able to save considerable funds in transportation because of the established and thriving freight business of Banning, they competed with devastating effectiveness against Beaudry and other rivals. After only six months, Beaudry was forced out of business; Newmark and Banning dissolved their short venture, and Newmark became a wholesale grocer, operating as H. Newmark and Company.

Emil Harris, seated fourth (circled) from the left, wearing a few of his marksmanship medals. He was one of the organizers of the Turnverein, a rifle club which was founded in 1870. Photograph taken in 1885

Newmark, with some satisfaction, describes the conclusion of this "mimic war in which Phineas Banning and I engaged…and to tell to what an extent the fortunes of my competitors were influenced, and how the absorption of the transportation charge from the seaboard caused their downfall. O.W. Childs, in less than three months, found the competition too severe and surrendered 'lock, stock and barrel;' P. Beaudry, whose shortsighted boast had stirred up this rumpus, sold out to me on January 1st, 1866, just a few months after his big talk."

In the midst of this economic revival it is important to note the influence and participation of businesses operated by Jewish women. Mrs. H. Cohn pursued a feminine trade in "fashionable millinery, dress cloak maker and dealer in fancy goods," as did Mrs. Mathilda Kremer. Flora Cohn petitioned for the legal right to function as a "sole trader." Mrs. Goldstein operated a private boardinghouse, popular as a meeting place for organizations and parties. She joined

The Merced Theater, next to the Pico House, opened in 1870

Ephraim and his wife Ernestine as proprietors of the newly opened White House Hotel in 1875.

The social life of the Jews in this period was one of whole-hearted social acceptance, and they participated in great numbers, although Jewish social activities were not totally commingled with the general community. In the 1870s there was a line of social assimilation beyond which the Jews did not go, being comfortable to pursue their own traditions and family mergers. Overt social exclusion would not surface for some decades however, not until the turn of the century.

The Jews enthusiastically enjoyed the social pastimes of the community. The forerunner of all social clubs in Los Angeles was organized in 1870, the Los Angeles Social Club, whose officers were predominantly Jewish. The Los Angeles Social Club's members' activities included a huge picnic at the Rancho Santa Anita. Another of the popular events that the press reported on was a ball that had "one of the most brilliant assemblages of youth, beauty, and fashion which has ever gathered in Los Angeles."

The grand social occasions for the city's Jewish families were weddings, bar mitzvahs, confirmations, and celebration of the religious holidays. The wedding of Rachel Edelman, daughter of Rabbi Edelman, to William T. Barnett as reported in the local press, reflects some of the wedding traditions of the day. "It was scheduled for three o'clock in the synagogue, but guests began to arrive at noon; by three o'clock only ladies could be seated. The groom wore a black dress suit with white cravat and kids, and walked down the aisle with the mother of the bride, as was the popular custom of the day. The celebration afterwards was held in the residence of the bride's father."

Fannie Benjamin graduated from Los Angeles High School in 1877. She enjoyed a successful career as a ceramic artist, opening her studio in 1902, which was located in the Downey Building

Picnics and outings to the beach or canyons were also very popular social events. A social outing, according to Harris Newmark, was a much more complicated undertaking than one might imagine. He speculates that the "residents of Los Angeles today have but a faint idea of what exertion we cheerfully submitted to in order to participate in a little pleasure." In his book he describes a typical journey to Catalina. A group of fifty or sixty men and women met at five o'clock in the morning at someone's home, and after a light breakfast rode in stagecoaches to the harbor in New San Pedro. In San Pedro they boarded a small steamer, which took them to the outer harbor where they transferred to a United States Coast Guard survey ship for the two-hour trip to Catalina. On board the passengers were given a substantial midday dinner before they went ashore. They strolled the beaches until about four o'clock when the guests reboarded the government ship which returned them to San Pedro after sundown. They again boarded the coaches for the final leg of the journey, arriving back in Los Angeles at around ten o'clock at night, the one-day excursion to Catalina taking about seventeen hours.

The attractions of the beach and surf were beginning to be appreciated as well in Santa Monica, which was perceived as a potential summer resort. In the summer of 1871 less than twenty families, many in tents, camped out in the canyon where there was a bar and "refreshment parlor." An amusing story describing a typical day at the beach in Santa Monica in February 1884 is told by Rosalie Meyer later in this chapter (page 97).

The religious life of the Jews in pioneer Los Angeles was simplified by necessity, since it was essential that they adapt to the rustic conditions in which they were living. Jews were prominent and respected citizens among the residents of Los Angeles, they were seen as hard working and strongly motivated to prosper. Vorspan

Horse drawn cars appeared on the streets of Los Angeles in 1874 and ran through 1901. This car operated from Exposition Park, Main and Jefferson Streets

In the 1870s and 1880s most of the elegant residences were located on Main Street in downtown Los Angeles

writes that in 1853, in early anticipation of the yet unknown Zionism, the *Star* reported, "remarkable change is in progress among the Jews in every country, owing to a manuscript being largely circulated by an influential rabbi, proving from the scriptures, that the time has come when the Jews must set about making preparations for returning to the land of their fathers."

According to Vorspan, the *Star* continued reporting its interest in Jews when it went to great lengths to explain to its readers the difference between the terms "Israelite, Hebrew, and Jew. After mentioning that 'Hebrew' came from 'passing over,' and 'Israel' from the 'wrestling of the Angel with Jacob,' and 'Jew' from 'Judah,' it [the article] concluded that 'Hebrew' today refers mostly to the language, and that 'Jew' is generally a term of reproach, while 'Israelites' is used in 'a respectful address to the nation.'" What emerges from this example is that the Jews were respected members of a community that was eager to understand the different traditions that these immigrants transplanted into Los Angeles.

Jewish religious services in Los Angeles are thought to have begun in 1851 when the first *minyan* (ten men needed for public worship) was held. Friday night and Saturday morning services were held in different homes and occasionally at the adobe saloon owned by John Temple. It is generally believed that the Jews in Los Angeles celebrated the first Rosh Hashanah holiday on September 26, 1851. These religious services were informal until the arrival in 1854 of Harris Newmark's uncle Joseph Newmark and his wife and children, a devout family steeped in Jewish tradition. Joseph Newmark was an ordained rabbi and conducted formal services until the B'nai B'rith Congregation was established in 1862 when Rabbi Abraham Wolf Edelman arrived

Pictured above is Saint Vincents College photographed in 1868 and located at what is now 6th Street and Broadway. The college was one of the recipients of Jewish charity. Manuscripts preserved in several Roman Catholic archives provided important clues about the extent of Jewish philanthropy in pioneer Los Angeles. The early Jewish pioneers supported many of the Protestant and Catholic projects, which included the towns' first orphanage and college

Jacob Baruch photographed as a teenager in Worms, Germany in the mid-1860s. In 1871, when Herman W. Hellman left his firm to go into banking, Baruch moved to Los Angeles and became a partner, and the business was renamed Hass, Baruch & Company

and took over the rabbinic duties for the community. Both Edelman and Newmark were among the early leaders of the Hebrew Benevolent Society.

With the coming of Rabbi Edelman, organizing the religious life of the Jewish community began in earnest. When the rabbi reached the tiny pueblo that was Los Angeles in June 1862, he found a Wild West frontier town with an established reputation for gambling, lynching, murder, and prostitution.

Rabbi Edelman was a "foreigner," as most of the Jewish citizens were, but he was already acculturated to the American way of life. The eclectic elements of the Jewish inhabitants were reflected in the Rabbi's own background. Edelman came from a Polish Jewish home with an Eastern European orientation, a background typical of the Polish-Prussian Jews. The majority of the small Jewish community in Los Angeles was Western European, mainly from Germany. Among the population of Los Angeles, which was exceedingly diverse, the Jew was simply another "gringo" to the Mexicans and the Spanish-speaking Indians. Stepping into the disparate community that was Los Angeles, Edelman smoothed the rough edges that separated the different cultural groups, calling forth his experience and extensive knowledge of languages. Fluent in Spanish, Edelman was known as "padre" to the Spanish-speaking residents. He brought strong spiritual religious values into the relatively uncivilized town, and inspired the entire population with his commitment to civic and social activities and Jewish organizations.

Edelman served as both spokesman and ambassador for the Jewish community, especially important since the Civil War had surfaced some evidence of latent anti-Semitism. Since the Jews had voted the Democratic ticket in 1861, some of the local press maliciously sought to isolate the Jews as a "secessionist block" painting them as being politically pro-slavery. This slander was untrue and the respected and admired rabbi was well suited to the role of ambassador, a role much needed to settle the political dust that was still swirling from the hostilities of the Civil War.

Rabbi Edelman conducted services in various venues including a meeting hall in the Arcadia Block Building, Leck's Hall, and the Temple Court House. His home became a natural meeting place and he was often invited by the general community to lead civic and fraternal societies. He participated in the Masons, the Hebrew Benevolent Society, Gan Eden Lodge and the Orange Lodge. The Orange Lodge Number 224 was also the Independent

This 1873 lithograph lays out the basic pattern of Los Angeles streets showing Fort Street (Broadway) as well as Spring and Hill Streets. This view looks northeast towards the San Gabriel Mountains from Olympic Boulevard. Los Angeles was populated at this time by 6,000 people compared to 150,000 living in San Francisco

Order of B'nai B'rith, established in March 1874 in Los Angeles, and Edelman was elected its first president. These fraternal and benevolent societies formed the basis for Jewish philanthropy in the early West, as well as the foundation for social gatherings, and provided the enriched soil from which to grow and nurture Jewish leadership.

Opening day ceremonies of the Boyle Heights cable railways

Arriving in Los Angeles from Bavaria in 1859 as a fifteen-year-old, Herman W. Hellman became a successful businessman and banker. In 1874 he returned to Europe for a short time to marry Ida Heimann from a German Jewish family in Trieste. Their Los Angeles home (pictured above), was located at the northeast corner of Fourth and Spring, then a residential area of the city. Later the house was moved and the Herman W. Hellman office building (still standing) was constructed on the site, completed in 1903. Herman built a large three-story mansion for his family at 958 South Hill Street

As a vigorous and outspoken supporter of and leader in Jewish education, Rabbi Edelman held school classes in his "parlor." The students were taught both religious and secular subjects, learned Jewish hymns and Hebrew, and were prepared for bar mitzvah. Edelman was a vocal and effective proponent of education, especially Jewish education and personally recruited and trained teachers, including his son David. A local newspaper reported, "The teachers are some of the sweetest of the Jewish young ladies here, and then there is Mr. David Edelman, who besides being an excellent instructor, adds dignity and tone to the school. I have no desire to flatter anyone, but I think too much praise cannot be bestowed upon those few who labor so industriously for the welfare of the children."

As a pioneer in Jewish education in Los Angeles, Rabbi Edelman inspired disciples who would both learn and teach. Kramer writes, "He taught at home and in the classroom, at civic meetings and fraternal hall, at ceremony and in sanctuary, and in the language of his listeners. His being a teacher was validated by his own commitment to study. In the general culture he was an autodidact, acquiring the secular knowledge which exploded in the 19th Century. Jewishly, he sought to find teachers for himself."

Congregation B'nai B'rith — Los Angeles' First Synagogue

Among the community leaders that worked with Rabbi Edelman to build the first synagogue was the banking entrepreneur Isaias W. Hellman, president of Congregation B'nai

B'rith. His role as a respected leader and generous contributor to the building fund made him the perfect candidate to address the congregation and visitors at the dedication ceremony in August 1872. His remarks attest to his deeply religious character and Jewish spirit:

> We are assembled here today to lay the cornerstone of this our future synagogue. It is a happy moment for all of us Hebrews to be present and assist on this holy occasion, and also to know that the long and seriously felt hardship of not having a place of worship of our own will soon be at an end.
>
> Those of you, my Jewish brethren, who have so long battled for this one object, always full of hope, but rarely with a prospect of success; you for whom no sacrifice was too great, who should and have ultimately so well succeeded, to you it will always be a day of joy….
>
> You, Mr. Edelman (Rabbi), who has for the last ten years so ably performed all your duties as teacher to our children, chasen, shohet, and spiritual advisor to our society; you, always the first at any sick bed, or giving consolation to the afflicted—to you we can say, well done, faithful servant of God! May the All-Powerful compensate you; may all your days be days of joy, and may He keep you and yours well for many years.

A portion of Hellman's remarks were a direct appeal to the young men in the community, and his plea rang out to inspire young leaders in the late 19th Century, much as a similar message rings out in today's 21st Century communities: "I am sorry to see that the Jewish young men, who certainly should be the first ones to join kindred institutions, have so far not done it. To them I here appeal, and hope that they will prove by their example that the youth of Israel still reveres the ancient faith of their forefathers."

Joseph Newmark, community patriarch, spoke at the opening of the new B'nai B'rith synagogue a year later on August 8, 1873. The city council proceeded as a group to the ceremony where a large audience attended the celebration, including many friends who were not Jewish. It was described by an awed observer as "one of the grandest spectacles ever witnessed in Southern California." A local reporter wrote: "The Congregation of B'nai B'rith may well feel proud of their House of Worship. It is the most superior church edifice in Southern California."

Congregation B'nai B'rith, which was then commonly known as the Fort Street Synagogue (later the Wilshire Boulevard Temple) marked the

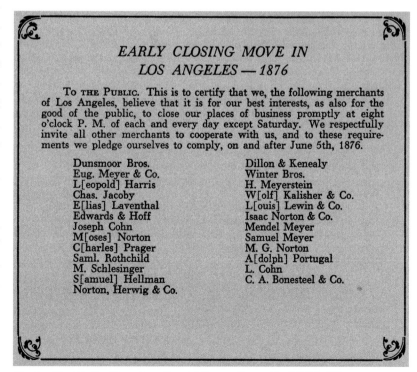

EARLY CLOSING MOVE IN LOS ANGELES — 1876

To the Public. This is to certify that we, the following merchants of Los Angeles, believe that it is for our best interests, as also for the good of the public, to close our places of business promptly at eight o'clock P. M. of each and every day except Saturday. We respectfully invite all other merchants to cooperate with us, and to these requirements we pledge ourselves to comply, on and after June 5th, 1876.

Dunsmoor Bros.	Dillon & Kenealy
Eug. Meyer & Co.	Winter Bros.
L[eopold] Harris	H. Meyerstein
Chas. Jacoby	W[olf] Kalisher & Co.
E[lias] Laventhal	L[ouis] Lewin & Co.
Edwards & Hoff	Isaac Norton & Co.
Joseph Cohn	Mendel Meyer
M[oses] Norton	Samuel Meyer
C[harles] Prager	M. G. Norton
Saml. Rothchild	A[dolph] Portugal
M. Schlesinger	L. Cohn
S[amuel] Hellman	C. A. Bonesteel & Co.
Norton, Herwig & Co.	

From the Daily Evening Republican, *June 3, 1876. Nineteen out of the twenty-five of this representative list of Los Angeles merchants were Jewish*

N. & H. JACOBY,

CANAL STREET,

WILMINGTON,

DEALERS IN

DRY GOODS, CLOTHING, HARD-WARE, PAINTS, OILS, GROCERIES, &c.

GOVERNMENT VOUCHERS BOUGHT

Hereafter no discount will be charegd on soldiers' final statements.   je3d1y

Nathan and Herman Jacoby's store located in the Port of Wilmington stocked a wide variety of general merchandise as displayed in this Los Angeles newspaper ad published in 1871. Nathan Jacoby arrived in Los Angeles in 1860 and by the 1880s the six Jacoby brothers (Nathan, Herman, Abraham, Morris, Charles and Lesser) were operating wholesale and retail clothing businesses in Los Angeles. By the 1890s they were involved in the manufacturing of clothing for men and boys. Their firm lasted into the 1920s

The corner of Main and Temple Streets looking south in the 1870s. Adolph Portugal's dry goods store in lower right. Portugal was born in Poland in 1832 and first appeared in the Los Angeles city directory in a full page advertisement in 1872. The advertisement described the store's clothing, boots and shoes, and dry goods and proclaimed "quick sales and small profits...competitors I defy"

Jews' religious imprint on the land in Los Angeles, the building representing a solid and beautiful symbol of their hopes for their children and future generations (Fort Street was later renamed Broadway). It had taken Newmark and his friends twenty years of hard work and enterprise to erect a structure in which they could worship peacefully and in freedom. Joseph Newmark may have envisioned bright years ahead for this small community—but it is unlikely that he could have imagined the Los Angeles of the future, which would proudly support more than 150 Jewish congregations by the middle of the 20th Century. Los Angeles in the coming years would be home to more Jews than anywhere in the world outside of Israel and New York City.

Although the majority of the members of Congregation B'nai B'rith were not observant and did not follow the Orthodox customs that many of them had been brought up to practice in Europe, they made valiant attempts to maintain their Jewish identity and traditions within the framework of the new community in the West. Vorspan writes: "If the piety of the members did not extend to eating only kosher food or suspending business on the Sabbath, on the Jewish New Year and Day of Atonement they were impeccable. They all closed their places of business, and some merchants from outlying areas moved into Los Angeles for the days." When the new synagogue was completed, the annual highlight continued to be the celebration of the Jewish High Holy days.

By the end of the 1870s there was no longer a kosher boardinghouse in town, and the "number of families who kept to the kosher diet had dwindled to an inconsequential minority. The members were getting wealthier but traditional Jewish life poorer." By 1880 the congregation was well on its way toward adapting to the more liberal environment, and adopting the Reform education of most of its congregants. The Jews and other members of the burgeoning town of Los Angeles were about to be juxtaposed and thrust into a new era—the time of "boom and bust" that characterized and molded the final two decades of the 1800s, a time that would lead them all into the new century.

Recalling the Opening Day of Los Angeles' First Synagogue — August 1873

Newspaper Article Edited by Norton B. Stern

For Jewish people, every Saturday is a holy day. But this week in Los Angeles, the Sabbath luncheon was even more important; Congregation B'nai B'rith was celebrating a sign of permanence. After twenty years of growth, the small Jewish community had built its first tall, stately synagogue. Those who feasted at Newmark's table had just come from the new synagogue on Fort Street.

Lifting glasses of brandy, the men toasted progress, made manifest in the new solid brick building with its leaded glass windows and heavy wooden doors. Within the new building, they and their families had assembled, men on the main floor and women in the balcony. They had come together like ingredients for the Sabbath stew, with an equally happy result.

An historian of the time reported:

> Over his dinner, Newmark remembered less cohesive times. Like other restless young men, he had come West in 1854, intending to raise his fortune by selling supplies to miners in the gold rush. Selling goods came naturally to many of the young Jewish pioneers, since their ancestors had also worked in the "backpack business," trading whatever goods they could carry — spices, furs, fabrics, precious stones—when persecution in Europe drove them from place to place.

But the American frontier was not

Joseph Newmark, patriarch of the Los Angeles Jewish community, arrived in 1854 and guided the spiritual life of Congregation B'nai B'rith until 1862

The first synagogue in Los Angeles was Congregation B'nai B'rith (now Wilshire Boulevard Temple) then located at 218 South Broadway (formerly Fort Street), 1873

organized around the young men's religion. For instance, because kosher butchers were rare, they had to learn to prepare their own food according to dietary law. They worked Saturdays, [ignoring the Sabbath restrictions] since the adobe shops of Los Angeles stayed open. They met for worship when their work allowed, in private homes or rented spaces. Even when they could not obey all the laws of their religion, Newmark and his peers kept the Sabbath by gathering on Friday nights to light candles and bless their shared wine.

✳ ✳ ✳

Just this year, the Jewish men had helped found the new Chamber of Commerce, and had been called the city's "best citizens" in the local newspaper. Together with their wives and children, they formed a Hebrew Benevolent Society and purchased lots for a Jewish cemetery. As Newmark himself was proud of noting, they shared a sense of upward mobility and a willingness to adapt.

The Jewish men and women of the City of Angels shared something else; a peculiarly American brand of freedom. In frontier Los Angeles, Jewish people were allowed to thrive, as they never had in the East or European cities. "The Israelites," as non-Jews called them, found a remarkable atmosphere of tolerance in Southern California. They were not persecuted as they had been in so many places, for so many centuries. Living side by side with

Catholics and Methodists, they became Americans and entered city government. Their names could be found on the pages of the local Blue Book, a guide to the booming town, and on the membership rosters of local societies.

Now, with the completion of the Fort Street synagogue, they had made their mark on the land too; the building was a solid and beautiful symbol of their hopes for the future. Newmark and the men at his table spoke of their new synagogue's beauty as they welcomed this day of rest. It had taken them twenty years of enterprise and hard work to build a place where they could worship. Like God, who rested on the seventh day, they felt the satisfaction of having been present at the creation.

Just after sunset at the *Havdalah* ceremony, Joseph Newmark started his new week. It was a gentle August Saturday evening and in an atmosphere rich with wine, spices, and the yellow flickering light from a candle, the patriarch of the Los Angeles Jewish community may have imagined that California would grow once trains reached it from the East. He may have pictured the arrival of more German and later, Russian Jews. In the room's dark shadows he may have foreseen the horrible World Wars that would bring even more of his people West. But in his best dreams he could not have imagined what would one day be true; that Los Angeles would have more than 150 Jewish congregations, and that by mid-Twentieth Century it would be home to more Jews than anywhere in the world outside Israel and New York City.

NAME-CHANGE IN LOS ANGELES

In the matter of change of name of Lewin Hirschkowitz, commonly called Leopold Harris. To the Hon. the County Court of the County of Los Angeles, State of California.

This petition respectfully represents that the petitioner is of the age of 36 years; that his place of birth was Loebau, Prussia; that his residence is at Los Angeles City, in this county; that his present name is Lewin Hirschkowitz; and that he desires to have the same changed to Leopold Harris; that the reason for the change is, that his true name being a difficult one for American lips, pens and postoffices, he long since adopted the use of the easier one of Leopold Harris, and by that name and that only, is known among the merchants and customers with whom he deals; and to avoid all question and suspicion that may attach to the voluntary and unauthorized assumption of a new name he desires to have such assumption validated by competent authority. That his father is dead and was named Feibush; that the near relatives of petitioner, now living, are his mother, named Hannah Hirschkowitz, residing at Loebau, Prussia, one brother named Moritz Hirschkowitz, residing at Lautenberg, Prussia, and one sister, named Rosa Summerfield, residing at Loebau, Prussia.

And petitioner prays order of this Court, setting this petition for hearing and that in such hearing after due notice the change of name prayed for may be decreed to be made.

Lewin Hirschkowitz
May 24, 1872

Document announcing a name change

Well-known street minister, the Reverend Johnson, preaching in downtown Los Angeles

The parents of the Baruch brothers, Mr. and Mrs. Jacob Baruch, came to Los Angeles in 1871. Their four sons, all born in Los Angeles in the 19th Century were (clockwise from the right) Clarence, Milton, Edgar, and Herbert. Milton and Herbert became building contractors, and built such structures as the Wilshire Boulevard Temple, Vista Del Mar, Beverly Hills City Hall, Hershey Hall at UCLA and many Los Angeles public schools

Slightly less than 500 Jews called Los Angeles home in 1880. The vast majority of Jews old enough to work in 1880 were foreign born, as 87% of all Jews 25 and over were born outside the United States. The majority of the Jewish foreign-born came from areas that became part of a united Germany in the course of the nineteenth century: 39.5% from Prussia, 36% from Germany (or various German states), 7.4% each from Poland and France, with the remaining few scattered among England, Switzerland, Russia, Italy, Canada, Mexico and Central America. Many of the Jews listed as having been born in Prussia were actually in fact from Posen and Pomerania, provinces of western Poland annexed by Prussia during the late eighteenth century, and had been nurtured in the more traditional Eastern European Jewish culture.

Almost three-quarters of Los Angeles' Jews in 1880 lived in a fashionable neighborhood directly south of the city's business district, bounded on the north by First Street, the south by Sixth Street, on the east by Los Angeles Street and the west by Spring Street. Boasting most of the city's few wooden, Victorian homes, these Jews clustered along the 100 and 200 blocks of South Main, living alongside other native and foreign-born whites. Virtually none of the city's colored minorities lived there. Two blocks south of First Street on Broadway (then Fort Street), stood Congregation B'nai B'rith, erected in 1873.

The remaining 25% of the Jewish community, with the exception of eleven individuals, resided in the second ward in two districts; first, north of First and a few blocks immediately west of the business district; and second, north of First and south of Aliso, between Los Angeles and Vignes. The Jews living in the latter two districts tended to be proprietors who had not yet accumulated any real property and blue-collar workers. These sections were among the most densely populated in the city, where white and blue-collar workers lived side by side and different nationalities clustered along certain streets: Latinos on Castelar, Germans on Sansevain, and French on Aliso.

Santa Monica Beach and its North Beach Bath House and Arcadia Hotel, a popular resort

A Day in Santa Monica

by Rosalie Meyer
February 1884

This small though interesting town is situated in Southern California, on the Pacific Ocean, eighteen miles west of Los Angeles. In order to describe it well let us pay an imaginary visit, or rather suppose that I was living in Los Angeles and a friend from this city [San Francisco] came to see me, and among other summer resorts, I take her to Santa Monica. We arrive at the depot just in time to take the half past nine o'clock train. After riding for about three quarters of an hour, we feel the fresh, cool breeze and know that we are near the ocean. In a few minutes more, the train stops, and we alight at a small house, which is the depot.

After walking a few yards toward the sea, we find ourselves at the top of a cliff seventy feet high, and looking down see below us a pure white, sandy beach. Before us lie the blue and peaceful waters of the Pacific. And right and left, we see that the land projects far out and half enclose the waters that lie between, forming what is known as Santa Monica Bay.

But we are wasting time; let us go down to the beach, for already I can see the little black dots above the water, which I know to be the heads of the bathers; so descending a gentle slope we find ourselves on the sand. I have often been there before as I have always spent my summer months in this way. I can hardly resist the temptation of joining the merry crowd, who are already paddling about in the cool, fresh water. But on account of my friend I do resist, and we sit down quietly and look on.

Here is a man, who looks, by the way he runs down the bank, as if he intended to swim over to China, but no sooner do his toes touch the water, than he gives a jump, turns around and runs up again. This performance, of course, sets all the spectators to laughing, which does not please his lordship, so he thinks to regain his honor by some wonderful achievement.

So ready! And away he bounds head foremost in the surging deep (as he thinks), but alas, by some mistake of nature, the water here is only an inch deep and the poor man strikes his head against the hard sand, and coming to the conclusion, by this time, that his bathing suit is a little damp and he might catch cold, he thinks it best to sit down on the sand and dry himself.

We see many other timid bathers and some good swimmers, who (as the saying goes) scare us half out of our lives by their daring. By this time we feel a slight gnawing inside of us and thinking the best way to remedy this is by eating something. So up to the hotel we go. After appeasing our appetites, we send for saddle horses and by the time we are ready to start, it is two o'clock. Again descending to the beach, we ride along for about a mile, when we come to a great sand hill.

I have often been told that in the year 1876 when all the country was in want of rain, the mustangs, or wild Mexican horses abounded in such great quantities that they ate all the grass and left none for the more useful animals. So, in order to get rid of some of them, they were killed by being driven over the cliff. The sand, in high tide, was washed over them and formed the sandbank now before us.

We ride on for about fifteen minutes, when we arrive at Old Santa Monica, generally spoken of as the old canyon. This always looked to me like a dried up river bed, but it must be many years since water flowed over it, for trees of oak and horse-chestnut which we see around, are many years old. Here and there scattered among them, we can see white canvas tents, there being very few wooden houses. The butcher shop is in the open air under the trees, the meat being fastened to the boughs by means of large hooks. This answers every purpose as the canyon in only inhabited during the summer months.

We now take another road home and arrive there just in time to watch in quietness, from our window, the magnificent sunset. The sun is just sinking behind the hills, and its bright beams fall in many colors upon the water, contrasting strangely with the dull gray of the sky.

In the evening as it is moonlight we go again to the beach, where we find many people already assembled in order to watch the highest tide of the year. We sit down on the steps of the bathhouse, which are quite high. At first the waves creep slowly and softly toward us, but as the tide rises they dash upon the sand in a way that makes us well realize "the anger of the sea."

> See the sun's red light
> On the waves flash bright,
> As in tranquil beauty they stray,
> Or break on the shore,
> A wild, angry roar,
> Down, down by the beautiful bay.

CHAPTER FOUR

A Golden Land of Sunshine and Opportunity: 1880-1899

1869. ⟶   ⟵ 1882.

Rev. Mr. & Mrs. A. W. Edelman,

Respectfully request the pleasure of your company to the

✦ BAR ✦ MITZVAH ✦

OF THEIR SON,

David W. Edelman,

At the Synagogue, Fort Street, on Saturday, February 11th, 1882, at 10 o'clock A. M.

*At their Residence corner of Main and Sixth Streets,
From 2 to 6 P. M.*

Bar Mitzvah invitation for David Edelman, son of Rabbi and Mrs. A.W. Edelman, 1882

The Jews in Los Angeles had achieved considerable success by 1880. Eighty percent were employed in white-collar occupations...

The Jacoby Brothers' store located on Temple and Main Streets (looking south), 1884

Golden oranges, golden sunshine, the return of economic prosperity, land as far as the eye could see, a climate that healed the sick and infirm, a blossoming agricultural industry, and books and promotional pieces that painted a glorious picture of this "golden" land—this aptly described the City of Angels as the country approached the dawn of the 20th Century.

A famous book at the time, *California: For Health, Pleasure and Residence* (1872), was written by Charles Nordhoff, a journalist and public relations man hired by the Southern Pacific Railroad. His book was considered a guidebook that "launched a thousand trips," and is credited by many with starting the California tourism industry. The book helped to erase the Hell Town image of Los Angeles, and in the opinion of writer Carey McWilliams, "had a more far-reaching effect on the fortunes of Southern California than anything that has ever been put into print."

To the despairing Americans languishing after the depressed economic circumstances of the mid-1870s, the word pictures in the book describing the sunny land that could grow anything, gave them hope—a place to run to and escape from the depressed and depressing gloom of the Midwest and East Coast. The agricultural benefits tempted men to travel with their families and take up farming, an enterprise that would soon replace the collapsed cattle industry. The perfect climate and plentiful land with its rich soil offered a formula guaranteed to succeed. Author and historian Gordon DeMarco asserts there was also "the belief, the dream, the self-mythology, that farming in the Southland would be dramatically superior to the backbreaking drudgery that characterized farming in so much of the rest of the country."

In addition to the sunshine, Southern California had another commodity that would radically jump-start the agriculture industry—the orange, a product that would come to define the region. In 1870 the orange industry was born in a pioneer colony in Riverside established by J.W. North. The area from Riverside to Pasadena to San Bernardino became known as the "citrus belt," and shortly, with the introduction of the Valencia orange, also included Whittier, Anaheim, Fullerton, Orange and Santa Ana. The sociological implications of the orange industry were enthusiastically outlined by Carey McWilliams:

> Basically, the orange tree is the key to an understanding of the social life of the citrus belt…it is the living symbol of richness, luxury, and elegance…it is the aristocrat of the orchards [and it has created] a unique type of rural-urban aristocracy…to own an orange grove in Southern California is to live on the real gold coast of American agriculture.

In Southern California, the golden sweet orange essentially replaced the hard glittering mineral gold that had originally lured the pioneers to the west coast of the country.

The slogan "Oranges for Health; California for Wealth" became popular and could be heard from coast to coast. Not many could resist the allure of this land of plenty. With a gift of Southland fruits to the New Orleans Exposition, the Los Angeles Booster Club invited the public to "see with their own eyes the exotic bounty that came from Southern California." "Boosterism" became an integral part of the Southland lexicon, a catalyst for activities announcing to the country that California was the quintessential place to visit and take up residence.

Boosterism poster promoting the land of opportunity

Another significant aspect of the advertising blitz attracted many who came to the sunny Southland for healing. Those people facing health issues came in great numbers, arriving in the golden state to "take the cure." The climate promised curative power from the sun and mild balmy temperatures. Promotional information coming from Southern California promised "cures for all ills." The literature declared that the superb climate "could cure chronic pneumonia, tuberculosis, liver disease, 'functional female disturbances,' the ills of old age, and insomnia." This health-seeking group added considerably to the increasing surge in population, which began in the 1870s and continued uninterrupted into the 21st Century.

The boosterism campaign began to take hold as people from all over the country and abroad were being tempted to travel and relocate to the golden

In 1896, the Young Men's Hebrew Culture Association was established by Congregation B'nai B'rith. Rabbi Michael G. Solomon was the advisor of the fourteen boys in their late teens (twelve pictured above). Almost all of them became active members of the Jewish community. Left to right, top row: Abraham Kremer, Samuel Behrendt, Marco H. Hellman, Leo W. Barnett, Isaiah M. Norton and the bottom row: Henry M. Newmark, Isaac O. Levy, George N. Black, Albert M. Norton, Edgar Baruch, Robert Newmark and Samuel T. Norton

land of Southern California. There was however, another obstacle to overcome that was an impediment to arrival in the golden state. A crucial element was required in order to tempt travelers—an easier mode of transportation was urgently needed to carry people overland so they could have uncomplicated access to this new land of opportunity. The loud and vocal demand for access to the western region of the country was quickly addressed—the challenge was answered by a miracle of innovation—one that would provide a safer and faster way to travel the country.

Now came the groundbreaking and novel roadway that was made of iron rails. A new form of transportation was introduced to the frontier—an impressive and massive wondrous machine that the American Indians with a sense of awe named the Iron Horse. Painting a dramatic picture upon the majestic land, and thrust with startling impact into the pristine environment, came the rumbling dark noisy monsters spewing thick swirls of black smoke—the locomotive had arrived. The railroad lines would soon revolutionize transportation in the country and make California one of the most sought after destinations to travel to and embark upon a new life.

This single innovation—the railroad—would explode the economy to new heights and propel the Western frontier into the industrialized era that was already in full swing throughout the country. New inventions were emerging all over the world. Alexander Graham Bell invented the telephone in 1876 in the United States, while in the same year, Nikolaus Otto invented the internal combustion engine in Germany. The first telegraph linked Los Angeles and San Francisco in 1860, and in 1879 Thomas Edison invented the electric light. The industrial revolution put the wheels of progress into a fast forward mode and the railroad accelerated the pace as this modern form of transportation began to take center stage. Building the extensive railroad lines would take enormous resources and man-power, providing both travel and work opportunities to grateful immigrants coming from other countries, as well as to all Americans struggling to recover from the aftermath of the Civil War.

North Broadway (originally called Buena Vista) during the 1880s. The pueblo characteristics of the city continued into the mid-20th Century

After a spirited and dramatic political debate, the Southern Pacific Railroad had been directed by Congressional mandate to lay tracks from San Francisco directly to Los Angeles. A feeling of celebration was apparent as Los Angelenos enthusiastically welcomed the news of the coming of the railroad. As the trains arrived on the scene and began operation, the railroad companies embarked on a massive promotion and advertising campaign to encourage tourists, families, adventurers, farmers and immigrants to travel the newly laid tracks and come to sunny California. Mountains of publicity found their way to the East and Midwest.

The publicity generated by the massive marketing campaign inspired the land booms of the 1870s and 1880s and filled the trains with paying customers. Boosterism was called the new "homegrown religion" of Southern California. It was *deju vu* for those who had witnessed the gold rush; the pioneers and adventurers came now, enticed by the new "gold" in Los Angeles. Billboards displaying beautiful golden orange orchards and comfortable homes were erected—the billboards themselves establishing a brand new method of communication. The city was promoted as "a vacation destination, a place of health, vitality and grand entertainments, surrounded by natural wonders and bathed in year-round sunshine." The exotic orange was a colorful symbol of the region and flourished well in the Mediterranean-like mild climate.

Electricity was introduced in Los Angeles in 1881 and produced at the Banning Street plant (above). Gas had been introduced to the city in 1869

In tandem with the coming of the railroad to Los Angeles came the streetcar, the first on Temple Street, and the next on Second Street; operations of the streetcars began in October 1885. The Southern Pacific made transcontinental connections with other railroads, opening up Los Angeles to the eastern United States. Southern California boosterism exploded when the Southern Pacific Railroad linked Los Angeles and San Francisco.

Los Angeles High School at Fort Moore Hill, 1908

Railroads represented an exciting new adventure for the country and many were eager to ride the huge Iron Horse; the masses waited impatiently for the ticket prices to be affordable. The competition for customers among the railroads triggered a rate war in March 1886—fares that were one hundred dollars a ticket from Kansas City to Los Angeles, dropped in the ensuing price war to fifteen dollars, then twelve and finally to one dollar! The crowds were in a frenzy to purchase tickets and find their way to Los Angeles. Although the one-dollar ticket lasted only one day, it did ultimately produce an economical five-dollar fare that lasted for nearly a year.

Harris Newmark reflects on the surprising events surrounding the fare war and the unexpected benefits that he witnessed:

> A falling out between the Southern Pacific and the Santa Fe railroads brought on a rate-war, disastrous enough to those companies but productive of great benefit to Los Angeles. Round trip tickets from points as far east as the Missouri River were hammered down to fifteen dollars, and for a few days established a tourist rate of just one dollar! When normality again prevailed…the fare was fifty dollars for first-class passage and forty dollars for second-class. The low rate during the fight encouraged thousands of Easterners to visit the Coast, and in the end many sacrificed their return coupons and settled here. In a sense, therefore, this railroad war contributed to the Boom of a year or two later. Freight rates were [also] slashed during this spasmodic contest, and it was then that the ridiculous charge of one dollar per ton permitted me to bring in by rail several carloads of coal, which I distributed among my children. Such an opportunity will probably never again present itself to Los Angeles.

Golfers at Los Angeles Country Club, 1900s

The booming 1880s led to huge increases in population. According to Karen Wilson, "While the embryonic tourism industry seduced vacationers to visit, land promoters dazzled them with visions of spacious lots and beautiful homes in dream towns. Tourist and native alike became consumed with the local pastime—land speculation. Property values in the city soared from seven million dollars in 1880 to thirty-nine million dollars in 1885. At the end of the decade, more than 50,000 people lived in Los Angeles, including approximately 500 Jews."

DeMarco declared that the first wave of immigration was "middle-aged, middle-class, middle-west." Most of the immigrants coming to the United States from Europe were workers and peasants and they tended to settle first on the East Coast. The new pioneers to the West, on the other hand, were coming from an established social standing in the East and Midwest; they were grounded in stability, and able to bring money and goods with them. They had made a living, owned property, possessed bank accounts. They came from small towns and farms in the Midwest, not the more developed urban cities of Detroit, Chicago, or St. Louis. They were conservative, self-righteous, law-abiding and God-fearing Protestants bringing their own customs, traditions and languages, and they soon became the dominant majority in Los Angeles.

These Midwesterners became known by the term "Iowans" which was simply a generic term for this wave of arriving pioneers. As they settled they built Protestant churches and Americanized the pueblo. One historian wrote that one of the significant aspects of the boom was that it "wiped out forever the last traces of the Spanish-Mexican pastoral economy which had characterized California since 1769."

Following this boom period, which peaked in 1887, came the letdown, the inevitable "bust." As banks tightened their loan policies, people who had owned land for speculation and investment, found themselves overextended and their land seized through foreclosure. The economy bottomed and many of those who had come to "get rich quick" found

Isaias W. Hellman's Farmers & Merchants Bank at Commercial and Main Streets in downtown Los Angeles, 1883

Kaspare Cohn (left) moved to Los Angeles in 1859, merging in business with Harris Newmark until 1885. Cohn donated the building for the Kaspare Cohn Hospital (later became Cedars-Sinai Hospital). Leopold Harris (right), one of the leading commercial developers in Los Angeles, constructed buildings in large sections of downtown Los Angeles.

themselves broke and disillusioned and many left Southern California to return home. The population that had rapidly expanded to 80,000 in 1887, dropped precipitously to 50,000 by 1890.

The hearty souls that remained however, those that survived despite the hardships—the immigrants who stayed to make Los Angeles their home—were the eventual beneficiaries. They knew that as long as the sun was shining and oranges continued to grow, they were well ensconced in the golden land of opportunity. Some of the principal boosters in this group, understanding the value of what California had to offer, organized and created a permanent sales campaign to promote the city—thus was born the Los Angeles Chamber of Commerce in October 1888.

During this time of rampant real estate speculation and rapidly rising prices for land—the boom years—Newmark amused his readers with stories about advertising for the land:

> If every conceivable trick in advertising was not resorted to, it was probably due to an oversight. Bands announcing new locations were seen here and there in street cars, hay and other wagons and carriages (sometimes followed by fantastic parades a block long); and for every new location there was promised the early construction of magnificent hotels, theaters or other attractive buildings that seldom materialized. When processions filled the streets, bad music filled the air. Elephants and other animals of jungle and forest were gathered into shows and used as magnets….

> As competition waxed keener, dishonest methods were more and more resorted to; thus schemers worked on the public's credulity and so attracted many a wagonload of people to mass meetings…arranged to make possible an ordinary sale of real estate. Despite all of this excitement, the village aspect in some particulars had not disappeared: in vacant lots not far from the center of town it was still not unusual to see cows contentedly chewing their cud and chickens scratching for a living…. Tricksters could exercise their mischievous proclivities; and the unwary one…the tenderfoot, was easily hoodwinked. Land advertised as having "water privileges" proved to be land under water or in dry creeks….

Communication now became much easier and more main stream thanks to the railroad and the telegraph. A new campaign, "California on Wheels," was created as a byproduct of boosterism and the growth of the railroad. Southland products traveled by rail on exhibit to communities throughout the country. "Soon, every major fair in the Midwest had experienced the wonders of Los Angeles." In 1893 the Chamber of Commerce organized the Southern California Fruit Growers Exchange, which packed, shipped, and marketed the orange nationwide.

Van Nuys Boulevard, 1911. When this photograph was taken the San Fernando Valley was an open, semi-arid desert devoid of trees or buildings with the exception of the Southern Pacific Railway line that passed through at Oxnard Street. On February 22, 1911, William Paul Whitsett invited hundreds of visitors to an opening-day barbecue at this location. Visitors to the opening could see the beginning of the development taking shape. Home lots began at $350 and business property at $660. The town of Van Nuys was formally annexed to the city of Los Angeles in 1915. By 1920 Van Nuys was considered the center of the San Fernando Valley

Magazines and newspaper conglomerates sent reporters to write about the wonders of the Southland. Among the many positive stories that were covered, reports were also written about the punitive system that contributed to the physical and cultural demise of the California Indian. These early articles and books served an important purpose—they provided Los Angeles and Southern California with a history, a documenting of the stark realities of the new West.

The surge in disseminating information through magazines, press, books, and literature, had an unexpected benefit for the women of the times. A popular magazine in the region, *Land of Sunshine/Out West*, featured local fiction, reviews, Indian culture, photographs, manners and morals, and poetry. The magazine was mainly written for and about women, among them were feminists like Charlotte Perkins and Margaret Collier Graham. Many new female writers found opportunity also in writing for the magazine, including Mary Austin and Nora May French. The feminist movement had many supporters in Southern California—even in pioneer times the region was considered advanced in its liberal outlook and innovative spirit. DeMarco commented, "Women had more equal access to college in the West than was the case in the East. Women were also active in the formation of cultural and social clubs in the Southland and were quite active in the temperance movement and suffrage campaigns of the 1890s."

Two names that are a part of the fabric of this era and the growth of communication in Los Angeles history are Harrison Gray Otis and Harry Chandler, joint owners of the *Los Angeles Times*. Otis arrived in Los Angeles from Ohio in 1882 and went to work for the *Times*. He was joined by Chandler, who married Otis' daughter; Chandler was reputed to be the brains behind the *Times*. David Halberstam wrote in his book, *The Powers That Be*, that the two men were:

> ...the chief architects and the chief builders of the new society, men who did not merely aid in the growth but in effect invented the city, not just a growing community of which they were a vital and important part, but rather an extension of their will...they did not just speak for the city, they 'were' the city. The act connected the *Times* to the upper level of Los Angeles society, and it marked the real beginning of the *Times* as the paper of the Los Angeles business establishment, the paper of the powerful and the rich, the voice of Los Angeles money.

These two dynamic entrepreneurs had their hand in politics, land syndicates, water rights and laws, and the beginning of the aircraft industry in Los Angeles. They built the *Times-Mirror* dynasty and had shares in many large properties including banks, railroads, and food market chains.

First Wave of Jewish Immigration from Eastern Europe Begins in 1880

The Jews in Los Angeles had achieved considerable success by 1880. Eighty percent were employed in white-collar occupations, nearly half of these in wholesale or retail businesses. As a group they achieved greater wealth proportionately than the general population. Mitchell Brian Gelfand in the *Social Mobility of Jews in Los Angeles, 1900-1920*, documents that forty-five percent of the Jewish work force owned real or personal property in 1879, compared to twenty-five percent of the non-Jewish population. The magnitude of Jewish property acquisition impressively reflected their success: "The 1894 tax digest listed two Jewish firms as the country's two largest personal property taxpayers...Herman Hellman, $89,125, and Charles Prager, $59,765." Other names listed among the top taxpayers were Kaspare Cohn, M. A. Newmark, Ralph and Hulda Leon, Mrs. Johanna Meyer, Leopold Harris and Simon Nordlinger.

Harris Newmark's Capital Milling Company, near Chinatown, 1889

The new City Hall, 1888

Many of these immigrants had come from the same towns in Prussia and Poland and brought their family members over to join them in the golden state. "Once these Jews arrived in Los Angeles they transplanted and enhanced Old World ties through business partnerships and extensive inter-marriage." This tradition carried over into their social, fraternal, and religious organizations.

Another major influence on Jewish mobility materialized from the cultural and social differences between the German Jews and those from a Polish-Prussian background. Yiddish-speaking Polish-Prussian Jews, emerging from a history of the rigid atmosphere of Orthodox and traditional Jewish religious practice, had a more difficult time adjusting their beliefs to the norms of the general population.

On the other hand, immigrant Jews of German origins were viewed as more cultured, better educated, socially mobile and more western, thus becoming more easily Americanized. They fit homogeneously into the population of Los Angeles, and were perceived as more assimilated. Gelfand writes: "The early 19th Century Jewish enlightenment had touched Jews more deeply than their Eastern European coreligionists. Germans found Reform Judaism, which sought to diminish the barriers between Christians and Jews. The Germans' religious learnings and Germanic cultural background helped them to mix well with the city's overall population, which included a large group of non-Jewish Germans. As the Polish-Prussians came from the more traditional Eastern European milieu, the Germans considered themselves above the Polish-Prussians."

In an effort to be accepted as Americans, the Polish-Prussian Jews sought to blend in and "pass" as Germans, since the German Jews were perceived to be more conventional and fit smoothly into the established social hierarchy. In Los Angeles, the Polish-Prussian Jews and their spiritual leader, Rabbi Abraham Wolf Edelman, thus embraced "Reform" habits and customs before Congregation B'nai B'rith openly called itself Reform. Rabbi Edelman "conducted a congregation with a Sunday school, mixed choir (both male

The Hellman home at Fourth and Broadway

and female, Jewish and gentile), an organ, mixed seating, and the addition of English prayers…. During some portion of the service male heads could be uncovered…. His wife cooked on the Sabbath!" The social and economic pressure to adapt and be assimilated into the culture motivated the Jews to alter their religious traditions and adopt customs that more closely resembled those followed by the non-Jewish population.

After nearly twenty-five years of devotion and commitment to the Jews in Los Angeles, Rabbi Edelman gradually became an innocent victim of his own success. He was gently eased out of his position by what was euphemistically called a "myth" in an effort to protect his feelings. Harris Newmark, president of Congregation B'nai B'rith from

The home of Leon Loeb, who arrived in Los Angeles in 1866, photographed in 1886. Loeb worked for Solomon Lazard in his dry goods store and was later his partner in the "City of Paris" store. Born in Strassburg, Loeb succeeded his relative Eugene Meyer as the French consular agent in Los Angeles. He served the French government until 1898 when he resigned because of the attitude of the French in the Dreyfus case

1881 until 1887, was credited with being the literary inventor of the myth. Newmark wrote, "In 1886, when local Jewry instituted a much more liberal ritual, Rabbi Edelman's convictions induced him to resign." Edelman was reputedly too "Orthodox" for the liberal congregation (despite all evidence to the contrary), a tale that was easily contradicted in a newspaper article some years later when it expounded upon the "Reformed Church" which the newspaper called the "Israelite Congregation."

The evidence, according to Gelfand, indicates that

> Rabbi Abraham Wolf Edelman was never a hard line Orthodox rabbi and Congregation B'nai B'rith was never part of a truly Orthodox establishment. Rabbi Edelman became a casualty of the times—the rough pioneer times were ending and the population looked to new social stratification, new and vigorous interest in the arts, opera, education, changing fashions and new political agendas. The Jews were now seekers of change and evolving with the times. Reform [Judaism] came to the West Coast not as a new movement, certainly not as a cause, but as the slow reforming of Orthodoxy. The adaptive process of a living faith accommodating to the new life of the West.

In 1885 the Congregation B'nai B'rith board of directors replaced Rabbi Edelman with a younger, more stylish leader, a "reverend doctor." Many in the Jewish community were uneasy with the termination of Rabbi Edelman and reluctantly agreed to the change to avoid a split in the Jewish congregation. Harris Newmark's "myth" succeeded in protecting the unity of Los Angeles Jewry at least for the short term. (Rabbi Edelman's spiritual tradition was carried

Opening ceremony of electric train which ran from Hollywood to Santa Monica beach, 1896

on into the early years of the 20th Century when his son, Dr. David W. Edelman was elected president of Congregation B'nai B'rith in 1910.) The Jewish population was striving for the same benefits and rewards of career and home that the non-Jewish population was seeking, and the Jews were willing to embrace significant change in order to accomplish their goals. In their efforts to be in accordance with the times, the Jews were eager to attain middle-class values and the status and image that would have them fit in, be upwardly mobile and blend in as part of the American culture.

With the start of the boom years in 1880, population in Los Angeles exploded, commerce mushroomed, and the town continued to divest itself of the last vestiges of the Mexican frontier and emerge as a bustling American city. One of the events that marked the unofficial end of the 19th Century in Los Angeles was the death of the last governor of Spanish California, Pio Pico, politician, *ranchero*, city-builder and Californio. He died in 1894 at the age of ninety-three. When Pio Pico passed away, it was said that he took the 19th Century with him.

University of Southern California Established with Land Gifts from a Jew, a Catholic, and a Protestant—1880

Isaias W. Hellman wrote to his brother-in-law, Mayer Lehman, in the spring of 1882 that the hard years of the 1870s were finished. According to Vorspan, he expressed his confidence in the future of Los Angeles and his own work:

> Business is very fair with us. I am making up for former losses. Los Angeles County is being filled up very rapidly with the best people from every part of the United States. Thousands of persons of wealth have come here since the Southern Pacific Railroad has been completed and have bought homes already improved or have bought land and are improving the land. Real estate has increased greatly in value and is still rising. Capital is accumulating here to such an extent that interest has come down below Eastern rates….

> The Southern part of California out of its beautiful climate and the great richness of its soil is destined to become the garden plot of the country. Nevertheless I am making all preparations to have enough ready income laid aside to change our domicile should we feel at any time like doing it. At present we are perfectly contented here, our beautiful home is the site [sic] and pride of the city. My own standing financially, socially, and politically is as good as I can desire.

One of the most far-reaching and philanthropic actions taken by Hellman and his contemporaries was to have an enormous impact on the future of education in Southern California. In 1880 the Methodist University of Southern California was founded on three hundred acres of land donated by a Jew, Isaias W. Hellman, a Catholic, John Downey, and a Protestant, O.W. Childs. This college, which grew into a prestigious university, was one of the first schools of higher learning in Southern California.

The gift of land donated by the three businessmen was comprised of three hundred and eight lots and given to the trustees of the foundation established to create the university. At the time, the *Express* published this editorial:

University of Southern California (USC), 1880

> In our local columns of today are set forth the provisions of a deed executed by Messrs. O.W. Childs, John G. Downey, and Isaias W. Hellman, transferring for the purposes of endowment a large and valuable tract of land in West Los Angeles to the Trustees of an educational institution to be established here and known as "the University of Southern California." This munificent gift…insures the execution of the university project…We trust that a prosperous educational institution may come into existence, which will not only prove a benefit but an honor to the southern part of the State.

Interest in education, a vital part of Hellman's Jewish heritage, caused him to be deeply involved in the affairs of the University of Southern California (USC) as well as other academic institutions of the day. Another university honored Hellman, when, in 1881, he was appointed a regent of the University of California, Irvine, the first Jewish regent selected by the university. His tenure as regent from 1881 to 1919 is the longest on record. *The Herald* was enthusiastic and complimentary in its endorsement of Hellman:

> The appointment of Mr. I. W. Hellman, President of the Farmers and Merchants Bank of this city, as one of the regents of the University of California…is an act which reflects credit upon [the] Governor. The appointment will be accepted as quite a compliment to Southern California, which has been too much neglected in the past in all lines. It is more graceful because Mr. Hellman has for years and years been one of the most enthusiastic, unflagging and liberal Democrats in the State…. Mr. Hellman, in addition to his sterling and sagacious business aptitudes…has many notable qualifications for the trust. Many…may not know that he is a gentleman not only of vigorous intellect but of very considerable research…and a quite accomplished linguist…. In Mr. I. W. Hellman, the University of California will have an energetic, capable and indefatigable conservator of its interests.

When Hellman was appointed to the first of two sixteen-year terms, the local press congratulated California's Governor George Stoneman's selection: "Mr. Hellman is a gentleman who has shown by the management of the institutions whose affairs he has directed with such marked ability…that he will carry to the deliberations of the Board of Regents an experience that will be invaluable in the handling of the numerous financial trusts…. We congratulate Governor Stoneman on his selection, and the Board of Regents on a collaborator so well qualified."

In a generous gift reflective of the Jewish commitment to philanthropy, Hellman donated fifty thousand dollars to create a scholarship fund at the University of California, Berkeley (1916) for students needing financial assistance. This generous gift was lauded in a UC publication, which attested to and underscored the impact that Isaias and later his family made on higher education: "The Isaias W. Hellman Scholarship Fund…perpetuates the name and memory of a man and family who have contributed more of their time, thought, and means combined, to the development of the institution, than any others on record."

By 1899 there was already significant development at the Los Angeles Harbor. Today the port is second only to New York in total tonnage handled

As further testimony to his respected status as a businessman and banker, Hellman was recruited in 1890 as president of the Nevada Bank. The bank was in serious financial trouble at the time and needed an experienced banker. He moved to San Francisco to take over operation of the bank and was welcomed as "the wealthiest Hebrew in America." The rush to buy stock in the newly reorganized bank demonstrated the strength of Hellman's reputation, and stockholders were urged to hold the stock and watch their money double in the next two years.

In 1905, I. W. Hellman merged the Nevada Bank with Wells Fargo and Company Bank, to forge the Wells Fargo Nevada National Bank, where he continued as president. The Union Trust Company, another enterprise organized by Hellman, merged with the bank to become the Wells Fargo Bank and Union Trust Company in 1924, and became known as the Wells Fargo Bank in 1954. This bank stands today as one of the most successful banking companies in the country.

E. S. Heller, Isaias' son-in-law said in describing his father-in-law, "From the time the City of Los Angeles was a frontier village to the present day of its marvelous progress, he was in the foreground of the chief enterprises undertaken in the work of development." When Hellman died in 1920, Rabbi Martin A. Meyer of Temple Emanu-El, eulogized him as a man who "remained true to his people and true to their faith. He had a mighty pride in all that being a Jew implied, for he not only understood the glory of it, but he no less understood the implications of duty and obligation which that placed upon him."

Celebrating the 400th anniversary of the discovery of America on Columbus Day, Second and Spring Streets, 1892

Looking west on Third Street toward Hill Street in the residential district, 1898

Anti-Semitism Begins to Surface in Los Angeles

The period following Hellman's move from Los Angeles to San Francisco in 1890 coincided with (but was unrelated to) the beginning of the economic downturn in Southern California. The "gay nineties" began with little gaiety for natives or immigrants, according to Vorspan, as a nationwide depression began to take hold in 1893. Unemployment was rampant, banks closed; many who were overextended in land speculation could not cover their debts and were wiped out. Seeking some relief from the depression, most of the immigration in the 1890s came from the Midwest as farmers and people from small towns sought a new environment and a way to start over.

These struggling pioneers to the West arrived from Iowa, Kansas, and Missouri, "the merchant, the uprooted professional man, the farmer with an invalid wife." Jewish immigrants continued to trickle in from Eastern Europe, but sadly did not receive a warm welcome from the established Jewish community. The Eastern Europeans were at the lower end of the economic scale and laboriously sought to build their own businesses, starting with rudimentary secondhand and junk businesses. Vorspan writes "the members of Congregation B'nai B'rith were deeply embarrassed by some of the newcomers, whose struggle to eke out an existence in a pre-industrial community during hard times forced some of them to unacceptable methods of doing business."

Perhaps this unstated but transparent stigma contributed to the social exclusion of the general Jewish population, which began to surface in the late 1890s. An effort was made by the Jews to establish their own social club in the face of the social segregation by the increasingly conservative Protestant population transplanted from the Midwest. The Concordia Club was organized by the Jewish community in May 1891 for the "social and mental culture" of its members. The group soon built its own clubhouse on Figueroa Boulevard which became

Dr. Daniel Cave arrived in Los Angeles in 1897 and became one of the city's prominent dentists. He was affiliated with Congregation B'nai B'rith, friend of the Herman W. Hellman family, and a supporting member of the Jewish Orphans' Home. Photograph taken in 1898

the "inner sanctum of high Jewish society." Vorspan quotes the *Los Angeles Times*:

> With the growth of Los Angeles as a metropolis, has come a demand for social clubs, as are found in all large cities. No social club will be a thorough success which accepts anyone as a member who merely dresses decently and is able to pay the dues.... No person should be admitted as a member of the club whom the average member would refuse to admit as a guest in his home.... Only such clubs as are exclusive in regard to the character of the members, can expect to be permanently prosperous. This philosophy was coupled with a policy of exclusion which was to extend to all Jews except the few who had joined in the early years. It is doubtful that there would have been a Concordia Club if it were not for this policy of social exclusion.

The economic depression that hung low over the city coupled with a spiritual depression in the Jewish community resulted in religious services that were poorly attended. The old Fort Street Synagogue—Congregation B'nai B'rith—was sold in 1894 by a community that needed funds to survive. It was also difficult to attract qualified rabbis to this remote territory, and the community struggled until the arrival of Rabbi Moses G. Solomon in 1896. Rabbi Solomon was the first graduate of Hebrew Union College, the Reform rabbinical school in Cincinnati, to obtain a position in Los Angeles. Coinciding with the rabbi's arrival, the congregation also decided to build a new synagogue, laying the cornerstone on March 15, 1896, and dedicating the completed temple six months later in September 1896. A capacity crowd of Jews and Christians attended the gala ceremony to celebrate what was "long regarded as the finest church edifice in Los Angeles." This temple served the Jewish community until 1928 when it was sold for $500,000, and the funds that were generated were used to erect the new Wilshire Boulevard Temple.

Joseph Newmark Recalls Events at the Time of Building the New Synagogue

After worshipping for more than fifteen years in the old Synagogue on Fort Street, and five years more after that name was changed to Broadway (from 1881 until 1887 it was my privilege to serve as President of the Congregation) ...the reformed Jews of Los Angeles built in 1896, the Temple B'nai B'rith on the corner of Hope and Ninth streets....From the early part of 1895, Rabbi M. G. Solomon held the office until 1899. It was during his administration, and while Herman W. Hellman was President, that the present Temple was consecrated.

Rabbi Sigmund Hecht replaced Rabbi Solomon in 1899, and he was to lead the congregation into the new century. The new Reform rabbi's arrival marked a milestone in the development of the city's first synagogue—it completed the early pioneering of Jewish religious life in Los Angeles. Vorspan paints the picture of the Jewish community at the time:

> As the twentieth century opened, Los Angeles Jews had the communal apparatus found in most cities: a synagogue, now Reform; a B'nai B'rith lodge; a Hebrew Benevolent Society and its ladies auxiliary group; an upper-level social club. As was common, membership in the groups overlapped and leadership interlocked....
>
> One other fixture was added to the Jewish community shortly before the century closed. In January 1897 the first issue of the *B'nai B'rith Messenger* appeared. It was named in honor of the congregation which was the principal Jewish institution in the city. The *B'nai B'rith Messenge*r tended indirectly to create the community for which it unofficially spoke. The news of a community numbering little more than two thousand, and the tidings brought from the larger Jewish world far away...did much to overcome the feeling of remoteness and lack of involvement in greater than local affairs.... Once in existence *B'nai B'rith Messenger* became an important source of communal self-awareness.

The physical blueprint of the region radically altered as farmland was converted into downtown business areas, and the agriculture-based city slowly metamorphosed into a commercial city, destined to become one of the most dynamic and energetic metropolises in the country. The small Jewish population of 2,500 at the opening of the new century would expand to over 450,000 by the middle of the 20th Century. The tiny community that had been defined by family and business ties grew vigorously and needed the network of functioning Jewish organizations to keep the developing community intact and in contact. Participation by Jews in every facet of the growth of the city was in evidence, their contributions crucial to its development and extremely important in the social and economic structure of the city. They participated in real estate and building, banking and commerce, and especially in the creation of the film industry that was to come.

As the Jews rose in economic prominence, they experienced an inverse waning in their social acceptance. Their robust activity in politics and government declined and they were confined to more appointed, advisory, and technical positions. According to Vorspan "Jews ranked high within the dominant Anglo-Saxon minority in early Los Angeles society, but a pattern of social exclusion, noticeable during the 1880s, became complete in the twentieth century. Exceptions could be made still to include old Jewish settlers, but even their children were kept outside the father's clubs.... New cultural motifs became prominent—regional exoticism, evangelical uplift, Hollywood glitter—and only in the latter did Jews figure. On the other hand, the anemic cultural quality of local nineteenth-century Judaism was enriched notably by the extensive later development of Yiddish, and by the modest growth of Hebraism and traditional learning."

"I Am A Citizen of Los Angeles!"— Harris Newmark

The family oriented Jewish community of the 19th Century evolved into a larger, more assimilated group in the 20th Century, dependent upon highly structured organizations needed in order to engender a sense of community. Vorspan expands on this concept:

A Laventhal family photograph. Standing, left to right: Isidore Laventhal (1865-1920); Mrs. Lesser Hirschkowitz, nee Hannah Laventhal (1868-1943); Edward Laventhal (1861-1929); Mrs. Michael Voorsanger, nee Rebecca Laventhal (1863-1945); Seated, middle row: Elias Laventhal (1831-1903); Mrs. Elias Laventhal, nee Bertha Reich (1832-1909); Mrs. Isaac Kauffman, nee Ernestine Laventhal (1860-1936). Seated front: Mrs. Jacob Stern, nee Sarah Laventhal (1870-1933); Joseph Laventhal (1877-1907); Mrs. Leon Himmelstein, nee Florence Laventhal (1872-1946)

> The nineteenth-century Jews of Los Angeles have been called the "cornerstone Jews," but "foundation Jews" would be a still better term. They imparted of their own dignity and self-respect to the name and repute of the Jew. They were not intellectuals or artists or scholars, but businessmen and men of affairs. Honest and inventive, and courageous also, they were charitable for all sorts of causes. The Jewish pioneers were a civilizing and energizing force, quick to join and also to lead. They established and maintained Jewish life…. Theirs was the steadfastness of men in a frontier environment who could easily have dissolved into the Christian majority, yet instead built a synagogue, established organizations, and voluntarily upheld their Jewish faith in a remote corner of America. The multitudes who followed their footsteps to Los Angeles in the twentieth century built upon these achievements of the nineteenth-century "foundation Jews."

As the 19th Century came to a close, there was tremendous excitement and anticipation by the country as they welcomed the turn of the century and entry into the 1900s. The Industrial Revolution was expanding the scope of industry and inventions were emerging at a breakneck pace to keep up with the rapid developments in the economy, and social, cultural and political progress. Perhaps the man most qualified to render his editorial opinions describing the end of these pioneer days, and the transition from a tiny dusty pueblo into the developing city of Los Angeles, is the man who lived as part of the community for sixty years of his life, Harris Newmark. In a closing retrospective to his book, *Sixty Years in Southern California: 1853-1913*, Harris Newmark is eloquent in his final reminiscences, "ruminating on the past, and attempting a prophecy for the future." History is fortunate to possess his final words in which he praises the "Western spirit:"

It would be presumption on my part to make complaint against the inscrutable decrees of that Providence which guides the destinies of us all; I dwell rather, on the manifold blessings which have been my lot in this life—the decision of Fate which cast my lines in the pleasant places of Southern California. When I came, Los Angeles was a sleepy, ambitionless adobe village with very little promise for the future. The messenger of Optimism was deemed a dreamer; but time has more than realized the fantasies of those old village oracles, and what they said would some day come to pass in Los Angeles, has come and gone, to be succeeded by things much greater still. We possessed however, even in that distant day, one asset, intangible it is true, but as invaluable as it was intangible—the spirit popularly called "Western,"

Marco H. Hellman with his daughter and son

but which, after all, was largely the path of transferred Eastern enterprise. This characteristic seized upon a vast wilderness…and within this extensive area it builded [sic] great cities, joined its various parts with steel and iron, made great highways out of the once well-nigh impassable cattle-paths, and from an elemental existence developed a complex civilization. Nor is there today in all this region a greater or finer city than fair Los Angeles.

'Westward the course of empire takes its way.' When Bishop Berkeley so poetically proclaimed this historic truth, even he could hardly have had in mind the shores of the Pacific; but here we have an empire, and one whose future is glorious. This flourishing city stands, in fact, with its half million or more human beings and its metropolitan activities, at the threshold of a new era. The Southern California of the coming years will still possess her green hills and vales, her life-giving soil, her fruits, flowers and grain, and the same sun will shine upon her with the same generous warmth, out of the same blue sky as ever. The affairs of men, on the other hand, change rapidly. After gigantic labor initiated but ten short years ago, the Panama Canal is dedicated to the use of mankind, and through its crowded waters will come the ships of every nation, bringing to the marts of Los Angeles choice products to be exchanged for our own. For this and other reasons, I believe that Los Angeles is destined to become, in not many years, a world-center, prominent in almost every field of human endeavor; and that, as nineteen hundred years ago 'the humblest Roman'… would glow with pride when he said, "I am a Roman!" so, in the years to come, will the son of the metropolis on these shores, wheresoever his travels may take him, be proud to declare,

"I AM A CITIZEN OF LOS ANGELES!"

Celebrating Thanksgiving dinner in 1896 is the Harris Newmark family. Seated in the front are Mr. and Mrs. Newmark along with their children and grandchildren, in the dining room of their home at South Grand Ave and 11th Street

Achille Levy—Bean King

by Rabbi William M. Kramer and Norton B. Stern

The rich agriculture market in Los Angeles expanded to the surrounding areas into communities as far north as Ventura County, with the Jewish families extending their social and commercial relationships into these neighboring communities. Achille Levy was a pioneer merchant, agricultural economist and creative and successful banker. The Ventura Star-Free Press *wrote, "The establishment of commerce, particularly in the Hueneme harbor area, by Jewish merchants, was the real factor in the building up of Ventura County as a viable economic entity…. The role of Achille Levy and his family in creating the commercial and mercantile establishments enabled the products of the rich Ventura soil to reach markets throughout America."*

Achille Levy was an excellent example of the mercantile-oriented, Jewish immigrant who, along with others of different backgrounds, contributed to the growth, development and prosperity of the American West, by relating local productivity to distant areas of consumption. Many of these pioneers of commerce have been forgotten, but Achille has remained widely known through the Bank of A. Levy.

✳ ✳ ✳

Achille Levy was one of those who convinced the majority of ranchers in the Pleasant Valley area to go into the raising of lima beans. Previously they had raised grain and moved quickly to lima beans when they found out that the beans were easier to handle than barley. In addition, the climate and soil of southern Ventura County were ideal for the bean crop. An 1890 report indicated that beans paid 150 percent better than barley. The authority for this intelligence was Achille Levy, who also estimated that given favorable weather conditions, Ventura County would produce 1,250 carloads of beans that year.

Levy acted as broker and purchaser of much of the lima bean crop and is to be credited with developing more and more new markets. In 1889, the Hueneme newspaper noted generally that, "A. Levy is shipping beans from here to a number of Eastern points." In 1890, it was reported that Levy had an order for six cars of pink beans to be shipped to Mexico. That same year, other reports listed markets including Denver, Kansas City, Chicago, Lincoln (Nebraska), Altoona, and New York City. By late October 1890, the Hueneme growers had provided nearly 16,000 sacks of beans, "most of them shipped by A. Levy of this place." A year later, he shipped a carload of beans to New Orleans for transshipment to South America, and in 1892, a carload of beans from Levy opened up a new market at Juarez, Mexico.

The fame of Hueneme as a port, the fame of Ventura County as the lima bean center of the world, and the fame of Achille Levy as the "Bean King," were dramatically established in October 1890, when two trains traveled from the Pacific to the Atlantic emblazoned with banners bearing the words: "Beans from A. Levy, Hueneme, Cal." The first shipment was carried by the steamer Silver Spring, from Hueneme to San Pedro, where its 2,984 sacks filled ten freight cars of the Union Pacific Railroad. The second shipment was even larger, filling twelve freight cars of the Santa Fe line. Both trains were exclusively made up of Levy's beans, easily identified by the signs, which "were 20 feet long and 3 feet high, and could be read while the train was in motion." Five years later, the Ventura paper observed that:

> Mr. Levy... wanted to advertise the resources of Ventura [County] abroad and took this method of doing it. Ventura County thereby gained a great reputation as a producing section of country, and Mr. Levy is justly entitled to the credit of it.

Achille Levy's successful efforts in lima bean marketing brought him detractors as well as admirers. He was accused of being a speculator who controlled the market. The implication was that Levy, along with other "speculators," depressed local market prices by claiming that there was an oversupply of lima beans and insufficient demand for the produce.

On May 6, 1909, the farmers formed the Ventura Lima Bean Growers Association, in order to more directly control the distribution of their crop. They engaged as the manager of the association, Julius M. Waterman, of Los Angeles, who was a grain broker. He and his partner Jules

Achille Levy became the leading banker in Ventura County (adjacent to Los Angeles) towards the end of the 19th Century. The Bank of A. Levy flourished throughout the county as well as into the San Fernando Valley through the 1980s

President of the Bank of A. Levy, its founder Achille Levy at the front window of his thriving financial institution, around 1910

Kauffman were among the leading Jewish commission merchants of Los Angeles. Their brokerage business operated from 307 West First Street. Interestingly enough, Julius Waterman was a brother of William M. Waterman, who in 1902 had married Achille Levy's oldest daughter, Anna. The farmers' lima bean marketing organization had as its vice president, Adolf Camarillo, who was a director of the Bank of A. Levy. The farmers and Achille Levy maintained close working relationships in the community and in banking over the years. It was not long before the farmers realized through their own cooperative marketing experience, that what they had thought of as speculative profiteering was in reality the reward that the American economic system gives to those who creatively employ risk financing.

The Name of Los Angeles' First Jewish Newspaper

by Norton B. Stern

The first issue of the first Jewish newspaper in Los Angeles appeared on March 10, 1897, and it was named *The Emanu-El*. It was established by Lionel L. Edwards, publisher, and his friend, Victor Harris, editor, and it appeared every two weeks. Edwards had been brought to Santa Ana, California as a child of nine in 1883 from San Francisco. As a youngster, he became interested in printing and in 1894, at the age of twenty, he founded a weekly newspaper in Santa Ana, which led a struggling existence for more than two years. In late 1896, this venture was given up and young Edwards came to Los Angeles to found a Jewish paper.

Edwards was fortunate to find Victor Harris, a talented writer with a fine Jewish background, whom he appointed to the editorship. Harris was a dedicated Zionist, "a brilliant person," and a year and one half after becoming editor of the new Jewish paper he was elected secretary of Congregation Beth Israel, Los Angeles' Orthodox synagogue. Later he also became the secretary of the Los Angeles Hebrew Benevolent Society; Victor Harris was to serve as editor for over nineteen years, until autumn of 1916. During these formative years he was the heart of the new publication.

It is difficult to know why the name, *The Emanu-El*, was chosen for the new Los Angeles publication. A year and one half before, in November 1895, Rabbi Jacob Voorsanger of Congregation Emanu-El of San Francisco, had established a Jewish newspaper in that city. He named it *Emanu-El*, in honor of the congregation he served. His newspaper, a weekly, became very well known, principally because of his editorial abilities and the fact that his congregation was the most prestigious in California. San Francisco was the center of Jewish life for the entire West. It seems likely that Edwards and Harris picked *The*

Los Angeles City Hall at Second and Broadway built in 1888. The Romanesque style building was surrounded by a residential neighborhood, a stark contrast to the City Hall which was to follow

The Sofia Women's Group received significant coverage in the local Jewish press

Looking down Spring Street in 1895

Emanu-El as a name, in the hope that their paper would become the voice of Los Angeles Jewry as Voorsanger's *Emanu-El* had become the key organ of the San Francisco Jewish community. Later, however, Victor Harris was to remark editorially that the prior use of the name *Emanu-El* in San Francisco had been "unintentionally overlooked."

Rabbi Voorsanger did not deign to notice the establishment of the Los Angeles paper, which had adopted the name of his own publication, for nine months. In fact, he was to claim that he had not been sent copies from Los Angeles. We may be sure, however, given his keen knowledge of Jewish events in all parts of the West, that the existence of the new paper was known to him almost immediately. When he did condescend to acknowledge its existence, he wrote:

> We learn… that Los Angeles is now blessed with a Jewish newspaper called *Emanu-El*. The anonymous editor and publisher have not sent us a copy of his sheet; hence we cannot tell what this Southern *Emanu-El* looks like. But why this anonymous gentleman had to purloin our name is a question. The name of a newspaper is not copyrighted, we believe, and we suppose we must wish the gentleman welcome to his little share of the grab bag. But were there no other names in the dictionary? The Southern *Emanu-El* will please let us have a look at him. If he be but a decent fellow no great harm is done.

This editorial critique had its effect and Edwards and Harris sought a new name for their paper. The *B'nai B'rith Messenger* was the name chosen, and it was used as the masthead for the first time on April 12, 1898, which was the first number of volume two. Victor Harris wrote that the reason this name was chosen was "because B'nai B'rith signifies 'children of the covenant,'" and that according to the Bible the "Almighty has entered into a compact with Abraham for the perpetuation of the Jewish race, which, despite the arguments of agnostics and scoffers at the holy writ, has so far proven true." Twelve years later the same gentleman was to editorialize that the new name was selected because "the B'nai B'rith Congregation [now known as the Wilshire Boulevard Temple] was the only one at that time that was permanently established in its own building, and we named it in its honor." It is this latter explanation, which has been generally accepted as the correct one.

At the time of the adoption of the new name, *B'nai B'rith Messenger*, the paper was enlarged and copies widely distributed to the Jewish and secular press. The *Los Angeles Herald* reported that the "change in name was made because a paper in San Francisco had already appropriated the…name to itself." The *San Diego Vidette* observed that the Los Angeles Jewish paper would not be "an organ of any particular order… however, anything of interest regarding the Order B'nai B'rith: or any other Jewish order to society, will be faithfully reported."

Needless to say, Rabbi Jacob Voorsanger heard of the change in name almost at once and a week later, he editorialized in a none too gentle fashion:

> Our neighbors of Los Angeles, tired of unintentionally pirating our name, has hauled down its standard and flung a new one to the advertising winds. It is now called the *B'nai B'rith Messenger*.

Interestingly enough, Dr. David W. Edelman, who served as the president of Congregation B'nai B'rith of Los Angeles from 1910 to 1933, in his annual report to the congregation ren-

Pictured in front with his guitar and young friends is Mannie Lowenstein (1857-1939). On the back of the picture the photographer wrote, "Yiddisha Picnic." His rubber stamped imprint reads, "Joey Laventhal, Photographs, 1151 Hope Street." Their home was the residence of the Elias Laventhal family and Joey was the youngest son, born in 1877. He was a traveling salesman for the family wholesale liquor business and also had a small photo business. This photograph was taken in the late 1890s

Dr. David W. Edelman had a long medical career in Los Angeles from 1891 to 1933. He was born in Los Angeles in 1869, the youngest son of Los Angeles' first rabbi, Abraham W. Edelman

dered in 1924, recommended that it change its name. He pointed out that "because of its identity with the name of a Jewish fraternity, and Jewish publication… much confusion… is constantly arising." But it was not until after the move from the Ninth and Hope Streets synagogue location in 1929, to the new Congregation B'nai B'rith building on Wilshire, that it became better known as the Wilshire Boulevard Temple.

Though we cannot know for certain the reason for *The Emanu-El* being chosen as the name of Los Angeles' first Jewish newspaper in 1897, or the full extent of those motivations that resulted in the change of the name to the *B'nai B'rith Messenger* in 1898, we can know that Lionel Edwards and Victor Harris planted the seed of Jewish journalism well. They nurtured it through its early years with wisdom and foresight, and it has continued to serve the Los Angeles Jewish community for over three-quarters of a century.

Westwood Hills-Beverly Glen 1927. This view of Santa Monica Blvd looking east at Beverly Glen shows the Pacific Electric trestle over Beverly Glen. This area between Westwood and Sawtelle was originally a part of the Spanish Rancho San Jose de Buenos Aires which was granted to Mexico Alanis in 1840 and later transfered to the Wolfskill family. By the mid-19th Century the area was subdivided into farmland and with the coming of the 20th Century, subdivided again into home sites. Santa Monica Blvd was one of the oldest major railway corridors to the ocean, and the Pacific Electric system connected all parts of Los Angeles

CHAPTER FIVE

The Turn of the Century—A Small Village Becomes A City: 1900-1916

Born in 1882 in Little Rock, Arkansas, Max Aronson became actor Gilbert M. Anderson, better known as Broncho Billy Anderson, the first real western movie star. He started the tradition of the cowboy hero who fought for justice. His film career began with "The Great Train Robbery" in 1903, which was one of the first dramatic American films. It set the pattern of crime, pursuit, and retribution, which became the basic elements for all westerns. Aronson had been in vaudeville up to 1903, but he had never been on a horse before that time. He starred in almost 500 short westerns, for many of which he was also the director. In 1907 he was a founding partner of the Essanay Film Company. His long series of Broncho Billy movies began in 1908, and continued for eight years. In 1957, at the age of seventy-five, he received an Academy Award

This handful of Jewish immigrants, who were mostly from Russia, played a crucial role in the development of the motion picture business...

Principals at Jesse Lasky's studio, shortly after the opening of his Hollywood riding stable, Lasky sitting in center

Oil derricks on the hills surrounding Los Angeles dotted the skyline in the first decade of the 20th Century. They resembled big hammers penetrating the earth, a sight that seemed out of place in the sunny southland. Oil was discovered at the intersection of La Brea and Fairfax Avenues (bounded by Wilshire and Beverly Boulevards), and derricks and drilling equipment were actively in operation in people's back yards, with producing wells working outside their bedroom windows. At the time that Edward Doheny was bringing in his first oil well, Abbott Kinney was buying up property near the ocean. The marshy tidelands were to become a city, "an upper-middle brow Italianate chatauqua resort for greater Los Angeles."

Abbott Kinney's vision took twelve years to become reality and in 1904 the community of Venice "rose up out of the duck marsh." According to author Gordon DeMarco "it was an American replica of the Italian city that was also built on a marsh. Kinney's Venice was the most dramatic version of Southern California-as-Mediterranean-metaphor....Kinney wanted both high culture and Coney Island. He built a large theater in which he envisioned lectures, concerts and plays.... Venice shone for a few years and ultimately thrived as a beach town, but not as a temple of culture."

Established in 1905, Venice Beach was a popular seaside resort during the 1920s. Pictured above is the Hotel St. Mark at the corner of Ocean and Windward

The growth and popularity of Venice and the other satellite communities was due in large part to the interurban railroad, the Pacific Electric Railway Company. Historian Kevin Starr wrote, "Turn of the century Southern California grew because it had a remarkable rapid transit system. The railroad sported long wide red cars which served greater Los Angeles from Long Beach to San Fernando; from Riverside to San Pedro." New cities began to spring up along the routes of the mass transit system. As the new communities began to pop up on the landscape a new boom was underway—a real estate boom that followed in the wake of the electric red cars. Population in the Southland sky-rocketed and by the turn of the century there were more than 100,000 people living in Los Angeles with many more hundreds arriving each week. Rumblings were also being heard among workers, as labor and capitalists became embattled in a politically charged atmosphere that would continue until the beginning of World War II.

The popular Venice Beach, filled with sun umbrellas and bathers, 1900

Westwood Village displays its white towers beckoning travelers to come and patronize the businesses in the university town, 1937. Westwood was planned as part of an overall development by the Jenns Real Estate Company in conjunction with the establishment of the University of California, Los Angeles (UCLA), 1929. The university town would become known as "Westwood Village" and is considered one of the nation's best planned suburban real estate projects

Just as the railroads revolutionized transportation and prompted the huge influx of new settlers to the West in the late 19th Century, the beginning of the 20th Century would have an equally important catalyst for the developing young city of Los Angeles—water. At the rate of growth that the city was experiencing, water was crucial and there was an urgent need to find new sources of the liquid "gold" to support the quickly expanding population in the golden southland.

William Mulholland was born in Ireland and moved to California in 1877. He was a self-taught civil engineer, and while working as a ditch digger for the city he studied its infrastructure diligently. Mulholland worked his way up and was appointed chief engineer of the Bureau of Waterworks and Supply for Los Angeles. Later in his career, his idea to pave the crest of the Santa Monica mountain range that runs from Hollywood to the sea produced a highway that bears his name—Mulholland Drive.

Mulholland, in a scheme he felt would save Los Angeles, devised a plan to channel water into the San Fernando Reservoir across the desert and over the mountains from Owens Lake, which was in Inyo County some 250 miles away. Meanwhile, behind the scenes, powerful men working together bought up "worthless" land in the San Fernando Valley for very little money and formed a syndicate. To irrigate the land Mulholland and the syndicate targeted the Owens River and proceeded to "push the city of Los Angeles to 'steal' its water. The city

Hollywood Boulevard, which at the time was called Prospect Avenue, a country lane passing through a fruit orchard, 1899

moved through this valley like a devastating plague. It was ruthless, stupid, cruel, and crooked," wrote Morrow Mayo in his book, *Los Angeles*. Yet, after years of intrigue and political double-dealing, Mulholland won civic support to construct the longest aqueduct in the Western Hemisphere at that time. The aqueduct was considered to be an engineering miracle. Author DeMarco writes:

> Under the leadership of Mulholland, an army of 5000 men labored through blazing desert summers and freezing winters for 5 long years to complete the most gigantic and difficult engineering project theretofore ever undertaken by an American City.

In a startling conclusion to the project, which was completed on November 15, 1913, it was discovered that the plunging termination point of the aqueduct was not in Los Angeles as the population had been led to believe, but in the northwest San Fernando Valley, near the present-day site of the Golden State Freeway (Interstate 5). It was obvious that the immediate impact of the aqueduct would enormously increase the value of the land that had been grabbed so cheaply

Photograph taken at a dedication ceremony of the Jewish Orphans' Home in Huntington Park (known today as Vista Del Mar), November 28, 1912

The Concordia Club housed the family social organizations of Los Angeles' Jewish community and was organized in 1891. The building pictured above was erected on Figueroa and Venice Boulevard in 1902

by the land syndicate. It is estimated that the syndicate realized a profit of 100 million dollars at that time.

To assuage the anger and outrage of the citizens of Los Angeles, the city fathers annexed 100,000 acres of the San Fernando Valley to Los Angeles, thus, as Mayo cryptically comments, "taking Los Angeles to the aqueduct." The Owens Valley Water War raged on over the next thirty years, amidst political rhetoric, attempts to dynamite and damage the aqueduct, bitter negotiations and sit-ins. The water rights war concluded in 1941 when a reservoir—the Owens River Gorge Dam—was finally built.

The water rights issue was only one of the catalysts for growth during this first remarkable decade of the 20th Century. In addition, the orange provided the impetus for an enormous industry, beginning with the establishment of the California Fruit Growers Exchange (1905), which organized hundreds of citrus fruit growers into a cooperative. The growth of the industry from 1900 to 1920 was phenomenal, with a corresponding huge impact on the size and face of the work force that harvested the orange and other citrus fruit. The original workers were Chinese, then Japanese, then Mexican; this last group of laborers became the dominant labor force after 1914.

Another innovation, designated by many as the most significant invention of the 20th Century—the airplane—soared onto the scene and was instantly immensely popular in Los Angeles. For ten days in 1910 thousands of Angelenos gathered on a bean field for a look into the future. It was the First International Air Meet, which took place at Dominguez Field (formerly the Rancho San Pedro). Demarco describes the opening day crowd of 20,000 as they streamed onto the field to see a miracle

The Concordia Club was considered the "high society" of Jewish life in old Los Angeles

"The growing popularity of golf throughout the country will eventually bring thousands to live in Southern California," stated an advertisement to attract Americans to the Los Angeles area. Pictured above is the crowd along with 29 contestants who teed-off in the first golf tournament held on Washington's Birthday, 1900. Thirteen years later more than 100 teed-off at a Beverly Hills course. By 1925 there were 45 golf clubs in the greater Los Angeles area and the 29 golfers had grown to over 25,000

before their eyes: "They came to see Glen Curtis fly a bi-plane at an altitude of fifty feet for a half-mile. And return! It was the first powered flight in the West. They came to see the Frenchman Louis Paulham buzz the grandstand and do other amazing things. Like fly to Arcadia and back—a forty-five mile round trip. They came to see hot air balloons, dirigibles, and death-defying aerobatics." Aviation became a wildly popular sport in Los Angeles. These first men in the aircraft industry established the foundation of what was to come—including the first aeronautical club founded and organized by Jews in Los Angeles (Chapter Six).

A cornucopia of wonders was already being displayed in Southern California—the orange, the mild climate, abundant land, and accessible transportation via the locomotive and automobile—to this multitude of riches was added the airplane and the beginnings of the multi-billion dollar aircraft industry that would base in California. These early highflying pioneers paved the way for the companies of the future—Lockheed and Northrup. The arrival of the airplane provided romance and adventure and, in a more practical vein, jobs. The industry would mushroom and gain momentum as a key to the Southland's economy in the build-up to secure the planes needed for World War I.

California tourism also grew dramatically and exponentially in the early years of the new century. It seemed that everyone who lived in a cold and snowy city or town wanted to trav-

The Pacific Electric street car started service through the Cahuenga Pass to the San Fernando Valley in 1911

el to California and escape the bitter winters. As these visitors returned home extolling the wonders of the Southland, their neighbors and friends joined the throngs of visitors—many who came decided to stay and make Southern California their home. The population of Los Angeles which was 100,000 in 1900, tripled during the first decade of the new century to an incredible 320,000.

The huge surge in population led to the establishment of State Societies—organizations that were started to provide a support network and social interaction for the people arriving from various states throughout the country. They came from all over the Midwest: Kansas, Pennsylvania, Ohio, and Iowa. Each club offered their members a way to preserve their traditions and socialize with people from "home."

Along with the thousands arriving from the Midwest, many were coming from other regions that would also make their mark on the land. Among these groups, one of the largest was the Mexicans who immigrated to Southern California and numbered 25,000 by 1910, a number that doubled in the next ten years. The Mexicans took jobs as laborers in the desert mines, the citrus fields, and the cement and chemical plants. Large numbers had fled to escape the Mexican Revolution, a migration that caused great economic and social pressure to the United States. This influx of Mexican citizens also influenced the restoration of the Spanish-speaking culture that had once been an important element in the early Southern California environment.

Another large immigrant bloc was comprised of the combined Asian cultures, which were well represented in Los Angeles predominantly by the Chinese and Japanese. The Chinese preceded the Japanese and were the backbone of the labor force cultivating and harvesting the citrus fields. The first significant influx of Japanese arrived between 1900 and 1910, when they reached population figures of almost 15,000. "Little Tokyo" was the center of Japanese life on the West Coast. Like the Chinese, the Japanese began by working on the railroads, and then drifted into the agriculture industry. "Anti-Oriental" sentiment was strong and laws were enacted to bar the Chinese and Japanese from owning land as well as severely restricting their ability to lease land. But the Japanese prevailed in the developing industries of landscape gardening, abalone farming and the fish canning industry.

The Mexican and Japanese laborers attracted much of the racial hostility of the caucasian Protestant population. This ethnic bias relieved some of the pressure from the relatively small group of African American migrants to

Isadore Louis and his wife, Valentine, with their son, Henry, and Flora Rafalska, great-grandmother (at right). The family settled in Los Angeles in 1868. Henry Louis became a leading pioneer in the Los Angeles sportswear and garment industry and was active in Jewish community activities. Photograph taken in 1900

Southern California. Because of the city's strict segregation laws, blacks came in very small numbers and were restricted to certain sections: Central Avenue district, Temple Street area and Watts (known as Mud Town). An increasingly larger migration of the black population began prior to World War I, in response to the great need for workers. The same boosterism and prosperity that appealed to whites also attracted the black urban population to Southern California.

The Jewish Community Welcomes the 20th Century in Los Angeles

Author DeMarco writes, "The Jews of early Los Angeles were a 'hearty lot.' They established shops near the Plaza during the murder-a-day Hell Town era and survived—the Newmarks, Lazards, Greenbaums, Samuels, and Hellmans. Vorspan and Gartner state that Jews were generally accepted into the life of the frontier town. 'No evidence points to their exclusion from the American settlers community, nor does any sign indicate that the Jews were outsiders to those, who, after all, were themselves outsiders in the town of the 1850s....'"

As the Jewish community in Los Angeles entered the 1900s, dramatic increases in population marked their entry into the new century. Jewish population increased from 2,500 in 1900 to 20,000 by 1920. It is believed that one reason for this surge in Jewish immigration was boosterism—many came for the economic opportunities and the health benefits. Another big wave of Jewish immigrants came to the United States from Europe and found their way to Southern California as part of the great Jewish migration into the United States in the first two decades of the new century.

Jewish community leader and banker I. W. Hellman at his Farmers and and Merchants Bank, 401 S. Main Street, in downtown Los Angeles, 1905 (Photograph courtesy of Wells Fargo)

The Jewish community although small was extremely visible, especially in retail and wholesale commercial business, while also identifiable in religion and politics. The recent immigrants from Europe stood apart as a group, more foreign than American, arriving with virtually no money and speaking little or no English. As they began to trickle into the culture, many of their established Jewish counterparts in Los Angeles were embarrassed by their odd clothes and alien customs. These immigrants had difficulty adjusting to the conditions they found when they landed in the West and needed assistance to begin their assimilation into the culture.

Fortunately help and support arrived from a vigorous group of activists within the Jewish community—the Hebrew Benevolent Society. This organization, working in conjunction with the Industrial Removal Office in New York, helped Jews leave the congested Eastern cities that were unhealthy and overcrowded and assisted them to relocate and seek new opportunities in the open spaces of Southern California.

In the early years of the new century, Jewish families settled in the downtown area; some lived in the Westlake, Temple Street, and Central Avenue sections. The more prosperous Jews settled in the western part of the region—Wilshire Boulevard, West Adams, and Hollywood. According to DeMarco:

Large crowd greets President McKinley arriving at the Hotel Van Nuys in 1901

> Los Angeles was as strange a human mixture as any on the planet. It was like a lower east side of New York planted in the cultural cornfield of small town Iowa. It was rice cakes, corn tortillas, as well as matzo crackers on a plate of meat loaf and mashed potatoes. It was crazy. It was impossible. McWilliams called Los Angeles 'an archipelago' of social and ethnic islands, 'interrelated, but culturally disparate.'

Toward the end of the 1910s, the concentration of the Jewish workers and lower middle class began settling east of downtown in Boyle Heights. At the turn of the century, the Jews had been living in the "old Boyle Heights [which contained] the Hebrew Sheltering Home, the Talmud Torah, the Modern Social Center, the Day Nursery, the area around the Breed Street Synagogue," and the soon to be established Kaspare Cohn Hospital. The new Boyle Heights was distinctly different in that the residents were "Orthodox in their religious beliefs but in their daily life were people of modern ideas and tendencies… newcomers from the East and from Canada [and from] the Southwestern part of Los Angeles who wished to live in a community where their neighbors, like themselves, were Orthodox Jews," wrote Vorspan.

The first quarters of the Jewish Orphans' Home were in the old Charles Stern mansion at Mission and Macy Streets. The structure burned down in 1910. In 1912 a new Home was established in Huntington Park which subsequently relocated to its present facility in West Los Angeles

Other forms of Judaism and Jewish expression also flourished in Boyle Heights, where Jewish storekeepers built prosperous businesses. Yiddish was commonly spoken and the thriving neighborhood would become a large-scale Jewish environment, developing well into the 1920s.

While the foremost names in Jewish business in the late 1800s were Newmark, Hellman, and Baruch, as the new century opened some new names came to the forefront. Harris Newmark's nephew Kaspare Cohn ran a very

137

Hollywoodland was a planned development north of Beachwood Boulevard. Here many of the early film stars built their mansions and fantasy castles. This photograph captures the look of the land just prior to the building of this new neighborhood, 1923

successful hide and wool business and also operated as a local banker for the farmers and sheepherders. His two sons-in-law, Ben R. Meyers and Milton E. Getz, ran Cohn's bank, the Union Bank and Trust Company. The Hellmans remained active in the Farmers & Merchants National Bank of Los Angeles. Another leading Jewish businessman of the time included David Hamburger, proprietor of the large People's Department Store. Haas, Baruch & Co., a wholesale grocer was established, descended from the earlier grocery business of Hellman, Haas & Company.

Jewish immigration to Southern California established a substantial Jewish working class in Los Angeles. Most Jewish families were occupied with simply making a living as shopkeepers, workingmen, clerks or artisans, and some few professionals. A small percentage were teachers and lawyers; shopkeepers were a relatively large group along with artisans, while the biggest labor pool was found in white collar work—clerks, managers, bookkeepers, accountants, and insurance men. Jewish shopkeepers generally sold food or clothing, and the manufacturers produced clothes, furniture, and cigars. Real estate was a valuable commodity and many Jews invested in land, either to build homes or to hold for appreciation of property values.

Many Jewish workers were involved in the garment and clothing business, and the city's Jewish tailors became organized as part of the International Ladies Garment Workers Union, founded in 1900. Union organizing and workers strikes would become more fully developed later in the 1920s and 1930s. Other occupations and trades included bakers, butchers and other food related specialties.

Hollywood: The Birth of the Motion Picture Industry

Just as the pioneer Jews of the 1850s and 1860s helped to build commercial Los Angeles, a small handful of Jews in the first two decades of the century laid the foundation for an industry that would someday designate Los Angeles as "the entertainment capital of the world." This handful of Jewish immigrants, who were mostly from Russia, played a crucial role in the development of the motion picture business.

The story of the emergence of the film industry in Los Angeles is as colorful and outrageous as the movie business itself. When Colonel William Selig sent his director Francis Boggs to Los Angeles in 1907 to complete *The Count of Monte Cristo*, one might think that the reason was the good weather—they could not shoot outdoor scenes in their Chicago based studio in winter. But there was a bigger and even more significant reason at the time—they came to California to be one step ahead of the process servers and enforcers of the patent trust. To understand this aspect it is important to explain the origins of the film business starting with the earliest version of the "moving pictures."

The First National Studios, 1927. The First National Picture Corporation Studios were built on the site of the Burbank family ranch at the intersection of Olive Ave and Barham Blvd in 1926. The town of Burbank was founded in 1887 and was incorporated as a city in 1911. The first movie making came to Burbank in 1912 when the Universal Film Company used the foothills of Griffith Park as a filming location. Film maker D.W. Griffith made the ranch famous when he produced the epic The Birth of a Nation *there in 1915. First National built a modern sound studio on the site of the Burbank Ranch with four sound stages and facilities of the highest quality. In 1928, Warner Brothers Pictures purchased the assets of First National and took over the studio renaming it Warner Bros. First National Studios*

The Three Stooges were among the first Jewish comedians on screen

The movie business had its beginnings in the first "store shows" started on Fourteenth Street in New York City in a neighborhood packed with Jewish immigrants. These first "peep shows" and nickelodeons were soundless ten-minute reels that appealed to the common man, especially since these immigrants could not speak English. The young Jewish entrepreneurs were quick to see the possibility of this crude primitive early form of the moving picture and partnered with each other to gain a foothold in this developing industry. In an attempt to thwart these fledgling companies, in 1907 the Edison Company gave exclusive licenses to eight production companies to use the Edison technology of film processing and camera operation. (In 1890 Thomas Edison had developed and patented the two chief components of moviemaking, a camera and a projector.) The Motion Picture Patents Company known as "The Trust" formalized this procedure in 1909, requiring filmmakers to pay what many felt were unfair taxes on equipment and royalties on each foot of film.

The Edison Trust flexed its muscle, both literally and figuratively, and attempted to stop the young capitalists from making their reels longer than ten minutes through lawsuits and strong-arm methods—fortunately for the movie-loving public, they were ultimately unsuccessful. The audiences wanted more—longer and better films, and the young Jewish businessmen fought to give their public what they wanted. The "ransom" demanded by the heavy handed Edison Trust motivated the filmmakers to flee to the West Coast where they would be further away from The Trust—they relocated to a place where they would have the freedom to make movies the way that they wished. Adventurous showmen and restless creators sought and found a refuge in Southern California to make their feature films surreptitiously. As the law came closer in the East, the sunny, mellow weather in Hollywood offered a strong appeal. The development of films, which began in New York City, shifted to Hollywood between 1907 and 1912.

When the early filmmakers arrived to take advantage of Los Angeles' perfect climate and distance from The Trust's thugs, they at first received a very chilly reception from the people of Los Angeles. The movie people were referred to as the "movie colony" and signs were prominently hung on countless apartment buildings stating: "No Dogs or Actors Allowed." Despite the lukewarm atmosphere, the movie business arrived in full force in Southern California, pioneered by names like D.W. Griffith, Thomas Ince, and Mack Sennett—inventor of the Keystone Cops.

The real momentum of the motion picture industry began when three men came together in New York City in 1912—Jesse Lasky, a vaudeville producer; Sam Goldfish, Lasky's brother-in-law and refugee from Poland, also a successful glove manufacturer; and Cecil Blount (C.B.) DeMille, actor, playwright, and director. The three men raised the capital to launch a film company, the Lasky Famous Players Company, which bought the rights to *The Squaw Man*, a popular stage play, and the three men decided to shoot it as a film in Flagstaff, Arizona. Shortly after their arrival in Arizona, Lasky still in New York, working on distribution and marketing the film, received a telegram from C.B. Demille:

FLAGSTAFF NO GOOD FOR OUR PURPOSE. HAD TO PROCEED TO CALIFORNIA. WANT AUTHORITY TO RENT BARN IN PLACE CALLED HOLLYWOOD FOR $75 A MONTH. REGARDS TO SAM. CECIL

Fox Movietone Studios, 1927. The Fox Studio entrance in the Spanish colonial style on Santa Monica Blvd next to Beverly Hills. In 1925 the William Fox Film Corporation purchased a tract of land called the Fox Hills Tract where 20th Century-Fox is today. By 1926 several Fox productions were being shot including some Tom Mix westerns and What Price Glory*, an epic about World War I. In 1928 a new studio was constructed at the Pico Blvd entrance, Movietone City which would be one of the first sound film studios in the world. The William Fox Studio in Hollywood was moved to the new location. By 1931 most Fox productions were being made at the new facility. The 1935 merger of Fox with 20th Century Productions created 20th Century-Fox Studios*

The Marx Brothers appear to be "Jewish pioneers" of the Wild West

Goldfish (who changed his name to Samuel Goldwyn in 1915), responded:

> AUTHORIZE YOU TO RENT BARN BUT ON MONTH-TO-MONTH BASIS. DON'T MAKE ANY LONG TERM COMMITMENT. REGARDS. JESSE AND SAM.

Ironically, the horse barn that DeMille rented was in a tiny suburb of Los Angeles, a little hamlet known as Hollywood. Thus the motion picture business, born in a barn, found its real roots in a city that would soon be known for its celebrities, for its glamour and glitter; the city would emerge as a place of dreams, of breathtaking innovation, and enormous and highly visible wealth.

An amusing anecdote is told about those early days describing the primitive conditions under which the movie people were compelled to work. DeMille had agreed to share the barn with the owner, Jacob Stern, who kept his horses there. It was said that DeMille had to wear big black galoshes to protect his shoes from the water that was used to clean the barn and the urine from the horses that constantly spilled onto the floor.

Baby Snooks (Fanny Brice) playing around with Daddy Snooks (Hanley Stafford)

DeMarco chronicles the early days of the motion picture business:

> DeMille, Griffith, and Adolph Zukor were three giant figures that made major contributions to the development of the American film industry. They took it from a curiosity and made it an art form as well as a mass entertainment. From the nickelodeon they turned it into an industry. They were instrumental in taking Hollywood through its infancy and in a very short period of time delivered it a mature business, a creative assembly line whose product—dreams, romance, illusion, and entertainment—captured the imagination of the entire nation…. D.W.Griffith brought 'protean genius' to the Hollywood film. DeMille brought the showmanship and spectacle. Zukor brought the business savvy that was to build the empire.

Hollywood once again brought to Southern California yet another descendent of the Gold Rush—resulting in Hollwood's population increasing from about 500 residents in 1900 to nearly 8,000 by 1913. Fashionable clothing stores, boutiques, and restaurants appeared along Hollywood Boulevard and its side streets. Tourism flourished as hundreds came each day to stroll down Hollywood Boulevard and watch the silent movies being shot.

The tourists were attracted by the show and the "perpetual vaudeville" that entertained them. The show was a spectacle with teams of filmmakers using the streets and buildings of Hollywood as a vibrant backdrop, exploiting every element of Hollywood to their advantage. Paul Zollo, writing about the times, quotes Dr. Edwin Palmer, from Zollo's *History of Hollywood* book written in 1937:

> Their presence was dramatic and pervasive. Private homes were gratuitously used for elopements and domestic dramas. Banks were utilized on holidays, Saturday afternoons, and Sundays for hold-up scenes. Drug stores and other places of business were regularly robbed before the camera. Citizens were halted on the streets to augment mob scenes. Streets were roped off for automobile accidents, often hosed down to make autos skid and turn over…. An army of almost any nation or age marching down Hollywood Boulevard behind a camera on the rear of a car, with one over the hood of the car following, was a common sight…. Christies' Bathing Beauties in costumes many years in advance of the time would rush down the street to their favorite restaurant for a between-acts lunch. Face paint and lipstick were introduced to the rural maiden as the conventional thing.

1913 was the same year that an English vaudeville comedian named Charlie Chaplin came to California to make movies. Chaplin signed with the Keystone Film Company and developed one of the most beloved and timeless characters in film history, "The Little Tramp." This role led him to phenomenal heights as a celebrity; his earnings of $10,000 a week made him one of the richest men in the world, according to Zollo.

The movie industry quickly grew from a crude form of vaudeville into a "medium capable of capturing the beautiful mystery of our very dreams, and of aspiring to the realm of serious art." Thus began the seductive allure of Hollywood, armed with its capability of attracting thousands of would-be film stars, producers, and technicians from all parts of the East—they came and converged on Hollywood Boulevard.

Jack Benny (left) and George Burns enjoy a day at the beach

The cornerstone of the mega industry had been set—the streets that comprised the city of Hollywood were the locations for what would become the major film studios in the motion picture business. In 1919 Charlie Chaplin, Douglas Fairbanks, Mary Pickford, and D.W. Griffith joined to form United Artists. Harry and Jack Cohn, two brothers, teamed up with Joe Brandt to establish Columbia. William Fox, starting out in 1915 in the former Selig Studio, built a studio at the corner of Sunset and Western, which became 20th Century-Fox.

Another of the huge film studios, Warner Brothers, originated in 1918 when the four Warner brothers—Harry, Jack, Sam, and Albert, made their first feature *My Four Years in Germany*, at a massive studio they built on Sunset Boulevard. This studio would make technological history in 1926 when their first picture introducing sound effects and music, *Don Juan*, was produced. The following

George Jessel, performer and spokesman for the USO

year they released the first official talking picture, *The Jazz Singer*, a Jewish themed movie starring Al Jolson, the first film that incorporated synchronized dialogue. In 1928 Warner Brothers moved to Burbank to satisfy their need for the additional space that was required for the new equipment to make the "talkies."

The original Lasky Famous Players Company became Paramount Studios when they purchased United Studios on Melrose Avenue. Paramount was home to the big directors Cecil B. DeMille and D.W. Griffith, and a list of movie stars that included Mary Pickford, Clara Bow, Gary Cooper, and Marlene Dietrich.

The American film industry was founded, and for more than thirty years was operated by, Eastern European Jews. The storefront theaters of the late 1910s were transformed into the movie palaces of the 1920s by Jewish exhibitors. And when sound entered the picture, a battalion of Jewish writers poured into Hollywood, mostly from the East. Jews ran the most powerful talent agencies, Jewish lawyers transacted most of the industry's business, and Jewish doctors treated the stars' illnesses. At the top of the business pyramid, Jews produced the movies.

As the city of Hollywood became so successful at the heart of the new American dream called movies, the cultural composition of the area began to change as big numbers of Jewish New Yorkers and Chicagoans infiltrated this primarily Christian community. The city's original inhabitants grumbled at the changes in the neighborhood as they watched Jewish proprietors take the place of gentiles; new kosher and kosher-style restaurants opened and the first Hollywood synagogue—Beth-El—was established on Wilton Place, north of Hollywood Boulevard.

As Jewish names became synonymous with Hollywood and the film business, an insidious wave of anti-Semitism began to rise as an ugly torrent from a growing group of racist

Goldberg family celebrates at a seder in the early 20th Century

extremists and religious fanatics. This "anti-Semitic demonology" accused the Jews of undermining American values. As Neal Gabler wrote in *An Empire of Their Own*:

> Ducking from these assaults, the Jews became the phantoms of the film industry they had created, haunting it but never really able to inhabit it. What deepened the pathos was that while the Hollywood Jews were being assailed by 'know-nothings' for conspiring against traditional American values and the power structure that maintained them, they were desperately embracing those values and working to enter the power structure. Above all things, they wanted to be regarded as Americans, not Jews; they wanted to reinvent themselves here as new men.

Gabler points out that this first generation of Hollywood Jews were "a remarkably homogeneous group with remarkably similar childhood experiences." From Carl Laemmle, the eldest, to Adolph Zukor, William Fox, Louis B. Mayer, Benjamin Warner and his sons, Harry, Sam, Albert, and Jack—all were raised in poverty in Eastern Europe. Coming out of Germany, Hungary, Russia, and Poland, they were united by their Eastern European origins. More overriding than their birthplace and difficult early lives, they were tied by a common thread—their "utter and absolute devotion to their new country…. Something drove the young Hollywood Jews to a ferocious embrace of America. Something drove them to deny whatever they had been before settling here." They were anxious to erase their past—the European roots, language and accents, customs and religion.

These Jewish moviemakers wanted to be part of America, where they would be respected and attain prominent social status. Unfortunately these goals seemed to elude them. Gabler quoted one Jewish producer: "The motion picture hierarchy felt they were on the outside of the real power source of the country. They were not members of the power elite. They were outside of that New England-Wall Street-Middle West money." A large part of the appeal of the movie industry for these Jewish entrepreneurs was the hope that they could break through the barricades erected by the American gentile power structure that existed outside of Hollywood. Inside the film business the Jews encountered no social barriers or the typical impediments that were being imposed by other professions to keep Jews and other "undesirables" out.

Lauren Bacall, film star and actress (also first cousin of Israel's former Prime Minister Shimon Peres)

Adding to the attraction of the business, was the fact that the Jews, having come from compatible businesses in fashion and retail, understood the tastes of the public; they were "masters at gauging market swings, at merchandising, at pirating away customers and beating the competition. As immigrants themselves, they had a peculiar sensitivity to the dreams and aspirations of other immigrants and working-class families…a significant portion of the early movie-going audience." The Jews knew their audience because they themselves were the "mirror image" of their audience.

The primary appeal that sparked the Hollywood Jews was their hunger for assimilation—in making films they saw they could satisfy that hunger. They would "build an empire of their own creation," make it into the image they wished for themselves as prosperous and successful Americans. This was to be their America and their

legacy would leave behind a composite of "values and myths, traditions and archetypes." Thus the Hollywood Jews set out to reinvent themselves and in so doing built large lavish estates, formed and became members of an upscale country club—Hillcrest—when they were restricted from membership in the Christian dominated country clubs. They were socially, politically and culturally active, but at the same time they hid their Judaism by quietly removing themselves from outward displays of their religion. "Ultimately, by creating their idealized America on the screen, the Jews reinvented the country in the image of their fiction."

Congregation B'nai B'rith was a thriving synagogue when Rabbi Magnin arrived from San Francisco in 1915

Jewish Religious and Cultural Life Grows in New Directions in the Early 1900s

The life of the Hollywood crowd was quite separate and very different from the other residents of Los Angeles—the world of the diligent lawyer, worker, or businessman was far removed from the realm of "celluloid fantasy." The men in Hollywood were building an empire—the motion picture industry. The rest of the Jews in Los Angeles were busy building their own businesses determined to earn the respect and acceptance of the general community. In the early decades of the 20th Century, ethnic divergence in Los Angeles was a commonly accepted fact, while ethnic politics was virtually non-existent. Aside from the Mexicans, who were viewed as outsiders, Los Angeles was overwhelmingly white, Protestant, and Anglo-Saxon.

In other cities across the country, especially on the East Coast, anti-Semitism became increasingly more visible. Its relative absence in the undeveloped pioneer Southwest was considered another advantage to life in Southern California. The cultural life of the "average" Jew did not differ very much from that of his gentile neighbors. Theater, lectures, and musical evenings were the predominant entertainment elements at the time. A group of Yiddish writers in Los Angeles produced a significant body of literature. The Jewish community was linked to important events through their principal cultural news medium, the *B'nai B'rith Messenger*, which also transmitted news of American and world Jewry.

The religious life of the Jewish community remained stable. At the turn of the century two synagogues existed in Los Angeles, the Reform Congregation B'nai B'rith (which became the Wilshire Boulevard Temple), and the Orthodox Beth Israel. Conservative Judaism is said to have developed out of a conflict between Orthodox and Reform beliefs, although others speculate that Conservatism arose from a conflict among Orthodox Jews. This latter disagreement resulted in a group from Beth Israel splitting off and forming Sinai Temple, which remains the oldest and largest Conservative synagogue in Los Angeles, according to Mitchell Gelfand. By 1920, ten congregations existed in the city.

With the religious scene in Los Angeles divided between "stern puritanical standards and nearly Utopian religious liberalism" Jewish sympathies understandably swayed in the more liberal direction. At one end of the spectrum Jews were eager to assimilate, at the opposite end was the community of traditional Jews, comfortable with the Yiddish language and maintaining their orthodoxy.

Sophie Tucker, famous for her singing, acting and rendition of My Yiddishe Mama

A throng of opera lovers gather for an outdoor concert in the early 1900s in Pershing Square

Rabbi to the Stars—Edgar Fogel Magnin

Rabbi Sigmund Hecht was the religious leader of the largest congregation in Los Angeles, the Reform temple, Congregation B'nai B'rith and was the authoritative voice of the Jewish community until he retired at the age of seventy. In 1914 when Rabbi Hecht was sixty-five, the congregation hired a young assistant to help with temple business. The young twenty-five year old native Californian accepted the position of associate rabbi with an annual salary of $2,500. This new rabbi had an extraordinary destiny before him—one that would catapult him into a leadership position in the Jewish community for the next fifty-five years. The young man was Rabbi Edgar Fogel Magnin. Vorspan writes "the young colleague differed greatly from Rabbi Hecht in bearing: his speech in and out of the pulpit and his personal manner were forthright and direct. During the 1920s he gradually became the spokesman for Judaism in quarters where it was seldom heard. The radio, Kiwanis Club, and Hollywood

The famous "Angels Flight" as seen at the Hill Street tunnel in this 1907 photograph was the "shortest paying railway in the world." Its two cable cars carried residents to the fashionable Victorian neighborhood on Bunker Hill in downtown Los Angeles

Class Motto: "BE THOU A BLESSING."

CONFIRMATION
AT
Temple B'nai B'rith
LOS ANGELES CALIFORNIA

Shabuoth: The Feast of Weeks
5673

Wednesday, June 11, 1913
AT 9:30 A. M.

S. HECHT, D. D., Rabbi

MISS CELIA DAVIDSON, Soprano
MISS JULIE K. CHRISTEN, Alto
MR. HAYDN G. JONES, Tenor
MR. EDWIN HOUSE, Baritone
MR. ERSKINE H. MEAD, Organist and Director
MR. JULIUS KRANZ, Violinist

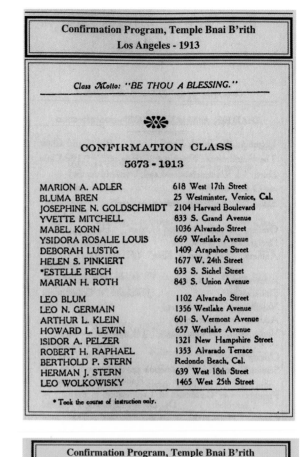

**Confirmation Program, Temple Bnai B'rith
Los Angeles - 1913**

Class Motto: "BE THOU A BLESSING."

CONFIRMATION CLASS
5673 - 1913

MARION A. ADLER	618 West 17th Street
BLUMA BREN	25 Westminster, Venice, Cal.
JOSEPHINE N. GOLDSCHMIDT	2104 Harvard Boulevard
YVETTE MITCHELL	833 S. Grand Avenue
MABEL KORN	1036 Alvarado Street
YSIDORA ROSALIE LOUIS	669 Westlake Avenue
DEBORAH LUSTIG	1409 Arapahoe Street
HELEN S. PINKIERT	1677 W. 24th Street
*ESTELLE REICH	633 S. Sichel Street
MARIAN H. ROTH	843 S. Union Avenue
LEO BLUM	1102 Alvarado Street
LEO N. GERMAIN	1356 Westlake Avenue
ARTHUR L. KLEIN	601 S. Vermont Avenue
HOWARD L. LEWIN	657 Westlake Avenue
ISIDOR A. PELZER	1321 New Hampshire Street
ROBERT H. RAPHAEL	1353 Alvarado Terrace
BERTHOLD P. STERN	Redondo Beach, Cal.
HERMAN J. STERN	639 West 18th Street
LEO WOLKOWISKY	1465 West 25th Street

* Took the course of instruction only.

**Confirmation Program, Temple Bnai B'rith
Los Angeles - 1913**

Class Motto: "BE THOU A BLESSING."

ORDER OF SERVICE

Processional .... Organ and Violin
(The candidates for Confirmation, escorted by the President and Vice-President of the Congregation, and by members of last year's class, enter the Temple.)

Greeting .... Rabbi and Choir

Invocation .... Mabel Korn

Hymn, "Prayer for Guidance," .... The Class
(Ritual Service, pp. 186-188 and 196-200, Prayer-book)

Opening Prayer .... Ysidora R. Louis

Ark Service:
    Reading from Micah IV .... Leo Blum
    Exaltation of the Torah .... Isidor A. Pelzer

First Benediction .... Leo Wolkowisky and Class

Reading the Scriptural Lesson from the Torah
    Berthold P. Stern and Helen S. Pinkiert

Second Benediction .... Robert H. Raphael and Class

Reading from the Book of Ruth .... Yvette Mitchell

Hymn, "Happy Who in Early Youth" .... The Choir

Floral Prayer I. .... Bluma Bren
(Floral offering, the members of the Class advance toward the open Ark, and deposit their flowers, organ and violin accompanying.)

Floral Prayer II. .... Marion A. Adler

**Confirmation Program, Temple Bnai B'rith
Los Angeles - 1913**

Class Motto: "BE THOU A BLESSING."

ORDER OF SERVICE—CONTINUED

Returning the Torah Scroll .... Rabbi and Choir

The Fundamental Teachings of Judaism .... The Class

Duet, " I Waited for the Lord," (*Mendelssohn*)
    Soprano and Tenor

Essay, "Philanthropy Among the Jews"
    Howard L. Lewin

Oration, "The Brotherhood of Man" .... Herman J. Stern

Declaration of Principles .... Arthur L. Klein

Anthem, "The Lord is King" (*F. Stevenson*)
    The Choir

Address to Parents .... Deborah Lustig

Consecration .... Josephine N. Goldschmidt

Valedictory .... Marian H. Roth

Address and Blessing .... The Rabbi

Violin Solo, "Album Blatt," (*Wagner-Wilhelmj*)
    Mr. Julius Kranz

Closing Prayer .... Leo N. Germain

Service Concluded, Prayer-book pp. 224
    Rabbi and Congregation

Presentation of Certificates of Confirmation to the
    Confirmed .... Dr. D. W. Edelman, President

Chorus, "Hallelujah" .... The Choir

Benediction and Dismissal .... The Rabbi

Postlude.

Program for confirmation ceremony in 1913 at Congregation B'nai B'rith, now known as Wilshire Boulevard Temple

Bowl were platforms for the vigorous, outspoken Rabbi Magnin. His reputation soon extended far beyond Los Angeles."

Many prominent Jewish members of the community supported Rabbi Magnin, among them was Dr. David Wolf Edelman (son of old Rabbi Edelman)—president of the congregation from 1910 until his death in 1933. Dr. Edelman was a "lay" leader who often took over in the pulpit during the absence of Rabbi Magnin. Rabbi Magnin's illustrious career began with a simple and eloquent statement of his philosophy as a Jew. As explained by Vorspan:

> Judaism as expounded by Rabbi Magnin did not have much theoretical cutting edge. It was viewed as that tradition…whose power and truth inspired all men to conduct good lives and erect the good society. Rabbis ought to lead in this greatest of enterprises, and Rabbi Magnin personally furnished an exemplar of meaningful civic endeavor.

Rabbi Edgar F. Magnin began his rabbinical career in Los Angeles in 1915. For well over half a century he was the spiritual leader of Wilshire Boulevard Temple (formerly Congregation B'nai B'rith)

When Rabbi Magnin arrived on the scene, the Jewish community in Los Angeles was philosophically and culturally divided into three basic groups—the German Jews, predominant and preeminent, they controlled the money, power and status in the community. They held themselves above the Russian Jews, who they viewed as immigrants from Eastern Europe, and who were more closely associated with Jewish religion and customs. The two groups rarely mingled and the German Jews often felt more aligned with gentile Americans and, according to Gabler, sought to emulate their Christian "gentility," many even celebrating Christmas while ignoring the Jewish holidays and traditions. Rabbi Magnin said the breach would be healed only when "the bright, upcoming young Jewish lawyers and doctors descended from [Eastern Europeans] marry the ugly girls of the Germans."

The third group, the Hollywood Jews, who were Eastern European in origin, German in attitude, was separate from both the other two. They were ignored by the Boyle Heights Jews and the German Jews critically referred to them as the "vulgar nouveau riche." Gabler writes,

> Such was the Jewish community over which Magnin would preside: wary, divided, status conscious. But to the gentiles in Los Angeles, all Jews, regardless of rank, were suspect, and their hands were to be kept from the levers of power. In 1909 there were only five Jewish attorneys in the city, in part because most firms proscribed hiring Jews altogether, and those that did hire proscribed making them partners, so that Jewish attorneys could really only serve the small Jewish community.

In Los Angeles the most thinly veiled anti-Semitism was reserved for the social country clubs, none of which accepted Jews. Even the prestigious gentlemen's clubs that formerly accepted wealthy German Jews refused them entry to be certain they were not invaded by the "rich, illiterate immigrant Jews of Eastern Europe." It was clear the Jews needed a new social ambassador, and Magnin gracefully stepped into the role. In June 1920 Magnin and a group of German Jews (most from the Congregation B'nai B'rith), formed the Hillcrest Country Club, purchasing 142 acres adjacent to Beverly Hills. "Within a year, in this essentially bar-

Al Jolson stars in The Jazz Singer

ren territory, they had erected something splendid enough to rival the bastions of the gentiles they envied and emulated."

Hillcrest was dominated and managed by the "power" Jewish families at the time—the

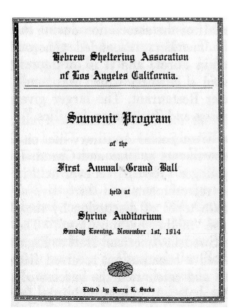

Front page of program for Hebrew Sheltering Association (Jewish Home for the Aging) event held at the Shrine Auditorium, November 1, 1914

Newmarks, Hellmans, Cohns, Loebs, and the Schiffs, the "Jewish court of nobility." At first they did not welcome the Hollywood Jews, though that policy changed after the Depression, and this illustrious group did join as members. While the German Jewish founders of the club were the financial and commercial seat of the Jewish community, the Hollywood Jews had a different use for their club membership— Hillcrest became a "sanctuary for their Jewishness." The Hollywood Jews never came close to commandeering Hillcrest; "they were there to enjoy the conviviality and the prestige. But whether by design or by nature, they did pierce the curtain of gentility. On Sunday nights there were loud and lively dinners, and afterward the movie Jews would show their recent films." At an annual golf event at which the members dressed in costume, Harpo Marx ran through the course in a gorilla suit. It was his brother Groucho who cryptically made the now classic statement: "I wouldn't want to be a member of any club that would have me as a member," a joking reference to Hillcrest.

Hillcrest ultimately forged an alliance between the two groups, which strengthened the Jewish community. This was critically important with the advent of the 1930s when the Jewish population, confronted with overt and vicious anti-Semitism, was urgently needed to contribute and raise funds for Jewish causes. As Gabler concluded:

> At Hillcrest the movie Jews and the German Jews who had originally ostracized them found they had more in common than wealth. They had their Judaism. They had their enemies. And they had their fear.

(A capsule biography highlighting plateaus in the career of Rabbi Magnin is included in this chapter, page 165.)

Establishment of Major Jewish Organizations: Jewish Home for the Aging, City of Hope, Jewish Federation, Vista Del Mar, and Kaspare Cohn Hospital

Alongside the slowly growing congregations fulfilling the roles of Reform, Conservative and Orthodox Judaism, philanthropy was also on the rise as the Jews in Los Angeles organized and maintained the charities typically found in Jewish communities throughout the country, including the Hebrew Benevolent Society (HBS) and the Ladies Hebrew Benevolent Society, and Congregation B'nai B'rith's Women's Society.

Vorspan summarizes this active and dynamic period in the Los Angeles Jewish community:

> A six years' flowering of new institutions demarcates the most significant period in the first century of Los Angeles Jewish philanthropy. Between 1909 and 1915, five major institutions were founded or transformed, and the transition from charity aid to systematic welfare was clearly discernible. Philanthropy became a central rather than peripheral interest of the Jewish community. The effort focused upon local deeds, with occasional collections and small Federation subsidies to a few national institutions.

New York's Industrial Removal Office continued to send workers to Los Angeles in an attempt to remove Jews from the crowded and impoverished New York City neighborhoods, many to escape the consumptive disease that was epidemic in the East. The city and Jewish community were overwhelmed, according to Vorspan, by "these pitiable victims of infectious slums and sweat-

Yetta Schlesinger, wife of Jacob, encouraged Kaspare Cohn to purchase a large house on Carroll Avenue in the Temple Street area. The home was remodeled to become the first location of the Kaspare Cohn Hospital, now the Cedars-Sinai Medical Center

shops. While it is not clear how many Jews came among the tubercular health seekers, there were evidently hundreds [that came] to find healing in the sunshine of Southern California. 'From one of the railroad stations, the poor consumptive hies to a lonely dark room in an illy [sic] ventilated cheap lodging house, where he remains until his scanty means are exhausted...the next recourse is the Hebrew Benevolent Society to be furnished with transportation home or supported here.'"

The resources of the Hebrew Benevolent Society were insufficient to take care of the Jews that came seeking relief from disease. Talk began to surface that a Jewish refuge should be established for "consumptives, those suffering from tuberculosis" similar to two institutions that had been founded in Denver. Into this void stepped the "richest Jew in town," Kaspare Cohn. A wealthy and generous highly respected member of the community, Cohn donated his home on Carroll Avenue to accommodate Jews suffering from disease. The Kaspare Cohn Hospital to relieve consumptives was established on July 11, 1902.

Kaspare Cohn was a key donor and willing contributor to many Jewish causes throughout the years, among them the Southern California Jewish Orphans' Home, and the Hebrew Sheltering Association (later the Jewish Home for the Aging). The press at the time noted that "as a philanthropist Mr. Cohn was one of the men who took a keen delight in helping every charitable institution that was brought to his attention. It was done quietly, and without ostentation, and the only philanthropic work which bears his name is the Kaspare Cohn Hospital." When he died in 1916, the *Los Angeles Evening Herald* said simply, "the death of Kaspare Cohn marks the passing of one of the men who helped to make Southern California what it is today...[he was] one of the men directly responsible for the development of Southern California."

Rough times, however, were in store for the newly established hospital. When local townspeople registered their disapproval at having tuberculars living in their midst, laws were

The first Passover Seder at the Jewish Home for the Aging, 1912

Another perspective of 19th Century downtown Los Angeles looking south on Spring Street from First Street. Photograph taken circa 1900 illustrates the extensive trolley system

passed that prohibited these institutions from being located within city limits. The Kaspare Cohn Hospital changed its policies to conform to the new laws and was used for other medical purposes, while the community once again urgently searched for an alternative solution to take care of the tuberculosis patients.

In 1906 cottages were erected on the grounds of the Barlow Sanitarium in Chavez Ravine to care for Jewish tubercular patients. Similar arrangements were made with three other institutions. There was a persistent need for better facilities, which led to the founding of a full-fledged tuberculosis sanitarium at Duarte. The Southern California Jewish Consumptive Relief Association (JCRA) was established on September 28, 1912; their goal was to create a facility to take care of those stricken with this debilitating disease. The JCRA spearheaded the purchase of ten acres of land at the Duarte site and despite the lack of water, telephones, or electricity, installed the first six patients in tent houses on the property. Two years later in December 1914, several hundred people on the "Sanitarium Special" of the Santa Fe Railroad visited the patients at Duarte and celebrated the dedication of the Sanitarium, which was seen as the little "Town of Hope" and later would officially be named the City of Hope.

Kate Levy, M.D., the second woman physician to practice medicine in Los Angeles was Jewish (the first woman physician, Sarah Vasen, was also Jewish, see article on page 161); Levy wrote a report about the new facility at Duarte that was printed in the *B'nai B'rith*

Messenger on January 23, 1914. Dr. Levy was passionate in writing an appeal for help and support on behalf of the Jewish Consumptive Relief Society (JCRA):

> All and everything will depend upon the support and help which the community shall extend to this, the first organized effort of the Jewish masses for an institution other than one for religious purposes only. There is involved not only the question of caring for the sick and helpless among us, but there is involved and unsolved another very serious question. Can all classes of our people assimilate and work harmoniously for one great cause? Is there a spirit of tolerance among the rich and the poor, the educated and uneducated, the agnostic and the believing Jew? In other words, is there a Melting Pot of reverence and respect for each other's various views and aims?

> Are we not all one in the brevity of our pilgrimage here on earth? Are we not one in human trial and weakness? We are surely one before the giver of all that makes life worth living, in the gifts of love and strength and health! Let us then devote what we have of these to one of life's best privileges, the helping of our weaker brother and sister while life and power are yet ours. What more beautiful tribute could you devote to the memory of dear ones gone before than a memorial tent or portable or concrete house at the Duarte Sanitarium for tubercular patients, with your dear ones names inscribed thereon? What a living monument!

While Dr. Levy was exhorting the Jewish community to give their support to the Duarte hospital, it should also be noted as a tribute to the inherent philosophy and humanitarianism of Jewish philanthropy that the Duarte facility was soon open to people of all religions—a practice that has been carried on throughout the years and operation of the City of Hope. An important impetus to the founding of the City of Hope was the fact that Jewish tubercular patients were generally excluded from non-Jewish medical facilities. Thus, the Jewish community knew on a very personal level how essential it was for patients to be treated with compassion and respect, regardless of their religious or ethnic background.

The Orphans' Asylum under the auspices of the B'nai B'rith lodge was instrumental in caring for orphaned or neglected children, many of whom came from impoverished families of an ailing tubercular victim. The B'nai B'rith group incorporated on October 3, 1908 as the Jewish Orphans' Home of Southern California, and was a success story from the very beginning of its operation. Jewish education and religious instruction were conducted in the Orphans' Home. The Jewish Orphans' Home evolved into the Vista Del Mar Child Care Agency in later years, and continues to operate with great success in guiding children of all faiths and backgrounds.

The first bus to the proposed site of Hollywoodland, 1923

Seventh and Spring Streets, now the heart of downtown

Another of the philanthropic enterprises being developed at the same time as the Town of Hope at Duarte and the Orphans' Home was the Kaspare Cohn Hospital. The newly transformed facility was now a general hospital giving medical, surgical and obstetrical care. Dr. Sarah Vasen, the first woman physician in Los Angeles, was the resident physician and supervisor of the hospital, managing a staff that included Dr. David W. Edelman, Adolph Tyroler and E. M. Lazard. Though Kaspare Cohn began as a charity hospital, after a few years it did collect fees from patients who could afford to pay for treatment. This tiny hospital that had its beginnings in a house on Carroll Avenue became the prestigious medical institution, Cedars of Lebanon Hospital, and ultimately Cedars-Sinai Medical Center in Los Angeles.

In 1909 Rabbi Hecht surveyed all the good work that had been accomplished by the Jewish community to care for the sick, the elderly, stranded children and other displaced persons. "We have now an Orphans' Home, a hospital for the sick poor, a society for the relief of consumptives, a Ladies Benevolent Society, a Fruit and Flower Mission, several Ladies Auxiliaries, a nucleus for settlement work and a number of other philanthropic and semiphilanthropic organizations in this city alone…. Nevertheless we do not achieve as much by way of permanent results as other cities do largely because we are scattering our resources instead of concentrating them; and Federation is the desideratum."

West Los Angeles near Kelton Avenue, 1922. A new boulevard was planned to run parallel with Santa Monica Blvd, which can be seen on the left

157

The Jewish Consumptive Relief Association began to build its campus in 1915. Today, known as City of Hope, it has become one of the world's leading medical and research centers

The idea and plan for a federation of Jewish charitable organizations would effectively institute a "united appeal" and promote an equitable distribution of funds that were raised for Jewish causes. This would alleviate multiple and separate appeals to donors and would eliminate the need for various institutions to raise their own funds. The idea would also lend itself to more efficient coordination and planning among the different groups.

California State Normal School (1905) was located downtown. The school which opened in 1881 moved to Vermont Avenue. In 1927 it became the University of California, Los Angeles (UCLA), and later relocated to Westwood

The Federation of Jewish Charities elected its first board of directors on December 23, 1911, and the new board held its first meeting of incorporation in January 1912. The leaders participating on the board included familiar names of prominent Jewish families and benefactors in the community: Ben R. Meyer (son-in-law of Kaspare Cohn), Dr. D. W.

Edelman, Louis M. Cole (a Hellman son-in-law), M.N. Newmark, Isaac Norton, and S. G. Marshutz. The Federation originally embraced six constituent societies: the Hebrew Benevolent Society, Hebrew Consumptive, Ladies Hebrew Benevolent Society, the Orphans' Home, Kaspare Cohn Hospital, and the Temple Sewing Circle. In 1929 the name of the organization was changed to the Federation of Jewish Welfare Organizations of Los Angeles, which by this time had added the following societies: Hebrew Consumptive Relief Association, Jewish Aid Society, Jewish Alliance of Los Angeles, Jewish Big Brothers, Jewish Loan and Housing Association, Jewish Committee for Personal Service in State Institutions, Jewish Mothers' Alliance Day Nursery, Los Angeles Jewish Dispensary, and Modern Social Center.

This organized federation of philanthropic institutions was to form a crucial foundation and platform from which to aid refugees and casualties and other victims fleeing Europe with the coming of World War I, a conflict already on the horizon in the first decade of the new century. The principal charity of the Jewish community was soon to become urgently needed war relief—this then became the next great challenge undertaken by the Jews in Los Angeles and Jews throughout the country.

Steve Broidy, a past president of the Federation, writing about the workings of the Federation, explained that the "Federation is a shirt-sleeve organization. It works quietly. It is the social engineer, the community planner, and comptroller—responsible for meeting the health, social welfare and recreation needs of the city."

One may begin to grasp the significance of Federation when recalling the Herculean task that confronted the Jewish community beginning in the early 1930s with Hitler's coming into power. The essential need for the Federation became compellingly clear during this time and again immediately after the war, as these philanthropic organizations attempted to cope in aiding the huge numbers of refugees and displaced persons trying to escape Europe and find new homes. The purpose of the Federation was to coordinate and constitute the planning arm of the community by bringing together all the welfare organizations concerned, and working out a planned strategy of teamwork. With the Federation in operation much of the confusion, duplication of efforts, and excessive costs and inefficiency were avoided. This resulted in the saving of much needed community dollars, and in implementing more effective and humane programs.

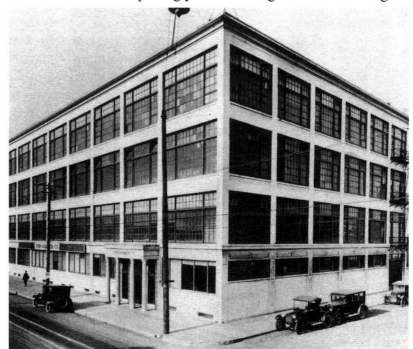

The Cohn-Goldwater Building which became a Los Angeles historic cultural monument, is located at the northwest corner of Twelfth and San Julian. It was completed in 1909 at a cost of $150,000 and it was the first "modern" factory building in Los Angeles to use all concrete and steel. The building is still being used for the production of clothing

A Forgotten Founder of the
Jewish Home for the Aging of Greater Los Angeles

by Rabbi William M. Kramer

A few years ago during research on the origins and early history of the Jewish Home for the Aging, a copy of the original document of incorporation was obtained from the Secretary of the State of California. It listed the names of the seven founders who had been elected as directors at a meeting in Los Angeles held on May 5, 1910. On May 28 attorney Emanuel F. Gerecht prepared and notarized the document submitted for incorporation. On June 1 that document was filed with the Los Angeles County Clerk and a copy was filed with the Secretary of State.

Seven men were listed as the incorporators and founders of what was then known as the Hebrew Sheltering Association. None were well-known members of the Los Angeles Jewish community, and of the seven, the identity of two of them could not be positively determined. Of those two, one was an "M. Goldberg," and because of the fact that there were several M. Goldbergs then residing in Los Angeles, further efforts to identify this founder were fruitless. The other unidentifiable founder was listed as "P.H. Blank." But it was evident that attorney Gerecht was not too careful in his spelling of the names of the founders, as he listed Jacob Epman as "J. Epner."

"P.H. Blank" has now been revealed to have been Philip Max Blank. He came to the United States from Kiev, Russia, probably in the late 1880s and settled in Los Angeles with his family soon after the turn of the century. His wife was nee Esther Molly Knepel and their son was Harry Gordon Blank. In 1910, when Philip M. Blank became a founder of what is now the Jewish Home for the Aging, he was operating a small furniture store in the Boyle Heights area of Los Angeles at 1335 East First Street. A year after the Hebrew Sheltering Association came into existence, on May 5, 1911, Philip Blank died. He was then fifty-nine years of age, and he was interred in the Beth Israel Cemetery of Los Angeles alongside of his wife, Esther, who died on October 9, 1909. Philip and Esther's son, Harry, took his father's place as an active leader of the Hebrew Sheltering Association.

Harry G. Blank, who had been born in Kiev, Russia, began his career in Los Angeles about 1902 as a peddler. By 1910 he was employed as a buyer for the Los Angeles Auction and

Mr. and Mrs. Phillip M. Blank, 1901

Commission Company, 730 South Spring Street. In 1912 he was a contributor to the first fundraising drive of the newly established Federation of Jewish Charities of Los Angeles. He gave his address as 208 Boyd Street, which was in the downtown section of the city.

From 1912 to 1914 Harry Blank served as the treasurer of the Hebrew Sheltering Association, and in 1919 he was elected the secretary and treasurer. Thus he continued his father's activity as a founding leader of the association. Later, Harry G. Blank became active in many Jewish community organizations, such as the Jewish National Fund, which he served as treasurer. He was the chairman of the loan committee of the Hebrew Free Loan Association and he was the president of that association from 1934 to 1936. And he was the president of the Mount Sinai Home in 1931 and 1932.

In 1901 Harry Blank had married Ida Arnovitz, and they had three daughters and a son. From 1918 Blank was the owner of a wholesale jobbing business. In 1949 Harry Blank was one of the members of the Los Angeles B'nai B'rith Lodge No. 487 and had been a member of that lodge for over twenty-five years.

So from the identification of a founder of a vital Jewish community service organization in Los Angeles has emerged the story of the important roles played by a father and son in that community.

———————◆◆◆———————

First Jewish Woman Physician of Los Angeles

by Reva Clar

This biographical study of Sarah Vasen, M.D. was written from the viewpoint of one who knew her and was a guest in her home many years ago in 1926, long after her retirement. This came about through my close association and warm friendship with the doctor's niece, Florence Vasen, daughter of Sarah's brother Nathan of Oakland. Both Florence and I were professional dancers working together on the West Coast Theatres circuit. I recall Dr. Vasen as a small, pleasant, gray-haired woman and her home on Central Avenue, Glendale, as a typical California bungalow of the time, with the dark, mission-style interior woodwork then very fashionable.

❋ ❋ ❋

Few of the thousands of people who drive past the huge Cedars-Sinai Medical Center in Los Angeles, or who enter its portals as patients or visitors, are aware of its humble beginnings soon after the turn of the century as the Kaspare Cohn Hospital, or of the role played in its development by a woman, Dr. Sarah Vasen, who served as its first superintendent and resident physician.

Sarah Vasen, the only daughter in a family of nine children, was born in Quincy, Illinois on May 21, 1870. Her father, George Vasen, born in 1835 in Prussia, worked as a "traveling agent," while her mother, nee Catherine Eschney, also born in 1835, was a native of Bohemia. The census for 1880 listed their children as follows: Benjamin G., 23, insurance company clerk; Aaron, 21, ship's steward; Abraham M., 17, bookkeeper; David, 15, clothing store clerk; Nathan, 13, apprentice painter; all of whom were born in Pennsylvania. The four younger children born in Illinois and still attending school were Phillip, 12; Sarah, 10; Jacob, 8; and Gustav, 6.

✳ ✳ ✳

Observing the results of female fertility in her own family Sarah may have decided on a medical career to aid those women who, like her mother, were producing the many children of that period: or to avoid marriage for herself and the prospect of years of childbearing with the attendant responsibilities during the proverbial best years of her life; or simply to assert her own individuality and resourcefulness after growing up with eight active brothers. Whatever her personal reasons, the choice was made and implemented.

Sarah received her training and medical degree in Philadelphia, where she began her professional life in a Jewish institution as indicated in this news item, which appeared at the turn of the century:

> Dr. Sarah Vasen, the resident physician and superintendent of the Jewish Maternity Home of Philadelphia has resigned these positions to resume the practice of her profession in Quincy, Illinois.

After practicing for some time in Quincy, Sarah was ready again for a change and in 1904 traveled to California where her brother Nathan had settled in 1896. Nathan lived in the small community of Aromas, near Watsonville in Northern California.

Dr. Sarah Vasen and her husband, Saul Frank

Seeking to investigate the opportunities in Southern California, Sarah proceeded to Los Angeles and in 1905 she became associated with the Kaspare Cohn Hospital. Because of her previous position at the Jewish Maternity Home of Philadelphia, she was well qualified to take over similar responsibilities for the Los Angeles establishment. Situated at 1443 Carroll Avenue in a house donated by Kaspare Cohn, the hospital (named for its benefactor) was organized in 1902 under the auspices of the Hebrew Benevolent Society as a facility for the care of consumptives. However, complaints by neighbors caused the city council to pass an ordinance that prohibited the treatment of tuberculosis victims within the city limits, so by the time Dr. Vasen became its superintendent, the hospital provided only for the needs of non-tubercular patients.

Dr. Vasen's superintendence brought her into a close and lasting relationship with Congregation B'nai B'rith's Rabbi

The confirmation class of 1904 (5664) of Congregation B'nai B'rith at Ninth and Hope Streets. The teenagers and their rabbi, from left to right, are: Laurence A. Lewin, Stella Cohn, Victor E. Hecht, Henrietta Hirshfield, Sylvan Cole, Rabbi Sigmund Hecht, Josef Citron, Milton J. Lesser, Alda Danziger, Nathan Malinow, Vivian Ancker and William Hellman

Sigmund Hecht, who had been a board member of the Kaspare Cohn Hospital since its inception in 1902. Additionally, the doctor and the rabbi shared a friendship through her membership in his congregation, which began soon after she assumed her position at the hospital and continued for many years. Since many of the officers of the hospital association and the doctors who provided gratuitous services to the patient were also members of Congregation B'nai B'rith, and since Sarah's achievements put her on an equal footing with the professional men she contacted, it was natural that she became a member of the temple where her friendships were extended to the wives of her associates.

✳ ✳ ✳

By the end of October 1910 it was announced that Dr. Sarah Vasen had "offered her services *gratis* in maternity cases to the poor who are recommended by the Hebrew Benevolent Society," which signified that by then she was already in private practice. Some weeks later the *Messenger* noted, "Dr. Sarah Vasen can be found at 935 West Temple Street. Practice devoted to maternity cases only. Phone Broadway 3049." Typical of the era was the fact that this "popular and efficient" woman physician who had superintended a hospital, and treated the various ailments of its male physicians, decided to restrict her solo professional efforts exclusively to obstetrics. Sarah's home and office were at the same premises, a mode of living that was a continuation of the pattern established during her years at Carroll Avenue.

Before the end of 1911 Dr. Vasen relocated her combined office and residential quarters to 1110 West Pico Boulevard, in an area of the city that was much favored at the time by the well-to-do Jewish families of Los Angeles who made their homes there and were the prime source of her practice. This move was much more significant, however, in affecting Sarah's personal life, for at the same address lived a newcomer to California, one Saul Frank, retired and a bachelor. The proverbial whirlwind courtship ensued and on January 25, 1912, Saul Frank, fifty-six, and Dr. Sarah Vasen, forty-one, were married at Temple B'nai B'rith by Rabbi

Children playing at the original Vista Del Mar location in Huntington Park, 1912

Sigmund Hecht. The ceremony was witnessed by Mrs. Sadie Radowitz.

⁂

Saul Frank was born in Holland on May 20, 1855, the son of Simon and Semilina Spanyard Frank, both of whom, natives of Holland were probably Sephardic Jews. Before coming to California, Saul had been in the dry goods business in the towns of Gobles and Kendall, Michigan for thirty years, where he had been "held in high esteem by all who knew him and was considered as one of the most popular businessmen in that section of Michigan." The couple's marriage certificate stated that Saul, whose occupation was listed as "stocks and property," was a resident of Kalamazoo, Michigan. So what began ostensibly as a retirement holiday for him resulted in another permanent resident for Southern California. The gregarious bachelor and the popular medical "maiden lady were ready for radical, albeit belated changes in their lives. For Sarah matrimony provided a reason for giving up her professional activities, [since] the companionship of a husband along with the financial security he could provide apparently outweighed any advantages or honors she had enjoyed as an independent woman.

In 1915 the couple settled in Glendale, and Saul Frank, retired, was listed in that city's directory for 1915-1916; his address was 1440 Sycamore Avenue. On November 1, 1919, Rabbi Sigmund Hecht went to Glendale at the request of Mrs. Saul Frank to organize a religious school. That Sarah took an active part in the nascent Jewish community of Glendale is shown by her concern for providing a religious education for the town's Jewish children. Saul also contributed to the needs of Los Angeles Jewry and is listed as a donor of $25 in the 1922 Jewish welfare drive. The popularity and sociability enjoyed by the Franks as individuals continued as the pair put down permanent roots in Glendale.

The pleasant existence shared by Sarah and Saul in their new home lasted only three years. On August 4, 1924, at the age of sixty-nine, Saul died suddenly of a heart attack. His only survivors were Sarah and a sister, Mrs. Sylvia Gregor, of Detroit. His obituary notice stated that during his nine years in Glendale, Saul Frank had "invested in real estate and transacted a number of business deals," and that he had made many friends there. Funeral services were conducted in an undertaker's chapel in Glendale by Rabbi Hecht, and the burial service at Home of Peace cemetery in Los Angeles was conducted by the Glendale Elks Lodge.

For the next twenty years the widowed Dr. Vasen lived alone in Glendale until a cerebral hemorrhage put her into the Glendale Research Hospital, where she remained until her death five months later on August 21, 1944. Her passing was reported in the Glendale newspaper by an obituary that referred to her as a retired physician, survived by her brother Nathan Vasen of Oakland, five nephews and one niece, Florence Vasen Kahn. Nothing appeared in the Los Angeles *B'nai B'rith Messenger*.

Thus passed from the scene Los Angeles' first Jewish woman physician—one of the first professionals engaged by the Jewish community and paid from community funds. These many years later it is a privilege to place her in her rightful niche in Los Angeles Jewish history as a pioneer woman in the medical profession of the city, a participant in the beginning years of one of the country's great medical centers, a contributor to Jewish welfare in the East and in the West, a woman of independence far ahead of her time, a devoted wife, a kind, generous and modest woman.

Rabbi Edgar F. Magnin and the Modernization of Los Angeles

by Rabbi William M. Kramer and Reva Clar

In an essay on "Hellenism and Hebraism" that Rabbi Magnin wrote, his closing words stand today as the watchword of his life's work towards which his energies were so successfully directed:

> Ours is the task of spreading the doctrine of religious ethics and of social justice until the earth is filled with the knowledge of God as the waters cover the sea. Let us be true to ourselves.

The story of young Edgar F. Magnin was not one to inspire a Horatio Alger novel. Far from being an exemplar of the rags-to-riches theme, Edgar was a member of one of the great pioneer mercantile families of the West, whose firm of I. Magnin and Company represented the ultimate in luxury merchandise for the wealthy. Despite being the child of a broken home, he was born, not with a silver spoon in his mouth, but with an entire silver service. Blessed with great intelligence and having been provided with the advantage of a fine education, he was destined for success from the time of his graduation from Hebrew Union College in 1914.

When Edgar Magnin left Stockton's Temple Israel near the end of 1915 and came to Congregation B'nai B'rith of Los Angeles as assistant to Rabbi Sigmund Hecht, he came to a congregation that was completely and efficiently organized. [The congregation] had enjoyed for sixteen years the dedicated leadership of Rabbi Hecht, who served beyond his own area and congregation as a Jewish religious leader and was active in the civic life of his community. Hecht was a respected writer, educator and lecturer, a force in interfaith relations, and an organizer of the Los Angeles Federation of Jewish Charities in 1911. Magnin did not come to a Jewish wilderness.

The young rabbi's year of service as spiritual leader of Stockton's Temple Israel was truly

Victory Bonds rally in downtown Los Angeles, 1916

a rehearsal for his Los Angeles career. When he arrived on the scene in Southern California, the stage was set and the audience was ready. Making his entrance at the side of the esteemed Rabbi Hecht, Magnin could have succeeded just by following the script outlined by his senior associate.

Many of the Reform congregations in the early years of this century were so lacking in Jewish knowledge that any young rabbi who could demonstrate signs of erudition, originality or intelligence in Judaism and general culture was much in demand. It was the pre-Zionist period when Hebrew had virtually disappeared from the services, when bar mitzvah had been replaced by confirmation and when a "sermon" often consisted of a review of a current book or the sharing of a poem. Thus, when Magnin burst on the scene with his goal of culturally educating and spiritually enlightening his congregants, with his sermons based on biblical themes, with his preaching on ethics, the effects were electrifying. Not only did he awaken his Jewish auditors, but Christians clamored for his appearance as well. From both the Jewish and general press notices of the period, it seemed that he never refused a request to teach and embarked on a continuous round of public lectures.

At Congregation B'nai B'rith's Friday evening services on December 10, 1915, "the junior rabbi" Edgar Magnin was inducted into his new post by the senior rabbi, Sigmund Hecht. In his first sermon, entitled, "The Stuff that Dreams Are Made Of," and heard by a large group of worshippers, he stated with characteristic fervor:

> Upon the summit of Sinai the Jewish dreamer heard in the thunder and the light-
> ning the message of justice and loving-kindness…the mighty man, Moses, saw

Harris Newmark breaking ground for the Jewish Orphans' Home (Vista Del Mar), circa 1911

the spiritual law that underlies all things and which if observed can alone preserve civilization and make life a thing worth possessing. It is the message of the Jewish dreamers that the world needs most.

Following his induction as associate rabbi, Edgar Magnin embarked on his many duties. He spoke at the B'nai B'rith Lodge's election meeting at the end of 1915. Early in January 1916, together with Rabbi Hecht, he addressed the regular meeting of the Council of Jewish Women at the temple. The weekly sermons were alternately delivered by the senior and junior rabbis, which indicated the congregation's desire to have Hecht share the authority of his position fully with the younger man. Hecht's name appeared as superintendent of the teaching staff of the religious school; Magnin was not on the list. Magnin's exuberance was infectious and it made him popular from the start in the pulpit and in his many varied speaking engagements.

✳ ✳ ✳

Magnin was warmly welcomed by the Menorah Club, an organization composed of young college students. Soon afterward, the associate rabbi spoke at a public meeting under the auspices of the Young Zionist Association. Unlike his senior rabbi, who was not an early sympathizer of the Zionist movement, Magnin was always pro-Zionist, though he favored cultural Zionism over political Zionism. Members of the Los Angeles congregation were leading supporters of the Zionist cause and were far more comfortable with Magnin's position, which he had made evident from the very beginning of his rabbinical career.

An article written for the support of Jewish causes demonstrated Magnin's strong sense of social responsibility. He wrote:

> And all the Jewry must work. The Jewish Federation Charities is not the activity of any particular congregation or group of Jews. It is the institution created by all the Jews of Los Angeles for all the Jews of Los Angeles who need it, and please God, the day will come when it will be able to help all who appeal to it irrespective of religious persuasion.

This exhortation was indicative of the spirit that pervaded Congregation B'nai B'rith and made it the most prominent Jewish institution in the view of the general community. Magnin's philosophy embraced all the agencies of the Federation in their goal to serve every Jew. Magnin challenged the secular nature of this Los Angeles institution and sought to correct the lack of a deep religious spirit that Rabbi Hecht sensed in his congregation. The rabbis wanted to be spiritual leaders but found themselves all too often Jewish civil servants dispensing ceremonies and vicariously doing Judaism for others.

Magnin saw the assimilated Jew not simply as one who had integrated into American culture at the expense of his Jewish past, but one who could find Jewish spirituality in a disciplined way in America and as an American without the medieval codes of the rabbis. He was not interested in displacing the codes, which he respected as Torah, for those to whom they were meaningful; he was instead offering an alternative path to the ultimate goal of Jewish spirituality. He considered being Reform no less worthy, no easier and no short cut.

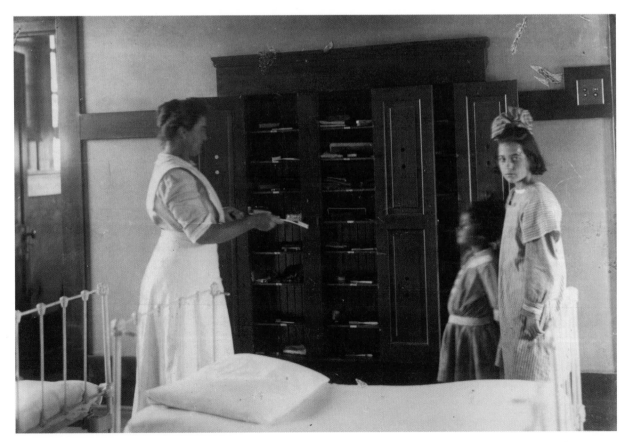

Photograph taken at the Jewish Orphans' Home (Vista Del Mar), Huntington Park, 1913

Old Chinatown, which was around Alameda Street, was torn down when Union Station was built during the late 1930s

An event of great importance to Edgar Magnin's personal life and career was announced to the public soon after his arrival in Los Angeles. This was his engagement to the socially prominent Miss Evelyn Rosenthal of Cincinnati, with the wedding planned for summer. It was reported that the romance began several years before, when both Edgar and Evelyn were attending the University of Cincinnati. News of the June wedding was reported in the society column in the *Los Angeles Jewish Weekly*:

> A telegram was received from Cincinnati of the marriage of Rabbi Edgar F. Magnin, junior rabbi of B'nai B'rith congregation, and Miss Evelyn Rosenthal, a society belle and daughter of one of the wealthy merchants of that city…. The couple will make their home in Los Angeles after August 1. The honeymoon will be spent at the summer home of the bride's parents in Michigan. A trip will be made through the Thousand Islands.

❋ ❋ ❋

In the *Congregation B'nai B'rith Annual* which recorded America's entry into World War I, Magnin attempted in his essay to analyze the causes of the conflict and its tragic consequences. He offered a light to dispel the gloom, dimmed albeit by prophetic misgivings.

> It is the future world tragedy we would avert the war after this one. It is the coming generation we would protect and make happy upon earth…. Where, if not in God's house, shall the grave spiritual questions of the hour be studied? Where, if not there, shall people attempt to reconstruct the world? When the synagogue is a force and not a farce, when the church performs its real function, then will such a tragedy and holocaust be impossible forever….

The military camps and centers in Southern California received the ministrations of both

By 1903 Leopold Harris and his two sons-in-law, Herman W. Frank and M. C. Adler, and his son Harry were established in their store pictured above, Harris and Frank. The men's clothing firm was located on Spring Street near Temple Street and covered 17,000 square feet

Magnin and his senior, who at different times during the year had visited the Submarine Station and the Naval Reserve at San Pedro, Camp Kearny at San Diego, the Artillery Corps at Fort Rosencrans, and the Marine Station at Balboa Park. There it was reported that they addressed "both the Jewish men and the men in camp regardless of their religious affiliation, and Rabbi Magnin has even done more by coming in direct touch with the men and to bring them the practical assurance of friendship and fellowship." Both rabbis spoke at the camps and for the fundraising drives, and also before church groups of various Christian denominations, thereby helping to "remove certain prejudices of long standing, prejudices that grew and grow upon the soil of ignorance."

✳ ✳ ✳

Rabbi Magnin, as editor of the *Twenty-Second Annual*, gave an account of the diverse activities of his career. A section headed "Outside Addresses" listed fifty-four speaking engagements and referred to other appearances too numerous to list. Groups addressed ranged from the Men's Club of Temple De Hirsch, Seattle, to the executive heads of the Canning Association, the Friends Church of Pasadena, and the American Indian Center Association. Mass meetings, cornerstone settings, church and school events were served, all of which in the rabbi's words, "made for a better feeling of understanding and friendship and have, on the whole, been delightful for the speaker at least." The latter point explains the reason for Edgar Magnin's immense personal success. His unfeigned enthusiasm and desire to reach out and touch every listener appealed to all. Religious boundaries were eradicated as Jew and gentile alike responded to the ardent young preacher's message of brotherhood and tolerance. He was truly an ambassador of good will.

✳ ✳ ✳

With Magnin spending many of his waking hours before the public, it follows that he came to the attention of the movie moguls of Hollywood. Film industry Jews were then in their most flourishing period. Expert in public relations, talent development and business, these men were attracted to the versatile Magnin, who afforded them an opportunity to practice Judaism in pleasant surroundings with a modest amount of religious pressures. Regardless of Magnin's support of many worthy causes, these were of secondary import to the public when he became known as "The People's Ambassador to the Movies." This title was given him by an interviewer from a Portland Jewish weekly in 1928. The journalist noted that

Kaspare Cohn Hospital (today is Cedars-Sinai Medical Center)

Magnin's temple was frequented by the "leaders of cinema land," and,

> Though his activities are of very broad and varied character and his popularity echoes through many walks of Jewish life over many rungs of things in Southern California, it is Hollywood first with which the average Californian mind associates the young rabbi whenever his name is mentioned.

✳ ✳ ✳

The climate was right at the congregational meeting on October 29, 1919, to authorize a new building [for Congregation B'nai B'rith], which was to "make of the B'nai B'rith Temple one of the show places of the nation, so far as Jewish religious institutions are concerned."

In speaking of the new venture to the local Jewish press, Rabbi Magnin said, "The matter of building a new temple had to come. Our congregation is one of the most rapidly growing in the United States and from present appearances will continue to grow still faster."

Magnin was described as having "some very lofty ideas concerning the new institution," which he visualized as "not only a great religious institution but a monument to Jewish aesthetic and artistic taste." His vision of a spectacular edifice was endorsed by the *Messenger*, which considered the matter from the standpoint of community growth and the many tourists who visited Southern California:

> It has long been conceded that the new structure is a necessity for Los Angeles, which has become a sort of Mecca for Jews all over the country and each year there is a great impetus given to the Westward movement. This Temple, it is stated, has become a sort of shrine and people come from Pasadena and other nearby cities, while tourists flock in from the various hotels. These are among the rea-

sons given for the splendor of the plans now being made, and officials feel that the new building should be creditable to the Jewish community of Los Angeles and uphold in a general way the dignity of the city as well as that of Jewry.

Abram M. Edelman, the architect for the Ninth and Hope temple in 1895 was again selected as architect for the new structure. In February 1927, the firm of Allison and Allison joined him as consulting architects. Sam Tilden Norton was an honorary consultant. Even before construction began Edgar Magnin made public his vision of the new temple as "an architectural gem," one to overshadow other major synagogues in the country, which he said he had inspected for himself. He felt it would be a "House of God that will stand out on the boulevard… as a sign of culture and spirituality, a symbol of Jewish idealism and good citizenship." He shunned false modesty in proclaiming his part in enhancing the temple's prestige and presented his vision of its future influence in Southern California.

> Our temple has stood out in this community as the leading Jewish congregation. Dr. Hecht took part in every form of activity in and around Los Angeles. I have addressed hundreds of meetings, assisted one organization after the other, participated in every movement for developing culture, art, music, philanthropy. Our temple is respected. It stands for Judaism and Americanism in their finest aspects. There on the great boulevard "the coming Fifth Avenue of Los Angeles" we shall stand like a beacon light, welcoming all. And even those who will never enter our portals will know that here we stand, Jews, sons of prophets and psalmists and priests and kings, descendants of a great race who gave the Bible to the world. Here we stand teaching and preaching and working today as our fathers did of old. Alive, energetic, dignified, hopeful, proud and unashamed, dedicating ourselves to something more that the acquisition of mere wealth. Here we will stand, an ornament, a power, a glory in God and humanity.

Rabbi Edgar F. Magnin wrote a glowing tribute to the officers and members of his congregation, the architects and builders of the magnificent temple, and his predecessors in the pulpit. He assessed the position of his congregation as a leading Reform institution in the country. His predictions, accurate as always, were well fulfilled during his long lifetime. With fervor, eloquence and deep emotion, the rabbi wrote in part:

> This is more than a work of art. Imprisoned in wood, stone, marble and canvas are the loyalty and faith of a great congregation. The souls of your loved ones, whom you have honored and our own as well, will live on in these walls, long after we have mingled with the dust. This imposing edifice will stimulate the imagination and awaken the spiritual consciousness of the hundreds of thousands of people who will be privileged to enter its portals. Those who pass by it daily will be inspired by its perfect proportions, by the vision that prompted its erection, and by a contemplation of the purposes for which it has been dedicated. They will know that the God of Israel still lives, and that the Jew has not lost the faith and the sense of religious consecration, that were so characteristic of his ancestors, and are so manifest on every page of its long, sad, beautiful history…And so, at last, Congregation B'nai B'rith is now housed in a manner befitting its dignity and importance.

And Edgar Fogel Magnin, a young man not yet turned forty who practiced what he preached, was destined to continue his leadership in Jewish life for the astonishing span of fifty-five more years at his beloved temple, as he rose to be the acknowledged dean of the American Reform rabbinate.

CHAPTER SIX

World War I—Rise of Anti-Semitism, the Roaring Twenties, and the Great Depression: 1917-1938

The winners of the first President's Cup Golf Tournament at Hillcrest Country Club were Laurence A. Lewin (left) and Herman A. Politz. Both men were charter members of Hillcrest Country Club (1923). Lewin was born in Los Angeles in 1890 and was a buyer for the Brownstein-Lewis Company, garment manufacturers and wholesalers. Politz operated a men's clothing store on Olive Street

Political life for Jews in Los Angeles was selective. While they were rarely found on the ballot, they were prominent in civic affairs and as political managers...

The 1920s era began with a real estate boom in Los Angeles. Population surged as the hunger for property reached epic proportions. As the land boom rejuvenated expansion, transportation also jettisoned to the next level. Just as the railroads had spearheaded transporting masses of new arrivals to the West in the late 1800s, the new "ticket to mobility" in the 20th Century was the automobile. Since Los Angeles was so spread out and so large the "car was king in Los Angeles in the Twenties, a position it has held ever since," according to author Gordon DeMarco. States William Deveril, "Certainly by the 19 teens and well into the 1920s and continuing into today, Southern California probably has the largest per capita ownership of automobiles in the world. The automobile changes transportation arteries and networks forever. And people in Los Angeles, like people everywhere, fell in love with their cars and the freedom of transit that cars offered. It's essentially a sociological phenomenon. People moved towards the automobiles and the embrace of the freeway system."

Jewish Aeronautical Association of Los Angeles was founded in 1933. The photograph above was taken at Mines Field (now Los Angeles International Airport) by Allen Brandes. Left to right: Milton Sharkansky, unknown, unknown, David Bushner, Allen Brandes, William Donner, Molly Mintz, Nathan Kluner, Leopold Shluker, unknown, Bernard Haines, and Al Dardick (see article on Jewish Aeronautical Association in this chapter, page 197)

San Fernando Valley, 1927. Lankershim Blvd in North Hollywood. The main street of this little town was in the midst of orange groves and ranch land

Los Angeles quickly overtook San Francisco in population in the early 1920s, and with the convenience of the automobile the population expansion extended into the suburbs of greater Los Angeles. As the demand for property mushroomed, and the land frenzy skyrocketed, another oil boom occurred. Oil, the "black gold," was discovered in Huntington Beach, Long Beach, and Santa Fe Springs near Whittier. Black gold prompted yet another California "gold rush" and oil wells projected themselves like tall trees into the Southern California landscape. DeMarco writes, "By 1924, the State of California was producing twenty percent of the world's oil and ranked first in the United States in the production of petroleum products." "Bonanza times" hit Los Angeles and everybody was trying to capitalize on the new opportunities for wealth.

It was an explosive era—the Roaring Twenties, the Jazz Age, flappers and raised hemlines, bathtub gin and gangsters, the land boom, the Model "T," get-rich-quick schemes, Mary Pickford and Charlie Chaplin. If the first two decades of the 20th Century in the City of Angels were exciting, the Twenties were wild with self-discovery and blazing new horizons.

DeMarco postulates that Hollywood portrayed a graphic representation of the dramatic and dynamic changes in Southern California and the rest of the country in the 1920s; he describes Hollywood in its early days:

> Hollywood became the metaphor for the Twenties. For the Dream. For the unreality of it all. In time, the metaphor consumed Hollywood itself. "You can't explain Hollywood," wrote Rachel Field. "There isn't any such place." Los Angeles and the rest of the country began imitating Hollywood—both its actual flamboyant, often scandalous lifestyle off-screen and its slapstick humor, romance, dress, and manners on screen.

> Hollywood was a narcotic on the public psyche. It had never been taken on such a trip of fantasy before. It was wonderful. Some dreamers, a little like lemmings marching to the sea, began swarming from their homes in drab, boring America to the sundown Sea of Hollywood. To be in the movies. To live their fantasies. Hollywood was mushrooming. Both the city and the industry. It was Los Angeles' leading industry by 1920 and remained so for twenty years. A fairyland

on a production line that had a payroll of 30,000-40,000 workers.

The land boom in Los Angeles dovetailed with the building and developing of the big Hollywood studios beginning as early as 1907. United Artists, Columbia, 20th Century-Fox, Warner Brothers, Paramount, RKO—all were blossoming and changing the look and character of Hollywood. As Paul Zollo chronicles in *Hollywood Remembered*:

> "Studios of unbelievable magnitude, erected at expenditures that stagger the imagination, are now far-flung in a circle that recognizes Hollywood as its center," wrote Laurence Hill in 1929. "Throughout the world, wherever the film flickers, the name of Hollywood is a household word."

The building boom extended to the construction of theaters, hotels, apartment and office buildings, restaurants, and classic "movie palaces." Of the latter, two of the most recognized are the Egyptian and Chinese Theaters, both of which were created by Jewish entrepreneur Sid Grauman. On May 18, 1927, Grauman opened the Chinese Theater on Hollywood Boulevard and it quickly became "Grauman's most lasting and cherished contribution to the mythic fabric of Hollywood life, and may be the most famous movie theater in the world." The first film shown on its screen was *King of Kings*, Cecil B. DeMille's religious extravaganza.

Even more famous than the theater is the fabled courtyard in front of the theater into which countless movie stars have placed hand and footprints and autographs memorialized in cement. This tradition has been carried on through the years and today the star-studded cement walkway attracts millions of tourists to Hollywood each year. Grauman's Chinese and Egyptian theaters were followed by the Pantages (originally the home of the Academy Awards), the El Capitan, the Hollywood Palace, and the Vine Street Theater (later the CBS Playhouse Theater), which ultimately became the Doolittle Theater.

Hollywoodland sign erected by the Hollywoodland Realty Company on Mt. Lee was advertising the development nestled in hills below. Four stories high, and a city block long, this unique landmark could be seen from most points in the city, 1923

Despite the tremendous growth of Hollywood in these early days, it retained its country atmosphere, replete with charming homes and splendid gardens. In 1924 a real estate development named "Hollywoodland" was built on 500 acres of land at the north end of Beachwood Canyon. Financed by Harry Chandler, *Los Angeles Times* owner, and the syndicate that bought up the land in the San Fernando Valley just before the aqueduct was built, Hollywoodland was envisioned as a "little storybook community." It was Chandler's idea to erect a huge billboard in the hills above the houses, spelling out in gargantuan letters, HOLLYWOODLAND. Each letter was thirty feet wide, fifty feet tall, lighted by 4,000 light bulbs surrounding each letter, at a cost of $21,000. The housing tract did not succeed, coinciding at the time with the economic crash of 1929, but the sign (slightly altered to read "HOLLYWOOD") remains today as a symbolic landmark of the entertainment capital of the world.

A new and exciting innovation in broadcast technology—radio—arrived in Hollywood in 1922, launched mainly to promote the new *Los Angeles Express* newspaper. In a promotional drive to sell newspapers, 1000 crystal wave radios were given away, introducing Angelenos to the new medium.

The first three stations were KNX, KHJ, and KFI. When KFI became part of the NBC Red Radio Network, NBC built a beautiful art deco studio in the heart of Hollywood, at Sunset and Vine. It had, as did the existing CBS structure, new broadcast studios built as live theaters that housed hundreds of audience members, who watched as various radio personalities entertained the listening masses. Harry Chandler owned KHJ (in addition to the *Los Angeles Times*); the station joined the CBS Radio network in 1927 with its format of educational, public affairs, and children's programming.

Max Factor, Russian-born Jewish entrepreneur and powerful film make-up innovator, renovated a building at the corner of Hollywood and Highland for his headquarters, and when the building opened in 1928 it became a Hollywood institution. As a result of a gift from Colonel Griffith J. Griffith, a large nearby parcel of land was donated and became Griffith Park; shortly afterward the Greek Theater, an outdoor amphitheater, was added. The Greek Theater was completed in 1930, and on adjacent property construction began on the Griffith Observatory, a Hall of Science to explore the heavens.

The world famous Sunset Strip came into prominence in the 1930s when the former horse trail leading to the ocean known as "Sunset" was transformed between Fairfax and Doheny. Many famous stars entertained the public in the illustrious nightclubs that populated the Strip. Among the clubs that glittered with celebrities and performers were the Trocadero, the Mocambo, and Ciro's (later re-

Library of the Jewish Alliance which was the first Jewish Community Center in Los Angeles

Horseback riding in 1923 in the Santa Monica Canyon are the Hellman brothers, natives of Los Angeles and political leaders Williams Jennings Bryan (Democratic presidential nominee in 1896, 1900, and 1908, and served as Secretary of State under Woodrow Wilson, 1913-1915) and William Gibbs McAdoo (Secretary of the Treasury, 1913 to 1918). Pictured left to right: Marco H. Hellman, Bryan, McAdoo, and Irving H. Hellman

opened in the 1950s as The Comedy Store). Also built during this era was the Palladium, which opened to the public in 1940. The building, which took up an entire block on Sunset at Argyle, was financed by *Los Angeles Times* publisher, Norman Chandler, at a cost of $1,600,000.

The Big Crash of 1929—the Great Depression Begins

The boom of the Twenties came to an abrupt end in 1927 marked, among other things, by the crash of Los Angeles' Julian Petroleum in that year. Eighteen months later, Wall Street crashed in New York City, turning the hopes and dreams of the country into stunned shock as the reality of the Great Depression began to set in.

The economic crash in 1929 hit Los Angeles as hard as it did the rest of the country. Along with Julian Petroleum, the Richfield Oil Company and the Guaranty Building and Loan Association also failed, and that was just the beginning. As brokers and bankers were jumping from tall buildings in New York, their counterparts in greater Los Angeles (having no sky-

City Hall opening dedication, 1928

scrapers) were jumping from bridges. Los Angelenos would not be cheered by the Olympic Games held in their great city in 1932, nor by the wishful thinking that the Depression would be short lived. The people in Los Angeles were angry and resentful of this down cycle of economic intrusion into their sunny paradise.

Los Angeles, along with the rest of the country, lost its idealism. DeMarco writes: "The Depression polarized, pauperized, embittered, and enervated a nation. People in the industrial North and Midwest where the concentration of workers was high, organized trade unions, and fought economic and human rights struggles from that fulcrum of power." In Los Angeles, however, things were different—unions were weak and the work force much smaller than the Northeast and the Midwest. In this city the population focused in two directions—social reform for the masses and spiritual fulfillment for the individual.

Metaphysics, yoga, a theosophical university, vegetarianism—all the pieces of the "new thought" movement said to have originated in Boston, gravitated west and found a home in Los Angeles. It was the beginning of the "cults and fads" reputation that Southern California would become known for, which continued to develop over time. The various elements—faith healing, the occult, vegetarianism, homeopathy—all were aimed at healing the spirit and the mind.

DeMarco speculates, "Many seekers were searching for a wizard at the end of the long yellow brick road they had traveled." One of those that stepped into the void was Aimee Semple McPherson, a box office "legend in her own time, giving Angelenos the fanciest theological entertainment they have ever enjoyed." She preached a gospel of physical healing and redemption. McPherson was symbolic of the times in Los Angeles—flamboyant, entertaining, passionate and sincere. When she preached she was the ultimate "showman," inspiring hope and optimism to those needing comfort or those in despair.

Southern California became a "veritable Celestial City," hosting a vast number of alternative churches and "cults," as well as astrologers and psychics. For many, these mystics and gurus with their positive promises, offered solace from untenable and unstable circumstances. The deeply felt resignation of the residents of Southern California, facing the total devastation and demoralization of the Depression, made them easy victims to the less ethical of the cult leaders and quacks who were quick to exploit the public's vulnerability. While individuals sought answers from the more reputable of these esoteric organizations, most of the populace realized that their problems had social roots and they sought collective action and political organizing.

In the 1930s, with ten million unemployed nationally, people were angry and rebellious, most believing that they had been lied to and manipulated by the politicians and the bankers and financiers. Bread lines were common and mini-revolutions were occurring in the major urban cities in the form of violent labor strikes. There was a change in thinking and ideas were forming to restructure society. This reorganization began by taking advantage of the skills of the engineers and technicians and increasing the use of machines—the idea was to let socie-

The Sephardic Jews from the Island of Rhodes in the Mediterranean are known as the Rhodeslis. They began to settle in the West, at first in Seattle, in the first decade of the 20th Century. Beginning in 1908 the Rhodeslis came to Los Angeles, and created their Peace and Progress Society. In 1935 they built the Sephardic Hebrew Center (pictured above), now a church, at Fifty-fifth and Hoover

ty work for everyone's benefit. Socialism, communism, technocracy, populism—all were being experimented with and touted by different groups of organizers and ideologues.

To further complicate the times, the drought in the Dustbowl of America in 1935 was the catalyst for another massive wave of immigration from Oklahoma, Arkansas, and Texas—most who came were poor, barely literate, and demoralized. They were met in Southern California with hostility and suspicion—there were already too few jobs for far too many people. These transplanted "Okies" as they were called, became underpaid and poorly treated migrant farm laborers. Relief money was quickly exhausted. Foreclosures were widespread among the people in California, and yet they were being forced to assimilate "an invasion of dirt-poor and busted Okies." Natural disasters added to the plight of those in Southern California, as they experienced the bursting of the San Francisquito Dam in 1928, killing 400, the earthquake in Long Beach in 1933, killing 118 with property damage of forty million dollars, an out of control fire in Mineral Wells Canyon in 1933, and the floods of 1934 in the mountain canyons. Although many believed it was the beginning of the apocalypse, somehow Los Angeles survived.

Jewish Community Civic and Cultural Activity — Political Upheaval and Factionalism

There were years of bitter politics in the early part of the 20th Century in California. The divisive issue of trade unionism erupted with the tragic bombing of the *Los Angeles Times* Building in 1910. The Progressives were united in supporting the right of labor to organize and bargain collectively, and spoke in favor of the break up of monopolies. The Progressive Party's onslaught against the Southern Pacific Railroad's political domination severely impacted California politics. Adding to the general apprehension, international rumblings

Beverly Blvd near Robertson Blvd in 1922, now some of America's most valuable real estate

were beginning to be felt from Europe as political factions began to mobilize in an uneasy prologue to World War I.

Political life for Jews in Los Angeles was selective. While they were rarely found on the ballot, they were prominent in civic affairs and as political managers, and held key positions on the Board of Education and the Board of Library Commissioners. Political campaigns for both parties were headed by Jewish chairmen, indicating that Jewish sympathies were divided between Republicans and Democrats. Jews were active in law enforcement and were represented in the city attorney's office by William W. Barman and the civilian police commission by Isidor W.

Sergeant Joseph Leon Kauffman(right), a Jewish soldier from Los Angeles, died in the Argonne Forest in France. A German high explosive shell killed him on September 26, 1918. He was attending the University of California, Berkeley in 1917, when war was declared. In 1919 a little less than ten months after the death of Sergeant Kauffman, "a slender shaft of white granite with a simple bronze inscription plate was dedicated to the memory of the soldier." It was the gift of Walter P. Temple, erected at the intersection of Monterey Road and San Gabriel, in Temple City

Birnbaum. Jews were also a prominent part of the judicial system, sitting on the superior court and holding federal judgeships.

Women in the Jewish community were very active participants in the cultural development of the city. Organizations such as the Women's Friday Morning Club, established for "cultural advancement and social betterment," included about eighty Jewish women in the total membership of fifteen hundred. They were also members of the local branch of L'Alliance Francaise, and the Council of Jewish Women, which worked to provide for Jewish immigrant youth.

The days of "home made" entertainment were long ended by the 1920s, with all of the attention now being given to the films and activity coming from the Hollywood moviemakers. Very little was taking place in the community in pursuit of the Jewish ideals of religious education, and Talmudic study was continued by only a handful of the pious.

On the other hand, the new cultural trends were being closely followed by many, and a rising interest was evident in the ideologies of Zionism, socialism and the revival of the Hebrew and Yiddish language. According to Vorspan:

> Distinctly Jewish cultural expression in Los Angeles reached its highest development in Yiddish, which flourished from the second decade of the twentieth century. For thousands of Jewish immigrants it was a native tongue, but to many Yiddish also represented a Jewish cultural ideal associated with the varieties of Jewish socialism and secularism. A substantial organization, the Arbeiter Ring (Workmen's Circle), gave Yiddish culture moral and financial backing, beside the fraternal benefits it dispensed to members. Socialist Zionists in the Jewish National Workers Alliance also had Yiddishism sympathies. Yiddish readers had the long-lived local edition of New York's Jewish *Daily Forward*, beginning in 1910.

Los Angeles' Yiddish writers were prolific and produced many literary works. Much of this literature reflected the times and the current history, such as Maurice Rogers' three act play entitled *Der Gayst fun Dew Tsayt* [*The Spirit of the Time*], a play about Jewish suffering during World War I in Eastern Europe.

A parade from the Los Angeles courthouse to the Coliseum which included flagbearers carrying American and Jewish flags

Palestine Mandate celebration, June 27, 1920, at the old Los Angeles Coliseum in Exposition Park. The event commemorated Great Britain's acceptance of the Balfour Declaration. The crowd was estimated at over 10,000 which made it the largest Jewish gathering in Los Angeles up to that time

Yiddish cultural life was "heavily political, shot through with the strife of the 1920s between sympathizers and opponents of Soviet Russia." Operating out of "rival" headquarters, the different political and cultural factions established their own clubs and separate theater troupes. "Side by side with its undesirable features, factionalism also had the effect of multiplying cultural media for the Yiddish public."

World War I Broadens International Horizon — Zionism Gains Momentum

At the start of World War I in 1917, citizens in Los Angeles were engaged in living normal lives while in the midst of an economic slowdown. They assumed the mantle of political neutrality along with the rest of America, cautiously noting the increase of Europeans immigrating to California through the newly opened Panama Canal.

At the conclusion of the war, however, Jews in the city were immediately caught up emotionally and financially in the post war ramifications. Many thousands had emigrated from Russian and Poland, and still had family and friends left behind who were suffering in the midst of the horror of wartime Europe. There existed a tremendous need for the Jewish community in Los Angeles and throughout America to assist their relatives and former countrymen. Human compassion was the dominant emotion and this concern, according to Vorspan, would have "far reaching effects in broadening the Jewish community's interests and stirring thought and emotion about Jewish destinies on a world scale."

Jewish thinking went beyond rescue and relief as the war recovery became prolonged. They studied the changes taking place in Eastern Europe and the impact on the Jews from the new global alliances and the restructuring of international coalitions. At this time, the Ottoman Empire ruled Turkey and Turkey controlled Palestine. Jewish pioneers and patriots aligned themselves with the British in fighting against the Turks for control of Palestine; this was seen as a way for Jews worldwide to reclaim their homeland. With Turkey's participation in the war, excitement was rising among Jews as they saw possibilities for Zionism and increased activity in Palestine. Vorspan writes:

> With the other major Jewish communities in the world engrossed in the conflict, the Jews in neutral America, numbering over 3,000,000 souls, assumed novel responsibilities. Even remote Los Angeles was affected by worldwide political storms as Jewish groups, especially the Zionists, became more active than ever before.... In two well prepared meetings [in Los Angeles], one at Congregation B'nai B'rith and the other a public luncheon, the famed Reform rabbi [Rabbi Stephen S. Wise] portrayed to a representative audience the current sufferings of Palestinian Jewry under the Turks and the future glory of a reborn homeland.

Representatives of the Jewish community in Los Angeles planned a congress of American Jewish delegates to meet and determine the needs of Jews in the post war era. Jewish community sentiment was intensifying, reinforced by the rapid increase in Zionism and "the future glory of a reborn homeland." An impassioned appeal went out to the Jewish community from the newly organized Federation of Jewish Philanthropies in Los Angeles. More than any

Los Angeles Jewish leadership at the cornerstone ceremony of the new Wilshire Blvd Temple, 1928. Front row, left to right: Rabbi Maxwell Dubin, Marco Newmark, Rabbi Edgar F. Magnin, Dr. David Edelman (president of the synagogue), George Mosbacher (building chairman), Mrs. James W. Hellman, and James W. Hellman

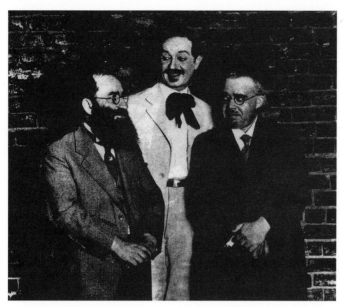

The renowned Cantor Yossele Rosenblatt on a visit to Los Angeles in 1928, with Yiddish actor Elia Tenenholtz and Rabbi Solomon M. Neches, who became Dean of the Western Jewish Institute of Los Angeles in 1935

other time in the city's short history, Jews were coming together and forming a cohesive and supportive unit. They were inspired and highly motivated to assist their compatriots to escape from war-ravaged Europe.

As Los Angeles Jewry strengthened in collective unity and their universal concern for Jews worldwide, Zionism became increasingly visible and gathered momentum. Groups of Zionists were needed to educate Jews about their history, to teach Hebrew, to explore ways to relocate displaced Jews to Palestine, to raise funds for land purchase and continue the development of Palestine.

Marco R. Newmark became the president of the new Nathan Strauss Palestine Advancement Society, which was established in Los Angeles as early as 1914 to "contribute and assist institutions whose purposes are the advancement of Jewish people in Palestine." The Nathan Strauss Society was considered one of the most effective early Zionist groups, and was organized by Harry Fram, prominent among Los Angeles' first Zionists. Marco Newmark spoke about Fram's contribution in 1927: "This history of our Society cannot well be told without complimentary mention of Mr. Harry Fram, our secretary, whose grasping of the situation and prompt action have made our Society possible." The group attracted a very large membership for its work in advancing free loans to small farmers in Palestine. Thus Los Angeles and its Jewish community were years ahead of similar organizations that were founded in other cities throughout the country.

Vorspan reports that a Zionist writer responding to the question of whether the new Jewish state was "religious," wrote that although Zionists were being divided between "national and political" and between the "ceremonial or Orthodox," they were "united on the moral laws of the Torah." The new Palestine "must be a country where the Jewish morals will be upheld and wherein Judaism shall have as its backbone, the Torah, the greatest of all teachers of morality and equality of mankind." On the same subject, a member of the community, Morris Kaufman, reinforced the distinction clearly when he said, "Judaism is nothing other than the national culture of the Jews, and simply requires as its basis a national territory like that of any other nation. Americanism concedes to every nation what it claims for itself: the right to live its own national life. In this respect, the Hebrew nationalists claim the sympathy of all American citizens, Jews and gentiles."

As soon as America entered the war in 1917 all of the various relief efforts were mobilized. Jewish young men went into the armed forces and those that remained at home continued with their efforts to raise money and raise people's consciousness of the sacrifices and struggles being undertaken. In 1918 Jewish young people were enlisting in the newly formulated Jewish Legion in the British army helping to fight for control of Palestine. The presentation of the Balfour Declaration, attesting to Great Britain's acceptance of Palestine as a Jewish state, was met with great celebration by Jews in Los Angeles along with the rest of the Jewish world. This enthusiasm was rekindled in 1920 when "an estimated ten thousand Jews (and three thousand automobiles) made their way to Exposition Park [adjacent to the USC campus] to celebrate the first anniversary of the British Mandate."

At the conclusion of the war, however, Jewish hopes were once again disappointed as America became more isolationist, retreating from foreign affairs. "Bloody pogroms" were spreading throughout Eastern Europe and the British were openly antagonistic to Jews and blocked their attempts to develop Palestine as a homeland for the displaced and persecuted European Jews. In Los Angeles, Zionists split into the labor faction (*Poale Zion*) and the religious (*Mizrachi*). As the last memories of the war were put to rest, Los Angeles entered the 1920s at the start of a new economic boom, which exploded into the "Roaring Twenties."

Post World War I — Social, Economic, and Political Ramifications

The end of World War I inaugurated a period of anti-Semitism in America felt by most in all walks of life. These anti-Semitic incidents set the tone after 1920. Among the more blatant events were "lurid accusations" in Henry Ford's *International Jew*, exclusion from universities and social clubs, and quotas based on national origins in the Immigration Act of 1924—

all combined to shock and disturb Jews. In Los Angeles, colleges and medical schools discriminated against Jewish applicants, and clubs were suddenly closed to respected Jewish businessmen. "Unknown in previous years, prejudice was by 1920 'gradually encroaching upon the confines of even this broad and splendid community,'" as reported by Vorspan.

As the concluding years of World War I heated up the political global climate, repercussions were far-reaching, extending across the continent into Los Angeles. Anti-Semitism became more deliberate and transparent as incidents against Jews increased. There was open refusal to hire Jews. Despite strong protests, plays that portrayed Jews negatively, like Shakespeare's *Merchant of Venice*, were produced in schools and designated as required reading. School authorities ignored petitions of protest by both Jewish and Christian members of the community.

Chaim Shapiro's political poster

Vorspan reports further on events of the time: "From time to time Jews were irritated by fundamentalist Christian detractions. The master evangelist Billy Sunday used Jesus' strictures against the Pharisees to assail the good name of contemporary Jews. Of a piece with

Adolphe Drabkin standing in the doorway of one of his pharmacies. This one was located at 100 South Grand Ave which today would be across from the Music Center, in downtown Los Angeles. Drabkin, from Montreal, spoke fluent French and was active in the French colony located in the Bunker Hill area

Sunday's attack were the implications of Mrs. West Stevenson's *Pilgrimage Play* depicting the last days and death of Jesus, produced by local volunteers. On this occasion, Rabbi Isidore Myers was invited by the Pilgrimage Club to give his answer to 'Who Crucified Jesus?' His endeavors to tone down the anti-Jewish features of the *Pilgrimage Play* were successful."

Some of the prominent Jewish leaders in the community were puzzled by the surge in anti-Semitism, and thought perhaps that use of Yiddish and other Judaic traditions were separating and alienating Jews from other Americans. In a determined effort to at least continue Jewish traditions in the home, much attention became invested in Jewish efforts to guide and educate children and young adults. The development of Jewish youth in Los Angeles became a Jewish communal concern, rather than solely a parental matter. In light of the revolutionary industrial progress that brought the automobile and films into the mainstream, parents and social workers were concerned about the impact of "progress" on young people. As more than one Southern California parent said in bewildered gravity: "I'm a father and am trying to set good ideals. As soon as the boy leaves home the influences tend to tear those down, so what can I do? We have a religious atmosphere in our home, but outside there are even anti-religious tendencies."

Los Angeles Jewish youth in the boom city of the 1920s joined their peers in trying to avoid European and earlier American restraints on their personal conduct. It was the "roaring twenties," yet they still felt the need for a meeting place inside the Jewish community. Temple Street and Central Avenue were emptying of Jews by the 1920s as Boyle Heights was growing, and the Educational Alliance was created to fill the gap. The new Modern Social Center opened in 1924, and operated as the Jewish "community center." The director, Jacob M. Alkow, was a young Zionist and Jewish educator. The center housed several dozen clubs organized for children and adults, and included meeting rooms, a gymnasium and playgrounds.

Jews interested in socializing and meeting with other Jews were attracted to "religiously neutral" organizations like the B'nai B'rith. Founded as a lodge in Los Angeles in 1899, it grew by absorbing other groups and appealing for recruits among recent Russian immigrants. The membership grew to 1,000 following World War I and by 1924 listed 2,000 men on its enrollment lists. The Los Angeles lodge was the largest in America.

Newly arrived Jewish citizens in Los Angeles found their social needs met by the "fraternal order." Vorspan writes, "If traditional Judaism weakened in the movement to the West Coast, the desire for Jewish companionship probably became stronger. The neutral, unphilo-

Sam Behrendt and Isaac Levy were the founders of Behrendt and Levy Insurance firm whose clients were among the founders of the early movie industry. The photograph is movie comedian Roscoe Arbuckle's birthday party at the Alexandria Hotel on February 12, 1917. Several celebrities are pictured as well as a number of second generation members of pioneer Jewish families

sophical environment of B'nai B'rith, resting upon humanitarian service and Jewish self-defense, attracted its thousands. The lodge was also a place where Jewish lawyers, insurance brokers, accountants, and dentists could find clients. B'nai B'rith became the representative Jewish organization in Los Angeles, rejoicing in its ability to mobilize Jewish energies for Jewish and civic effort." Other organizations that offered companionship and Jewish interaction included the Jewish Professional Men's Club, consisting of men in the professions—physicians, attorneys, engineers, dentists, and architects—and the Concordia Club, which hosted social events for both women and men, whose clientele eventually moved to the Hillcrest Country Club.

Jewish Philanthropy Increases As World War I Ends

Jewish philanthropic institutions developed rapidly in the second decade of the new century. Five major institutions had been founded or transformed between 1905 and 1915, with a discernible trend away from charity to "systemic welfare" with philanthropy a central interest. As a result of World War I this philanthropy turned its attention to relief overseas. Los Angeles Jews had been active regarding world Jewish assistance, especially during the Russian pogroms and revolutions in the early part of the century. When World War I broke out, the people in the community with close ties to Eastern Europe became very active once again. The synagogues and B'nai B'rith Lodge collected money on behalf of suffering European and Palestinian Jews. The newly founded American Jewish Joint Distribution Center in New York received funds from the Los Angeles Jewish War Sufferers Relief Society. War relief became the main charity of the Jewish community.

In the years following the end of the war this overseas aid diminished, coinciding with America's gradual withdrawal from foreign issues. Vorspan reports:

> After six or seven years of concentration upon the needs of world Jewry, philanthropic interests were again turned inward. The Federation of Jewish Charities sharply reduced its efforts, however. During World War I, the United War Chest was successfully established to support all local philanthropy, and included the Jewish institutions. It was renamed the Community Chest after the war. The Federation gave up its fundraising activities to the Chest, and became solely a planning and budgeting body.

Los Angeles County was the richest agricultural county in the country. Pictured above is the Union Terminal Market in downtown Los Angeles

Los Angeles Jewry Confronts the Great Depression and the Fragile Rebirth of the Community

The Depression that followed the boom years of the 1920s hit Los Angeles hard, and among the populace the Jews were among those hardest hit, specifically with the loss of jobs. The *B'nai B'rith Messenger* wrote, "The Jewish employee, in times of distress, is the first to feel the brunt of unemployment." Jewish wage earners and business entrepreneurs alike suffered as jobs disappeared and businesses went bankrupt. In one of the most extreme cases, the famous pioneer banking family, the Hellmans, were "virtually wiped out." Organizations and individuals in the Jewish community did their best to rally and take care of their own with welfare from the community. They gave milk to children to stave off malnutrition, cash to pay rents, and food to those who had no other source.

Jewish immigration continued in Los Angeles, following the trend of the general population. Despite the fact that people were coming in smaller numbers than previously seen, still the Jewish population rose from 70,000 in 1930 to 130,000 in 1941. Jews arrived both from Europe and cities throughout the United States. The German and Austrian Jewish refugees had a particularly difficult road. In addition to trying to make a living, they also were perceived as having a lower social status than transplanted Americans; nor were they eligible for public welfare.

When recovery slowly began in the mid-1930s, manufacturing and the resurgence of the trade unions played a primary role. The rapid growth of the Los Angeles garment business,

Members of the Jewish community "dressed-up" for St. Patrick's Day in Los Angeles in 1923. This photograph was taken at the home the Gilbert family at 4125 W. Pico Blvd. Pictured in the front row (far left) is Leonard Gilbert, nine years old, who eventually founded the Gilbert Variety Stores. In the second row, standing, second from the left, is Meyer Raphael, whose father was the founder of the third oldest corporation in California, Raphael Glass Company

Farmers and Merchants Bank in 1923 (lower left hand corner) between Main and Spring Streets at Fourth Street. Surrounding the bank is an office building built by and named after the bank's president, Isaias W. Hellman

whose trade union members were predominantly Jewish, strongly advanced their destiny since the apparel workers were among the strongest of the workers' labor unions.

The other primary benefit to the Jewish population during this recovery was the transition of workers from laborers and artisans to more professional and technical occupations. For Jewish physicians the focal point was Cedars of Lebanon Hospital, both for its medical excellence, and as a haven from the progressively increasing bias against Jews in the medical profession. In addition to becoming doctors, Jewish professionals became pharmacists, social workers,

President Woodrow Wilson visits Los Angeles as the nation prepares to enter World War I

nurses, dentists, attorneys, teachers and accountants. Added to this were the many hundreds of Jews active in the film business that were employed by the Hollywood studios.

Politically, Jews remained mostly behind the scenes during the turbulent Thirties, when corruption versus righteousness seemed to characterize the political battlegrounds. According to Vorspan, "Running a Jewish candidate for an elective office was an unrealistic thought in the Los Angeles of the 1920s and 1930s, even though appointive office was by no means rare. When that came, it was usually to the bench: Los Angeles had a string of Jewish jurists, some of whom achieved judicial eminence."

Despite differences in politics, Jews continued to cluster together in particular neighborhoods. Boyle Heights grew dramatically and was home to many synagogues, hotels, theaters, apartment houses, and kosher restaurants. Other more prosperous Jewish neighborhoods close by were City Terrace, Central Wilshire, the Wilshire-Pico district, and Hollywood, all combining to a Jewish population of nearly 100,000 by 1940.

Jews did not feel secure during this pre-World War II era; there was a sense of "external menace." It was too early for recognition of the Nazi peril fomenting in Europe—instead the insidious threat first emerged from the so-called "respectable" Southern California citizens actively operating Ku Klux Klan organizations in both Glendale and Inglewood. Vorspan reports, "They functioned by 'gentlemen's agreements' to exclude Jews from home ownership and social groups in their neighborhoods. Many areas were closed tight to Jews by means of restrictive covenants (agreements among owners not to sell to Jews or other 'undesirables') and other devices."

Even civic bodies such as the Chambers of Commerce colluded to keep the Jews out. The economically powerful Hollywood Jewish studio people might have challenged these "exclusivity" barriers, but they were content to stay within their own industry. According to Vorspan,

> To genteel anti-Semitism and crude Nazism were joined some of the uglier aspects of Protestant Fundamentalism. A belief that the Jew caused depression and war came all too readily to those who had accepted Christian myths about the Jewish 'Antichrist' in their crudest form. Radio listeners in Los Angeles of the 1930s could hear this type of preachment from the Reverend Martin Luther Thomas…. Myths about Jews could be found in such places as police records and probate reports, where a Jewish defendant might exhibit "typical tricks of his race in attempting to turn a deal wherever he can."

The most serious form of anti-Semitism was evident in the employment market. It was no secret that jobs in insurance, banking, and retail were not available to Jews except in "token" positions. Jewish doctors were not welcome to practice at most hospitals, and attorneys were not invited into the big white Protestant dominated law firms. With devastating unemployment widespread, Jews had to confront the additional discrimination of not being hired or considered for jobs because they were Jewish, once again pointing out the "deep stratum of latent anti-Semitism" that existed.

As a result of the hard times that had fallen in the Jewish neighborhoods, community life suffered. Jewish institutions could not find financial and social support necessary for them to flourish,

The northwest corner of Seventh and Spring Streets in 1926. The building had several names and was known as the Union Oil Building

and existing limited funds went to relief assistance. As international political tensions intensified in the pre-World War II years, responses began to emerge again from the Jewish community to help the Jews overseas. The religious life of the Jewish neighborhoods was inconsistent and somewhat apathetic except around the High Holy Days. "The 'Jewishness' of many neighborhoods exceeded their formal Judaism." One exception to the strain on synagogues with lagging attendance was the Wilshire Boulevard Temple, which survived relatively without incident, due in large part to the activities, charisma, and reputation of Rabbi Edgar F. Magnin. As Vorspan noted,

> It cannot be said that the religious sector of Los Angeles Jewry contained very much spiritual or intellectual power. Jewish religious traditions seemed unable to attract or hold the loyalty of younger people. Partly on account of emergency needs during the Depression, there was an undue taint of commercialism in many of the synagogues. However, the Depression years were basically not a religious age in Los Angeles nor in American life.

The unique success of Rabbi Magnin was the exception to the prevailing apathy that was underlying the lack of religious interest in post war Los Angeles. After World War I, Rabbi Magnin addressed overflowing crowds at Congregation B'nai B'rith, as attempts were made for a religious revival in the aftermath of the war. People were more serious following the war in Europe and its devastating ripple effects in the United States. They were trying to find comfort and turning toward more spiritual matters. Magnin, in an effort

In this 1931 photograph, Albert Einstein chats with founder and president of Universal Studios, Carl Laemmle. Einstein had come to Pasadena to work at the California Institute of Technology

Hamburger's Peoples Store located at Eighth Street and Broadway was the first large department store in downtown Los Angeles

to inspire his audiences, remarked, "The people are learning that life is something more than running after nothing. People are returning to religion."

Magnin focused on a particular lecture in the year following the war, entitled "Americanization." This speech gave him the opportunity to expand religion to interfaith patriotism and reinforce the positive feelings of nationalism with the triumph of democracy. Speaking on the subject gave him the chance to effectively facilitate and guide the assimilation of the newly arriving immigrants. This was also an especially important platform that Magnin seized in order to share his favorable views on Zionism, describing the ideals to both Jewish and non-Jewish groups that previously were not aware of the Jewish dream of a homeland. In a speech to a large group at the Los Angeles Ebell Club on "The Present Status of the Zionist Movement," he explained:

> It is not the political aspects of Zionism or the attempt to solve the problem of anti-Semitism that makes it so appealing…. It is the cultural aspect of the movement emphasized by Ahad Ha'am. For Zionism means the rebirth of Jewish values. But whether or not Zionism is realized in practice, it is a great ideal. It wakens in the Jewish heart pride and loyalty to the past as well as the will to live and give in the future. It makes Hebrew a living tongue.

The majority of members of Congregation B'nai B'rith were in large part descendants of Polish-Prussian and Eastern European Jews. This created a perfect backdrop for Magnin's dedication to Zionism, moving from the cultural Zionism of the poet Ahad Ha'am to the political Zionism of statehood, espoused by Theodor Herzl. Magnin spoke fervently about the necessity for Jewish people to be educated about their own history so that "the world might be enlightened concerning Jewish thought and Jewish life."

Jewish community life changed abruptly in the 1930s. Since so many of the Jewish leadership lost their

In 1929 the Hamburger's Peoples Store became the May Company. A few decades later the store branched out to the growing suburbs. In the mid-1980s this store relocated to Seventh Street and in 1993 merged with Robinson's Department Store.

World War I ends and Los Angeles celebrates

wealth during the Depression, they were unprepared to assist with the financial needs of the Jewish people overseas. With the establishment of the United Jewish Welfare Fund in 1929, combined appeals were made for both European and Palestinian Jewry. To this organization were added two more in the mid-1930s: the United Jewish Community, founded by the Federation to take care of internal matters in the community, such as youth organization and Jewish education, and the Jewish Community Committee, established for external issues such as confronting anti-Semitism and combatting the rising power of the Nazi regime in Germany. Many new names were prominent participants in these newly organized groups, among them were: Lester Roth, Isaac Pacht, Harry Hollzer, Walter S. Hillborn, Mendel B. Silberberg, David Blumberg, Mrs. Bertha Sieroty, and Aaron Riche.

Unfortunately, the same pattern of apathy that seemed to infiltrate synagogue attendance and membership re-emerged in the area of Jewish education. One new development that helped to reverse the downturn in Jewish education was the establishment of the Bureau of Jewish Education under the auspices of the Los Angeles Jewish Community Council. The critical importance of the funding for the Bureau of Jewish Education reflected the feeling that it was necessary for the community to take responsibility for revitalizing the education of their children.

A few years later, in 1937, the United Jewish Community and United Jewish Welfare Fund merged into a single organization, the Los Angeles Jewish Community Council (LAJCC), whose partial aim was stated "to coordinate and harmonize the activities [of Jewish organizations] and in particular [to] foster, develop and co-ordinate all phases of Jewish social service, relief, welfare, educational, recreational and community life." To accomplish their aims a centralized appeal for funds would be made. Vorspan writes, "Unprecedented and soul-stirring calls for overseas aid lay entirely within the province of the new leaders, together with many Los Angeles Jewish institutions which had never before received communal aid." Campaign funds gradually increased due to conditions abroad and by the end of 1941, the LAJCC had a membership of 156 Jewish eligible and functioning organizations, a solid representation of support for the needs of the Jewish community moving into an uncertain future.

Post World War I Recovery in Los Angeles— the Calm Before the Storm

By 1935, Los Angeles was starting to show signs of recovery from the Depression. Population had increased to 1.5 million and the county was ranked fifth among industrialized counties in the country. Motion pictures, oil refining, airplane manufacture, and automobile assembly plants were among the industries that kept Los Angeles listed among the top industrialized regions. Furniture, tires, and women's apparel were thriving manufacturing commodities, developing alongside the agriculture industry that helped build the Southland. Companies operating in Southern California included: Firestone, Goodyear, Goodrich, General Motors, Ford, Chrysler, Studebaker, Lockheed, Douglas, and North American.

Improvements were made in dams and aqueducts enabling Los Angeles to expand its water supply and improve its electric power. Despite the economic slowdown, civic buildings continued to be constructed, among them the new Federal Building and Post Office, Union Passenger Terminal, and Griffith Park Planetarium.

Asher Hamburger (L) at the Golden Jubilee of the May Company, 1931

Meanwhile, Hollywood continued to make movies, the industry gaining momentum in the 1930s, as people looked for a way to forget their troubles. The "dream" continued to stubbornly fight for recognition and was available to the masses on the silver screen. Hollywood in the Thirties, according to Matthew Ellenberger,

> …quickly became the synonym for the Los Angeles Basin. Like some frightening god of wrath, the motion picture industry remade the city in its image and transmitted that image to millions…. urban sophisticate, worldly, at home in the nascent 20th Century culture with its corporate, impersonal organization and the cult of personality.

With the introduction of "Busby Berkley, Betty Boop, Mickey Mouse and the 'screwball comedies,'" Hollywood provided an escape for the suffering masses.

Jewish Hollywood performed another service when they began to make movies about some of the social problems being faced by the country. They addressed issues like social injustice, coal mining conditions, underage labor, and bigotry, in films such as *Horses for Sale* (1933), *Black Fury* (1935), and *Black Legion* (1936). "The social message films of the Thirties were optimistic, simple and often sentimental," giving hope in times when it was desperately needed.

In an era that brought a wealth of literary writers to the forefront like Hemmingway, Steinbeck, and Huxley, one that emerged as an icon to the public, especially in Los Angeles, was Raymond Chandler. He wrote seven novels that were set in Los Angeles, and his Phillip Marlowe detective stories captured the imagination of the populace as the anti-hero crusaded against injustice. Liahna Barber wrote in Los Angeles in *Fiction*:

Chandler's Los Angeles is finally more than a portrait of a depraved regional society. The many falsehoods merge into a larger one and the city becomes a graphic symbol of The Big Lie—the cardinal deception of American civilization—that prosperity brings personal contentment and deliverance from the past. Chandler demonstrated with relentless consistency that money and privilege are traps and that the past is inescapable.

This was a difficult lesson that the City of Angels was also learning. In the 1930s, boosterism campaigns of the preceding fifty years came to an abrupt halt. As the citizens of Los Angeles had their illusions briefly shattered by the war and years of economic depression, they now realized that the sunny paradise that offered warmth and leisure, oranges and new vistas, opportunities for new lives and new beginnings had been unrelentingly tested in these trying years. As with most times of suffering and sacrifice, these encroachments on their idyllic city added to the strength and character of its inhabitants. They began to embrace their city with a new sense of reality and determination to revive the glittering golden days much as their pioneering parents and grandparents had in the generations preceding them.

The Jewish Aeronautical Association

by Sue Lipman and Norton B. Stern

In the early 1930's, the idea of flying as a sport was not as popular as it is today. Flying at that time provided a true challenge to its devotees, and in 1933, a small group of young Jewish men in Los Angeles decided to take on that challenge and learn to fly. The formation of this group owes its existence to an incident in 1933 when an aircraft mechanic remarked to Leopold Shluker, that in his opinion, Jews could not fly an airplane.

Leopold Shluker, one of the founders of the Jewish Aeronautical Association (JAA), 1936

Shluker, a prosperous Los Angeles businessman, was at that time spending a few hours each week working on aircraft at Mines Field. William M. Mines had established the airport in the midst of bean fields in the late 1920s. Today it is Los Angeles International Airport. Leopold Shluker did not know of any Jewish flyers or mechanics, but challenged by the notion that Jews could not fly airplanes, he contacted a few friends and interested them in forming a Jewish flying club. He then inserted a notice in the Anglo-Jewish press:

Ben Grobman (left) and Sam Lewis, members of Jewish Aeronautical Association, with the Piper Cub airplane purchased by the organization, 1940

Several Jewish young men interested in aviation have expressed their intention of forming a club in Los Angeles, which will be open to all interested in the sport. Leopold Shluker, who is a student flyer and has been interested in aviation for the past five years, is sponsoring the club project. Those who are interested in becoming affiliated with such an organization to learn to fly are invited to communicate with Mr. Shluker at Atlantic 8942. Social activities will be stressed.

This notice was successful in bringing several young Jewish men together and frequent notices thereafter in the *B'nai B'rith Messenger* of Los Angeles, informed the public of the progress of the club and gave it the publicity necessary to its growth. In September 1933, a notice appeared, which mentioned that two applications for membership had been received and that the club was under the direction of Leopold Shluker and A. Saul Alpert. By October, "Jewish Air Cadets," had been chosen as the name of the flying club. At the same time, the public was informed that "a few applications from girls are being considered" and that "plans for an air show are being discussed."

The name Jewish Air Cadets did not remain in effect for very long, for by December 1933, the club was known as the Jewish Aeronautical Association. In less than three months from the time of the original announcement, the group could boast of a roster of twenty-four members.

The young Jewish men, who comprised the initial membership, ranged in age from eighteen to thirty-eight years and were quite diverse in status and occupation. From its beginnings in 1933, until the club ceased operations in mid-1941, due to the activities and effects of World War II, about one hundred individuals belonged to the group. At one time, over sixty members were active.

The insignia of the Jewish Aeronautical Association was designed by member, Bernard Haines, and consisted of a pair of wings stemming from each side of a circle, in the center of

Jewish Aeronautical Association members gather in front of their Gardena clubhouse

which was the traditional six-pointed star, a *Mogen Dovid*. It was published for the first time on March 23, 1934, and was reproduced on the membership cards printed for the organization in the fall of 1934. This insignia is used today by El Al Israel Airlines. [The insignia is also used by the Israeli Air Force.]

❋ ❋ ❋

G. Willis Tyson and Marion West were well known throughout the country as skillful flying instructors. Because of their high standards of training, in less than eight years, about sixty-five Jewish young men and one woman were able to qualify for and receive private flying licenses from the Civil Aeronautics Authority. At first, student flyers could solo and take their test for a flying license whenever the instructor felt they were ready. Later, ten hours and then thirty-five hours of solo flying time were required before the examination for a license could be taken.

The first big event of the Jewish Aeronautical Association took place on Sunday, March 25, 1934, when the club made its initial formation flight over Los Angeles. This event brought the new group to the attention of the greater public. The *Los Angeles Herald Express* gave the unique affair advance coverage:

> Believed to be the first of its kind in the history of aviation, an all Jewish flying
> club, the Jewish Aeronautical Association, is to make its first formation flight over

The Los Angeles Municipal Airport (once known as Mines Field) was established in 1925 as a general flying field and military base on Inglewood's southwestern border. The Hangar No. 1 building that once housed the Curtiss Wright Flying Service was the first structure built at Mines Field in 1929. Designed by the architects Gable and Wyant, Hangar No. 1 was declared a Los Angeles Cultural Monument on November 16, 1966. The official dedication of the airport took place on June 7, 1930. In 1935 the Federal government granted a subsidy to improve the airport and three years later authorized additional work under the Work Project Administration. The City of Los Angeles purchased the entire site in 1937 and by 1939 the field had accommodations for 90 planes. At this time American Aviation Factory was located at the airport site with an entrance from Imperial Highway

> Los Angeles and Hollywood, Sunday, March 25, at 2 p.m. Twelve airplanes will be engaged in this novel flight, leaving from Los Angeles Municipal Airport. The planes will be piloted by Jewish fliers and observers, led by William Denels and Mel Wallack. A parachute jump is also planned by Abe Bradofsky, a member of the association.

At 2:15 p.m., twelve pilots and twelve observers took off "in perfect order, and for an hour flew over Los Angeles and Hollywood," the first flight of this type by an all-Jewish squadron. The pilots in this historic formation included: William Denels, Melton S. Wallack, A. Saul Alpert, David Becker, Sam Greenspan, Bernard Haines, Milton Sharkansky, Harry Harris, Arthur Wisen, Abe Bradofsky, and Leopold Shluker. While they were in the air, a heavy fog rolled in and they were "unable to fly over some areas originally scheduled." The fog caused the formation to break up, some of the pilots got lost and the aircraft returned to the field at different times.

Prior to the flight, Allen Brandes (then Abe Bradofsky), made his first parachute jump from "the height of 3,000 feet, and thrilled thousands of spectators while he fell through the air, purposely delaying the opening of his parachute." This delayed jump was said to be "the first recorded jump by a Jewish aviator." Brandes had had no prior training or experience.

❋ ❋ ❋

In 1936, at the urging of several leaders of the Jewish community of Los Angeles, the JAA changed its name to the California Flying Club. Three men, two of whom were Aaron Richie, long a leader in the field of community relations, and Ben Meyer, president of the Union Bank, attended a meeting to urge the change of the name, Jewish Aeronautical Association. Among the reasons given, were that with the increased worldwide anti-Semitism due to the Nazis in Europe, some might think that the group was an extralegal military organization of Jews. Also, there was the feeling that because of

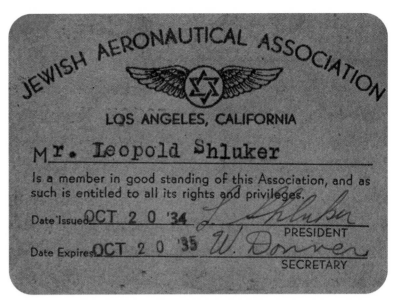

Membership card for the JAA. The emblem, the wings and the Jewish star, designed in Los Angeles in 1934, eventually became the official emblem of the Israeli Air Force and El Al Israel Airlines

the hostility of the Arabs in Palestine toward the Jews living there, no opportunity should be given them to falsely claim that American Jews were forming military organizations to help Palestinian Jewry. The members of the Jewish Aeronautical Association at first refused to change their name. They were proud of it. But later they acceded to the request and incorporated as the California Flying Club, on May 1, 1936. The directors of the corporation were listed as Leo Shluker, Nate Kluner, and Dave Bushner, all of Los Angeles. There can be little doubt, however, that to the members it remained the Jewish Aeronautical Association. The new name of the California Flying Club was published for the first time in the announcement of activities on May 8, 1936.

✳ ✳ ✳

The Los Angeles Jewish group believed, at first, that they were the only such club of its kind in the world, but they soon found out that there was also a Jewish flying club in Palestine. The two organizations began to correspond regularly, exchanging information and various items of mutual interest. The group in Palestine was eventually revealed to be part of the Jewish underground military organization there. In one of the regular announcements in the press, it was mentioned that the California Flying Club "is one of two Jewish flying clubs in the world. The other is located in Palestine."

✳ ✳ ✳

Nearly every member contributed to the war effort in the 1940s. The club wrote to Army headquarters in Washington, D.C., offering their services as a group. The authorities in their answer, thanked them, but explained that they had no policy for group enlistment, and could only accept the members individually. Thereupon, some of the members went to Canada to join the Royal Canadian Air Force, in order to get into action sooner. [Nearly all of the members of the club actively participated in the war effort, most of them as fliers.]

With the ending of the war, the Air Force had a great surplus of aircraft, which were to be sold for instructional purposes only and not for use in foreign countries. Sam Lewis and others purchased some of these airplanes and flew them to Panama, placed Panamanian flags on them, then ferried them over a long and roundabout course to Palestine, where they aided in the 1948 War of Independence of the new Jewish state. The airplanes were used to bring in supplies and arms and were also used in the battle itself. These aircraft had to be smuggled out of the country because of the United States' Neutrality Act. Those involved in this operation faced trial in Los Angeles during January and February of 1950. Sam Lewis was not convicted, for the jury felt that he acted as a pilot only, not as a conspirator.

Mary Pickford was forgiven by the community (opposite page)

After the 1948 war of Independence, Lewis remained in Israel and helped to form the El Al Israel Airlines. He has logged over three million miles as a pilot and he was the first to fly a multi-engine airplane across the Atlantic regularly. At one time he held the commercial speed record from London to New York at nine hours and twenty-three minutes. Sam Lewis is perhaps the most colorful member to come out of the Los Angeles Jewish flying club and he is quite a hero in Israel.

✳ ✳ ✳

The Jewish Aeronautical Association or the California Flying Club as it became, made a name for itself, not only through its activities, but also through the dedicated and patriotic service of its members. They found a challenging and constructive sport and their efforts went much further than simply disproving the foolish remark that Jews could not fly. Though the club did not officially disband, it was inactive by mid-1941, when a large proportion of the members had entered the armed forces. There was an attempt to bring the club back to life again after World War II, and a few meetings were held. But the effort to re-create the group was unsuccessful, perhaps because the members were leading such varied lives by then, with the added responsibilities of families and careers. Still, the feeling and interest of the former members for the association seems to be that expressed by the founder, Leopold Shluker, in 1942:

> The club will never die. It's meant too much to all of us. It gave us something to live for, and now it's given us a way to fight more effectively than if we were on the ground. And I think it's also proven that Jews can fly and are proud to fight for their country.

Mary Pickord: From A Moment Of Intolerance To A Lifetime Of Compassion

by Rabbi William M. Kramer and Norton B. Stern

The Los Angeles Hebrew Sheltering Association [now the Jewish Home for the Aging] was chartered on June 4, 1910, to provide temporary quarters for Jewish transients. Just before Passover of 1912 it was learned that there were coreligionists at the Los Angeles County Poor Farm. Among those who determined to provide a Seder for the Jewish indigents at the poor farm and permanent housing under Jewish auspices were Simon Lewis, Simon Shukin, Louis Glasband, I. Kaufman, L. Traub, Mrs. Ray Corenson and Mrs. H. Lew Zuckerman. Later the group was augmented by Ben R. Meyer, B. Forer, L. Eisner, Louis Isaacs and Max Brown. Simon Lewis served as the founding president of the Sheltering Association and continued in the office for the first six years of the organization.

Mary Pickford (far right) with residents of the Jewish Home. Miss Pickford was the honored chairperson for over three decades of the Ida Mayer Cummings Auxiliary

Years after the modest beginnings in a small rented cottage [as the Sheltering Association] in the downtown Los Angeles area, the Jewish Home for the Aging, as it came to be known, developed into one of the leading senior citizens residential programs in America. As the facility grew it came to enjoy the patronage of some of the Jewish members of the film industry. Foremost among them was Ida Mayer Cummings, the sister of Louis B. Mayer. It was on impulse that Mrs. Cummings sent an invitation to Mary Pickford, "America's Sweetheart," to attend and to speak at the first annual donors' luncheon in 1939, of the Junior Auxiliary of the home.

Mary Pickford, perhaps the greatest of the silent film stars, told in her autobiography of the incident which made her receptive to the invitation of Mrs. Cummings. She [Pickford] had been talking to "two Jewish friends of mine." One was Carmel Myers, the daughter of Rabbi Isidore Myers, who had served congregations in both San Francisco and Los Angeles. Carmel was an important film star whose career covered much of the silent era and into the beginning of the talkies. Miss Pickford described Miss Myers as "an actress, beautiful, talented and of rare intelligence and character…" She continued,

> "It is a source of great pride to me that she always calls me her sister." As Mary Pickford states it, "each of us has at least one moment in his life that stands out with a burning sense of shame and self-guilt, a moment during which we committed a grave, though perhaps unintended offense against a fellow human being. Some have the power to efface the pain of that moment from their minds;

others find solace in appeasing their consciences by one means or another; still others have known how to distill a deeper understanding of themselves and others from their honest remorse."

The 1939 incident occurred as the Nazi campaign against the Jews was unfolding. Miss Pickford said that she made "an intolerant remark," in which she blamed wealthy Jews for what was happening, on the grounds that they had "bought up German properties at bargain prices, after World War I… to exploit the depression in Germany." Carmel Myers gently reproved her, and Mary Pickford took it to heart.

> I am sure Carmel Myers has forgiven me that lapse from grace, inexcusable as it was. That she will ever forget it I doubt. Such jolts to the spirit, particularly when administered by a trusted and intimate friend are not easily put aside. Carmel, however, never knew this, but she will know it now: because of that intolerant outburst I was so ashamed of myself that I went home that night and got down on my knees. I asked God to forgive me and show me the right path to help these persecuted people. I repeated that prayer every night for several weeks. I made

Beverly Hills City Hall 1932. Beverly Hills began as small train station named Morocco Junction, until 1906 when Burton Green and his partners formed the Rodeo Land and Water Company after trying unsuccessfully to find large amounts of oil in the immediate area. In 1912 they built the Beverly Hills Hotel to attract prospective real estate buyers and incorporated the area thereafter known as Beverly Hills in 1914. By 1920 a migration of movie people and celebrities began to take an interest in the town publicizing it internationally. In 1927 Beverly Hills became a full-fledged city with a mayor and its own city council. The Spanish Colonial style Beverly Hills City Hall was under construction on Crescent Drive in 1932, and became the dominant landmark in the area. The main building and tower include the city office, library, police, fire and other city departments

up my mind that I would answer the very first appeal from the Jewish people with my whole being; that I would somehow make retribution for a baseless slander of a defenseless minority that was now being crucified as no other people has been in all history.

Not only did Carmel Myers forgive her, but she remained her close friend and visited her regularly during the years of her seclusion, and she stood by her coffin at Mary Pickford's funeral. Two weeks after Miss Pickford's death (May 29, 1979), Carmel Myers was asked by one of the writers, if she recalled the incident of 1939. Despite Miss Pickford's own account in her autobiography, the affection and forgiveness of the rabbi's daughter had completely blocked out the incident from her otherwise excellent memory, an act of exquisite Jewish charity.

❋ ❋ ❋

When the invitation came from Mrs. Cummings, Mary Pickford related that her "opportunity finally came" to do repentance for her thoughtless remark. She spoke at the luncheon and began an association in which she knew that she "was serving God." The donor luncheons became an annual affair in her life. Later many of them were held on the ground of Pickfair, the Beverly Hills estate which had been established by her and Douglas Fairbanks.

It was Mary Pickford who suggested that the Boyle Heights facilities of the Jewish Home for the Aging, which had been dedicated in 1931, be expanded. Nothing could be done until the conclusion of World War II, and then, in March 1948, the cornerstone of the five-story Mary Pickford Building was laid. It was dedicated in 1952.

After Mary Pickford's death the Ida Mayer Cummings Auxiliary held a memorial meeting in her honor. Rabbi Edgar F. Magnin spoke feelingly of his friendship with her and told of her "affection for the home," and said, "It was a huge source of joy in her life." Miss Pickford referred to the residents of the home as her "babies." She said, "I have never been a 'schiksa' to them, that is, a gentile woman." She took pleasure in the fact that they spoke of her as "little mother," mammale," and "mammochka." She remembered that when she had been ill many of the residents went to the "shul" to pray for her recovery. After her funeral they went to the new synagogue in the current San Fernando Valley facility, and there they said *Kaddish* for Mary Pickford, a woman of compassion.

Chaim Weizmann in Los Angeles Fifty Years Ago

B'nai B'rith Messenger, April 18, 1924

Arriving by train from Dallas on April 10, 1924, Dr. Chaim Weizmann spent a few hectic days in Los Angeles on a money raising tour for the Keren Hayesod. Born in a village near the city of Pinsk in 1874, Weizmann earned his doctorate in chemistry from the University of Geneva in 1900. In 1904 he moved to England, and after World War I his life was almost totally devoted to Zionism. He became the first president of the State of Israel in 1948, serving until his death in 1952. The following report of Weizmann's visit to Los Angeles was recorded in the B'nai B'rith Messenger, *April 18, 1924.*

The outstanding event of the past week in the Los Angeles Jewish community was the visit of Dr. and Mrs. Chaim Weizmann, who came here in the interest of the *Keren Hayesod* [The Jewish Agency], to help raise funds for the building of Palestine. Every honor due to the great leader of a great cause was paid by communal and civic leaders. Dr. and Mrs. Weizmann have traveled far and worked hard for the cause which lies so near to their hearts and were physically unable to attend the many social gathering which had been planned in their honor.

Two big events were planned. One was the banquet at the Biltmore where Mayor [George E.] Cryer, the British Consul and Dr. [Rufus] Van Klein Smid [President of the University of Southern California] were among those assembled to do honor to the World Zionist leader. Honorary President of the Los Angeles Zionist District, Marco R. Newmark, presided, while Dr. David W. Edelman [President of Congregation B'nai B'rith] acted as toastmaster.

The key note sounded throughout the entire affair was sympathetic to the cause of Zionism and the rebuilding of a Jewish homeland in Palestine, while a good deal was said by the various speakers of the "Brotherhood of Man" and as one speaker put it the "Fatherhood of God." The attendance was large, nearly 1,000 people being gathered about the banquet tables.

The feature of the evening, about which the deepest of interest centered, was the speech of Dr. Weizmann, the leader of the movement, which he himself designates as a national movement. When he arose to speak he was accorded an ovation that he acknowledged with appreciation. Dr. Weizmann in appearance proved to be more of the scientist than the orator. While only an idealist could occupy the position of leader of World Zionism, a position that

Weizmann addresses Zionist Congress in Basel, Switzerland with Nahum Sokolow (right) and Arthur Ruppin (left)

Weizmann (center) at Fifth Zionist Congress in Basel, Switzerland (1927)

he himself characterized as "prime minister of a country which does not exist and with an empty exchequer," still it is the practical presentation in figures and facts of the cold business-man that impresses.

Dr. Weizmann successfully presented the Palestine movement, which he declared, "represents more indestructible forces than the armies and navies of civilized nations" and asserted, "no force on earth will stop the up-building of Palestine."

Without the use of rhetoric or oratory Dr. Weizmann paid a compliment to Southern California, to the United States, to his "own beloved country Great Britain." He spoke of the Mandate and of England's good faith in the matter and the ratification of Palestine as a Jewish homeland by all nations "including your Republic." He spoke of the size of Palestine, saying that it is a very small country covering only 25,000 square miles. The speaker declared however that American standards as to size are different than the European standards and declared that it is possible to place 2,000,000 persons in this small space.

"Every year," said Dr. Weizmann, " we send some of our best boys to California to get information on agriculture." Dr. Weizmann said that during the past four years immigrants have come into Palestine at the rate of 1,000 per month, a considerable number for so small a country. These are young men and young women, pioneers—unmarried men many of them, ex-soldiers who have gone through the war. He told of the percentages that are farmers, artisans, professional men and unskilled laborers. The number of immigrants, he said, could easily be trebled if there were means of employment.

The immigrants, according to Dr. Weizmann, came largely from what was before the war the Russian empire, from Soviet Russia, Poland and other Central European countries. "Many came from No Man's Land, where Jews actually today lead a nomadic existence. It is hard to make it clear to Los Angeles people what the situation is in the Ukraine and other countries where half a million Jews have been thrown out—without protection or fixed abode. This

The Brown Derby was a famous night spot and restaurant frequented by Hollywood celebrities, 1937

calamity," he said, "will increase, not decrease."

The great Zionist spoke of Palestine as a means of salvaging the race but at the same time he made it distinctly and decidedly clear that he does not view Palestine as a means of "salvage," but as a national homeland.

Speaking of the physical problems to be met in the up-building of Palestine, Dr. Weizmann likened the work to that of France, where even the soil must be reconstructed. Palestine is pictured at a disadvantage even here as it has "no organized government in back of it," but the entire project is a "moral effort," an attempt unparalleled by human endeavor. "Palestine is a haven," the speaker said, "but this problem of refuge is incidental and does not touch the core of the questions. The up-building of Palestine is as important to those who do not want to go to Palestine as to those who do want to go there. It is a mere accident that you Los Angeles Jews are here tonight—and not there. Your being here sheltered under the wing of a great government implies responsibility."

Dr. Weizmann then launched an appeal for the National Homeland and gave his reasons for believing in such a necessity. He touched upon the old subject of the necessity of the Jew to be a little better than others so that he might stand equal with other in the eyes of the world and said: "In Palestine for the first time in history we will stand or fall by what we do or don't do—with no apologies."

He drew a picture of Palestine as it appears to him in its possibilities for culture and for national life and declared, "whether you want it or not, no force on earth will stop us." One interesting and little-known fact concerning Palestine was brought out in the Weizmann address—that the rainfall in Palestine is equal to that of London and coming as it does in torrents it works destruction to the soil.

Dr. Weizmann declares that Palestine is slowly being rebuilt and stressed the fact that the more money the more rapid the building. He spoke of its need for soil rebuilding, reforestation, and all the physical conditions, which he acknowledges, will have to be met with money and sacrifice and work. He has absolute faith and conviction in the feasibility and success of the plan. He was applauded to the echo at the close of his address and Dr. Edelman then made an appeal for funds, which resulted in the donation of $40,000 to the *Keren Hayesod* cause.

Monday night a mass meeting was held at the Philharmonic Auditorium at which time $25,000 more was pledged. A luncheon was held at the Biltmore on Monday after which Dr. Weizmann addressed a group of workers at the Paulais. An additional $4,000 was presented by a private group, while Mr. B. Platt made a $2,000 contribution to the fund. The Sinai Congregation contributed $15,000 and Beth Israel $7,000 at the Biltmore banquet.

CHAPTER SEVEN

World War II—Jewish Community and the World Stunned by the Holocaust: 1939-1954

Fairfax Avenue, a commercial and residential center of Jewish life in Los Angeles from the 1950s to the present

> *Jews left the armed services with components of their identities as Jewish Americans enhanced.... almost all came back from the war with a feeling of pride in their Jewishness...*

In Los Angeles, as in the rest of the country, the painful times of the Depression ended abruptly when Pearl Harbor was attacked by Japan in December 1941. It was a time when everyone gathered together, the country was unified and mobilized behind the war effort. With its burgeoning aircraft industry, Los Angeles became a key center of employment and manufacture in producing airplanes for the armed services. As Gordon DeMarco states: "World War II literally catapulted Los Angeles out of the Depression. In fact, it was one of the best things that ever happened to it. Sunny fortune was once again smiling on the City of Angels."

Unfortunately, times were not quite as optimistic for the community of Japanese-Americans. In 1940 nearly 40,000 people with Japanese heritage lived in Los Angeles, most working in farming. The members of this community, seen as a threat to no one, were notified and given five days to settle their affairs, sell their homes and property or lose them, and move to the assembly center. Over 100,000 Japanese Americans, two-thirds of whom had been born and raised in the United States, were stripped of their property, evicted from their homes, and placed in internment camps. They were transported from the assembly centers to "relocation" camps in the West, described as "barbed wire shanty towns in remote areas."

Executive Order 9066, the removal order, was implemented in Los Angeles in February 1942, and the Japanese Americans were interred until January 1945. Although the Federal government compensated for some property loss, it was estimated to be less than ten percent of their actual property holdings. "More than half a century of racial bigotry was packed into Executive Order 9066. It was national in scope and politically bipartisan. Its victims were predominantly Southland Japanese Americans. So went the war for democracy on the home front," wrote DeMarco.

Vorspan noted: "Although Jewish voices were heard no louder than others in defending the Californians of Japanese ancestry who were shut away in internment camps during World War II, relations between Japanese and Jews exhibited conspicuous warmth for years thereafter. The Nisei reportedly felt that Jews especially had befriended them with moral and material aid during the hardships of their resettlement and had helped in securing their indemnification. Jewish assistance meant

A look into the future

Myer Pransky, the man behind "the spirit of Boyle Heights." A World War II bomber was also named for the eastside Los Angeles Jewish neighborhood which flourished between World War I and the end of World War II

much at this time, for the younger Japanese generation was undergoing the difficult stages of quitting such traditional ethnic occupations as truck gardening and flowers in favor of business and the professions."

1942 was a depressing time in the United States; people were frightened, angry, and faced uncertainty because of the war that was now being fought on two fronts. The Nazis were in control of North Africa and most of Europe. Asia was being dominated by Japan. The bad mood of the country was clearly evident in Los Angeles. In times of stress and fear, minorities are usually a prime target, and this era offered no exception. In addition to the Japanese, another ethnic minority, Mexican American youth, demoralized during the Depression, organized into gangs and were "perfect victims." History documents that the Mexican American community was another persecuted minority in those years in which the country was fighting for the principles of democracy.

The Victory House of Boyle Heights was at the corner of Brooklyn Avenue and Soto Street

Morris Cohn established a men's clothing firm in 1889 and by 1893 began to manufacture clothing. His was the first garment manufacturing firm in Los Angeles and it became a national leader in the development of the sportswear industry. Pictured with Morris Cohn at the company's fiftieth anniversary (1939) is his partner Lemuel Goldwater (left)

One of the largest minority groups in Los Angeles, the 235,000 Mexicans, lived comfortably as neighbors to the Jews in Boyle Heights and City Terrace. Jewish organizations worked hard to repair conditions after the "wartime race riots" so as to avoid any reoccurrences. In addition to the growth of the Mexican population, there was a tremendous migration of "Negroes" coming out of the American South. Vorspan reports that the black population tripled from 1950 to 1960 increasing to an estimated 460,000. "Jews had Negroes as near neighbors…and in West Adams as well. At heart, the Negroes' needs were those of the Jews immeasurably multiplied: housing, jobs and opportunities for economic advancement, and a modicum of social acceptance. Lacking a business class and residing in faded Jewish areas, they bought largely from Jewish stores and often worked for Jewish employers."

Various large groups of minority populations were struggling for identity in Los Angeles in the post war era. Despite great differences in status among these groups, there were many who recognized common interests. The Jews, being well organized and economically strong, took the leadership role in the pyramid of minority groups, and aided local organizations in promoting and assisting intercultural relations.

Jewish organizations supported the efforts of the National Association for the Advancement of Colored People (NAACP) and both minorities collaborated in common causes. It was mainly through the actions of the local American Jewish Committee, and their diligent pursuit of the law, that the practice of segregation in public housing was abandoned by the populace.

Economic discrimination against minorities persisted, however, especially hurting the Jewish professionals. "The outlook for the aspiring Jewish physicians was bleak: of two medical schools in the city in 1948, one would take no Jews and the other had a *numerous clauses* [i.e., "limited number;" a discriminative anti-Semitic policy]. Moreover, during the seven years ending in 1949, only one of 323 internships in private hospitals went to a Jew. Residencies were particularly difficult to obtain, even in public hospitals. Since established physicians administered these policies in league with bigoted hospital administrators, the medical societies of Los Angeles were, predictably, anti-Semitic." Fortunately the Mount Sinai Hospital and Cedars of Lebanon arranged for internships and training for those victimized by medical anti-Semitism. Similar roadblocks needed to be circumvented in the other

Groundbreaking ceremonies for new classrooms at San Fernando Valley Jewish Community Center, 1957

professions like banking and insurance, petroleum refining, mining, and heavy manufacturing.

Housing A Priority in Post World War II Los Angeles

When the war ended in 1945 and young men were returning home, Los Angeles found itself in the midst of a housing shortage. It was estimated that nearly 300,000 people a year were arriving in Los Angeles, a population that predicted the emergence of an economic boom. They needed housing and so it came. Remi Nadeau wrote, "[It was] the biggest real estate boom the city had yet seen. It was so like Southern California. It was a boom of private developers, a boom for those who could afford to buy new houses, which included most vets with their G.I. loans, FHA, and VA to help." The crunch on public housing—housing for those who could not afford to buy a new home—was relieved somewhat with this surge in building and then subsequently put on a back burner where it would stay until the early 1950s. Suburban tract houses were built—ten thousand units were completed in two years.

With such a strong surge in the building of homes, post war Los Angeles seemed to have everything—jobs, housing, suburban San Fernando Valley, the orange and citrus industry, and the emergence of television in 1949. Aided by the massive construction of the freeway system, mobility was much improved and travel time was cut considerably. This was the start of the modern freeway system plan that developed aggressively into the 1970s. "America's love affair with the automobile is greater nowhere than in Los Angeles," wrote DeMarco. No matter how many roads and freeways were constructed, it always seemed there were too many cars for the number of freeways, and the traffic jam with its ubiquitous offshoot—smog—became a fact of life for those living in Southern California. Life in Los Angeles was returning to normal in the post World War II days—a housing boom was in place, the automobile stimulated the building of freeways, and a robust aircraft industry and agriculture business combined to enrich the lives of the Angelenos.

World War II Inspires Zionism: Jewish Communities Assist War Refugees and Survivors

Jews volunteered in huge numbers to fight for America in the war. During the war approximately 550,000 Jewish men and women served in the armed forces, a figure that represents the equivalent of "thirty-seven divisions," and about 11 percent of the Jewish population. This meant that nearly every Jewish family had someone in uniform fighting tyranny overseas. According to Deborah Dash Moore, this "widespread involvement in the military turned Jews into fighters. They became seasoned soldiers…the experience changed their lives, their perceptions of the world, and their self-understanding as Jews." Many of these young Jewish men and women were witness to racial discrimination overseas, especially directed against black Americans. Undoubtedly, this explicit display of prejudice prompted indignation and anger and inspired many to participate in the civil rights movement that began in earnest in the 1950s and continued into the 1960s.

Moore speculates, "Fighting for their country empowered American Jews. In the armed services they came to identify with America and its ideals…. Jews left the service with components of their identities as Jewish Americans enhanced…. almost all came back from the war with a feeling of pride in their Jewishness, with an awakened interest in Jewish life." This new feeling of identity with their Jewishness was emphasized when they viewed with horror the decimation of the Jewish people in the concentration camps. A heart-wrenching awareness also reached Jews at home in America, as they read and received reports on the extermination of European Jewry. American Jews responded to the crisis with speed and generosity and contributed greatly to the war effort, buying millions of dollars of war bonds, operating canteens for servicemen, participating in blood and scrap drives, and were especially magnanimous in contributing to Jewish organizations working to assist the refugees.

Jews in every social stratum and at every economic level, including many prominent in the entertainment field, responded in strength to the news of the mass murder of European Jews. Moore writes about the some of the contributions of the Hollywood celebrities: "Upon hearing of the Nazi extermination of the Jews [they] pooled their talents in 1943 to create *We Will Never Die*, a memorial to the two million murdered Jews [the number would increase to six million by the end of war] and a militant call for action to FDR." This pageant "called upon its audience to mourn its dead and affirm its future." A part of the performance portrayed

Bill Hertz, actor and founder of the Paramount Ranch filming facility in Agoura, 1952

Business thrived in post war Los Angeles

Jewish soldiers fighting under the flags of eighteen allied nations—representing many countries, but ironically not their own homeland. "We Jews of Europe are being killed as Jews. Give us the right to strike back as Jews...the Jews demanded: Let the Star of David be one of the flags that enters Berlin."

The aftermath of the war triggered an enormous tidal wave of Zionism, led by the American Jewish population, still reeling from the shocking revelations of the death camps. As the unprecedented genocide in Europe became exposed, "aghast at the ravages of anti-Semitism," Zionists demanded unrestricted Jewish immigration into Palestine and the establishment of a Jewish commonwealth. The message emanating at the conclusion of the war was clear—"if Jews could be targeted for destruction and could not rely upon the world's democracies for a timely rescue, then they had to rely upon themselves." This infusion of confidence unleashed the rising tide that was to help create the nation of Israel.

When World War II ended, an estimated 150,000 Jews were living in the 449 square miles of Los Angeles, an increase of 20,000 during the war years. Jews were a significant part of the new wave of immigration pouring out of Europe. Judge Harry Hollzer, president of the Jewish Community Council, as well as other leaders, had predicted this surge in Jewish population. According to Charles Brown, another Council member: "We in the Los Angeles Jewish community are living in a frontier which is as dramatic in its way as the original pioneer town of Los Angeles, which was the goal of the first movement of Americans westward. Jews are trekking westward to Los Angeles in one of the greatest waves of migration in Jewish history. Each day the urban centers of the East lose their Jewish citizens to the attractions of our climate and resources. Jewish people are coming from Chicago, Philadelphia, Boston, Pittsburgh, Detroit, Omaha and a hundred other places."

American Jews and Christians were all equal as migrants in their journey west. A substantial cross section of war veterans brought masses of young people in the prime of their working years; a high proportion of them were college graduates. In post war Los Angeles, an estimated 66,000 Jews moved to Southern California between 1945 and 1948. By 1951 this new wave of Jewish immigration increased to 105,000 Jewish households, thus the total of the Jewish population living in Los Angeles County had surged to 330,000. This flood of Jewish arrivals brought large numbers of young people, eager to start families and ambitious to discover and embark on new career opportunities.

World War II and its aftermath offered a dramatic turning point for Jews in Los Angeles, in America, and throughout Europe. The great migration brought many Jewish Americans to the West, settling in Los Angeles where Jews could be "whatever types of Jews they wanted to be." They could start new in a spacious, clean, sunny environment with an invitation to prosperity. As Deborah Dash Moore explains:

> The destruction of European Jewry ruptured American Jews' living link to their European past. The Holocaust shattered an era of European Jewish cultural innovation and religious renewal. The rich European Jewish community that had sustained American Jewish life through immigration and provided world Jewry with intellectual, moral, and religious leadership lay in ashes. The disaster left the New World as the remaining hope for a Jewish future in the Diaspora. American Jews, long considered exotic provincials by their European brethren, now confronted an awesome burden of ensuring Jewish security and survival. This task they neither anticipated nor welcomed. The end of World War II forced them to face their responsibility for world Jewry in a radically altered Jewish world. Having survived the war unscathed, American Jews forever lost their provincial isolation.

The immigrants continued to pour into America from Europe, and many of these immigrants were Jewish survivors of the war. The Jewish community felt responsible to assist these refugees to help them get settled. According to Max Vorspan, "In the midst of reportedly the

Observers in post World War II Los Angeles found the city expanding daily

217

most severe housing shortage in the United States and a keen search for jobs by an immense throng of returned soldiers, an effort to find homes and employment for refugees had to be most discreetly conducted. When housing in relation to the émigrés was discussed publicly, there were some bitter reactions from the general community since they felt that newcomers were being given more consideration than American citizens. The same danger affected public solicitation of jobs, many of which were quietly found in the garment industry."

Economic and Social Development in the Jewish Community

Until World War II, the base of the Jewish population was living in the eastside Boyle Heights area. The Boyle Heights Jewish community was working class and often militantly progressive in its politics. Jews were extremely active in the labor movement and organized some of the most powerful unions in the garment industry. Jewish support was critical to the election of the first minority city council member in the 20th Century, Edward Roybal, who won his campaign in the Boyle Heights area.

Domestic politics locally reflected the same fervor and unity that Zionism was generating nationally and internationally. Deborah Dash Moore writes, "When Los Angeles Jews went to the polls in November 1946, they voted overwhelmingly for a Fair Employment Practices Committee.... Whether they lived in Boyle Heights or Beverly Hills, Jews lined up in favor of the anti-discrimination proposal.... Although an anti-Semitic and anti-communist rabble-rouser like Gerald L. K. Smith drew crowds of ten thousand when he visited the city, Jews believed that he represented a vocal minority and that they possessed the means to defeat him and his supporters."

The 1950s ushered in a surge of cultural institutions in Los Angeles. Pictured is the Los Angeles County Museum on Wilshire Blvd

Slapsy Maxie's nightclub in Los Angeles

The massive in-migration after the war created a major Jewish community in Los Angeles. By the 1950s nearly half a million Jews lived in greater Los Angeles, making Los Angeles the second largest Jewish community in the United States after New York City, the third largest after New York City and Tel Aviv. At its height the Jewish population of Los Angeles represented 7 percent of the city's residents (today it is approximately 6 percent.)

In post World War II Los Angeles the number of jobs increased and the economy was on a steady path of expansion. The immigrants organized their 1939 Club, also known as the Association of American Jews of Polish Descent, in 1952, generating aid to their countrymen through a social outlet. Communal innovation was created as specific needs arose, and new-comers felt free to experiment. Many had left relatives behind and were looking to replant their "roots" in this new land that offered so much space and freedom. Moore writes: "not only were the newcomers constrained by few restrictions, but they also discovered that it was remarkably easy to get involved in Jewish life....Even old-timers, Jews who settled in Los Angeles before World War II, found themselves energized by the arrival of so many Jews and the opportunities created by their presence."

Popular boxer and personality Slapsy Maxie Rosenbloom, 1939

Union Station's opening celebration on May 3, 1939 which attracted over 100,000 people. During the salute Southern Pacific's No. 1 locomotive, dating from 1869, was driven down Alameda Avenue. Union Station became the welcoming spot for the new immigrants to the area and became known as the "Ellis Island" of Los Angeles

The city of Los Angeles was prospering and the Jews shared in this prosperity as Jewish incomes grew within this expansion in occupations that included managers, proprietors, and small business entrepreneurs. In the mid and late 1950s the number of Jews entering the professions also increased dramatically. Obviously as a result of the urgent need for housing, construction became a principal industry in Los Angeles. Jewish professionals with backgrounds in finance, real estate, and insurance bought land and built homes in the southern and eastern parts of Los Angeles and in the San Fernando and San Gabriel Valleys, accurately predicting areas that were growing rapidly.

Many Jewish entrepreneurs established businesses as a result of the surge in the construction industry. In areas such as building supplies, the firm of Familian Pipe and Supply Company, a business owned by David Familian and two of his sons, George and Isadore, became prosperous. Another old firm benefited during this era, the Southwest Steel Rolling Mills, a successful scrap business run by Ruben and Lester Finkelstein, originally founded by their grandfather. Jewish businessmen also played a dominant role in developing Southern California shopping centers and retail supermarkets. Many new opportunities were available to young Jews after the war that had been previously barred to them because of discriminatory policies. Now, openings were found in banking, utilities, insurance, real estate, aircraft companies, and other large corporations.

The automobile became a necessity in Los Angeles

Vorspan reports, "In 1948 'a comparatively small number' of Jews 'worked for seven large insurance companies,' and about the same time Jewish bank employees were reported 'very meager' in number. To be sure, there was actually one large 'Jewish' insurance company—the Beneficial Casualty Insurance Company, founded in 1940 by Edward D. Mitchell, Oscar Pattiz, and J. C. Earle. The firm evolved into the Beneficial Casualty Insurance Group, with Mitchell and his son Joseph N. Mitchell its principal officers. Both father and son were prominent in Jewish communal and philanthropic affairs."

In banking and finance some familiar names surfaced. The Union Bank, founded by Kaspare Cohn, and operated by his son-in-law Ben R. Meyer, was known as Los Angeles' "Jewish bank." The bank rapidly expanded approaching the 1950s and was ranked as the thirtieth largest bank in the country. This propelled the growing trend of Jewish builders investing capital in new banks and savings and loan associations. According to Vorspan, "the Jewish builder replaced the Jewish film magnate as the entrepreneur *par excellence*. Just as films were no longer central to the economy of Southern California, so the Jewish segment of that industry was no longer the financial pinwheel of Jewish communal effort."

Hollywood Jews, Communism, and Anti-Semitism

Meanwhile, Hollywood's movie community was facing its own political and social dilemmas. The late 1930s and 1940s saw a rise in anti-Semitism, stemming from both the Nazi menace and the start of the cold war following World War II. The irrational idea that communism and Judaism were synonymous was incomprehensively taking hold. As a result of the manifestation of this thinking, Hollywood Jews were scrambling to disassociate themselves from the old myth that linked Jews to political radicalism. Jewish Hollywood's hatred of communism was partially the fear that a small number of Jewish radicals would make all Jews suspect.

This trend of suspicion and paranoia had begun years earlier. Prior to the start of World War II, the global fight against fascism was being confronted in the Spanish Civil War, an early prelude to the larger war that was to come. The struggling Republican Loyalist government in Spain was fighting the incursion of the tyrannical Francisco Franco, leader of the fascist rebel forces. Many supporters of freedom journeyed to Spain to assist the Loyalists, arriving from a myriad of other countries including America. DeMarco states, "Hollywood became a haven for European exiles from fascism in the 1930s and 1940s. Many were writers who worked in Hollywood and most of them were political. And some…were radicals and socialists. They were all fervently anti-fascist…. The anti-fascist commitment found its political expression in the formation of the Hollywood Anti-Nazi League in 1936."

Lillian Hellman, Dorothy Parker and other celebrities established the Motion Picture Arts Committee to help Spain fight the encroaching tyranny. Hollywood film people continued to become involved in the political issues being generated in the election campaigns at home, as well as the turmoil brewing overseas. A key element at the center of this new ideological controversy was the organization of the union. Disaffected workers in the film industry wanted to organize into guilds so they could negotiate with the producers. Unions were getting more active and there was unrest among labor and guilds working in the studios. Strikes led to violence and confrontation when striking labor groups were attacked by management-hired "scabs" and thugs.

In the political environment of Hollywood, union busting was a way of life. To avoid potential conflicts, the formation of the Academy of Motion Picture Arts and Sciences (the Academy) was created in 1927. Author Neal Gabler states "the Academy was essentially a sweetheart union where producers invoked the sanctity of their common artistic mission with their creative employees and thereby deflected dissatisfaction that might have translated into genuine political action. Even the Oscar, which the Academy awarded to recognize artistic merit, was just another way of striking filmmakers where they were most vulnerable—at their vanity."

However, in the Depression years of the mid-1930s, the peace with labor shattered when studios could not meet their payrolls. After studio heads imposed strict pay cuts on the employees, a group of angry writers formed the Screen Writers Guild to represent their interests against management, intensifying left-wing political sentiment. Since many of the writers had come from eastern establishment careers as journalists, novelists, and were young men with college degrees, they also came with a social conscience. They had family members who had been loyally represented in the garment and trade unions and came from generations of socialists. These gifted young Jewish writers wanted to use their talent to "right wrongs, expose injustices, redress grievance, and create new worlds, and they brought this passionate commitment to Hollywood."

Jewish actor Melvyn Douglas, returning from a horrifying trip to Europe in the late 1930s, joined with other political activists that formed the Hollywood League against Nazism, later renamed the Hollywood Anti-Nazi League. The League was the primary vehicle proselytizing for condemnation of the Germans and was the main group representing the community's left-wing activism. The organization sponsored weekly radio programs, published its own trade newspaper, *Hollywood Now*, and "generated a number of subcommittees to address and educate specific constituencies—women, youth, labor, race, religion, professions—all of which led the right wing to accuse it of being a communist front."

Hollywood conservatives responded to the ugly union disputes by targeting communism. According to Gabler, "Communism has always been denounced as a philosophy that was alien and hostile to the 'American way of life,' but now the Soviet Union was seen as a formidable foe bent on actually taking over the world and the United States. And their American agents—the Communist Party—were just the ones to help them get away with it. An enemy without

Pious patriarchs, averaging 80 years of age, celebrate the traditional Succoth ceremony at the Los Angeles Jewish Home for the Aging, 1940

and within is one and the same. Convenient, that. It simplified things for people who were looking for simple answers. The cold war was on. A war against communism and for freedom. That's how it was phrased. The time was right that the opening should be fired on the movie lots of Hollywood. Joe McCarthy was still three years away."

The liberal Hollywood writers tended to merge their ideas with the communists, who were at this time simply trying to organize workers into unions. Thus, in fighting for workers' rights and ideas of the "liberal left," Jewish writers indirectly became the foundation of the Communist Party in Hollywood. Gabler writes, "In America, the Party was a group of committed intellectuals roused by the romance of the workers, and the workers were disproportionately Jewish." The Communist Party, eager to increase its ranks, began recruiting Jews actively and Zionism and anti-Semitism moved to the top of the Party's agenda, resulting in a large minority of the Party leadership being Jewish.

In the meantime, many of the Jewish studio heads were deciding how to retaliate against the minions of Nazi agitators in Hollywood, including a particularly threatening Los Angeles Bund, targeting the Hollywood Jews. Determined to counter the ugly attacks, the heads of MGM, Columbia, Twentieth Century, Warner Brothers, Fox, Paramount, and RKO joined together to form the Community Relations Committee, the political instrument of wealthy Los Angeles Jews.

Michael Greenberg (at age eleven, back row, second from right), stock broker and executive for Big Five sporting goods, visiting the home of Lester and Margie Greenberg (not pictured). Seated at left is Harvey Greenberg, one of the founders of the Harris and Frank clothing chain. Home located at 717 Hillcrest Road, Beverly Hills

This group of Jewish executives worked within generally defensive strategies, in contrast to the writers who were seen as more proactive and aggressive, and thus the two groups apparently questioned the actions of the other. Politically, the United States government was still trying to remain neutral prior to the United States entry into the war, and was strongly suggesting to the Hollywood film barons that "they refrain from all controversial subjects."

In a shocking incident late in 1940, Joseph P. Kennedy, the U.S. ambassador to England, and suspected Nazi sympathizer, met with the Jewish executives in Hollywood. Douglas Fairbanks, Jr., who attended the meeting, wrote the following summation in a letter to President Franklin Roosevelt:

> Kennedy stated that: "…although he did not think that Britain would lose the war, still, she has not won it yet. He repeated very forcefully that there was no reason for our ever becoming involved in any way. He apparently threw the fear of God into many of our producers and executives by telling them that the Jews were on the spot, and that they should stop making anti-Nazi pictures or using the film medium to promote or show sympathy to the cause of the 'democracies' versus the 'dictators.' He said that anti-Semitism was growing in Britain and that the Jews were being blamed for the war…. He continued to underline the fact that the film business was using its power to influence the public dangerously and that we all, and the Jews in particular, would be in jeopardy, if they continued to abuse that power." The executives were shocked. "As a result of Kennedy's cry for silence," Ben Hecht later wrote, "all of Hollywood's top Jews went around with their grief hidden like a Jewish fox under their gentile vests."

During the war, after America's entry, a time of peace reigned at home, since now everyone was simply an American. In fact, after the Japanese bombed Pearl Harbor, Roosevelt welcomed the assistance of the media in producing training and propaganda films. This gave Hollywood the opportunity to make patriotic films decrying Nazi atrocities, while heralding the bravery of our soldiers, and the "rightness of our mission." After the war, the State Department and military brought several film executives to Europe to view first hand the ravages that Hitler had wrought. The executives were shaken by what they saw, especially when viewing the concentration camps, but were curiously reluctant to speak publicly about their experiences.

One of the spiritual leaders of the Hollywood Jews, Rabbi Edgar Magnin, responded more forcefully. He felt that the Holocaust would not create sympathy for the Jews, but "would actually reopen the divisions between the Jews and the gentiles. 'All they talk about is the Holocaust and all the sufferings. The fools don't realize that the more you tell the gentiles that nobody likes us, the more they say there must be a reason for it. They don't understand a simple piece of psychology....They've got paranoia, these Jews.'"

Despite the threatening warnings by Kennedy and others with the same bias, Hollywood's producers were determined to make pictures condemning anti-Semitism. One of the first was made by RKO, *Crossfire*, about a psychopath who murders a Jew. Meanwhile, the rights to *Gentlemen's Agreement* were bought by Darryl Zanuck. The surging wave of confidence expanded to embrace a new and revitalized interest in Zionism and intense feelings reflecting the necessity to provide a homeland for the Jewish people. A number of Hollywood personalities, both Jew and gentile, formed a branch of the American Arts Committee for Palestine.

Gabler quotes film executive Robert Blumofe about the Hollywood Jews:

"Most of us...had a feeling that we were homeless, waiflike people who got pushed around, not really accepted. And suddenly Israel, even to the least Jewish

The California wine industry continued to flourish during the post war era. New machinery was introduced that provided for the expansion of the wineries

of us, represented status of some sort. It meant that we did have a homeland. It meant that we did have an identity. It meant that we were no longer the stereotype of the Jew: the moneylender, the Jew businessman. These were fighters and they were farmers and they revived the land there…. All of this was terribly, terribly uplifting."

Deborah Dash Moore explained the non-ethnic nature of the political divergence among the Hollywood Jews:

> Among the substantial numbers of acculturated east European immigrants and second-generation Jews in the motion picture industry could be found all political stripes, from communist to left-wing liberal to Democrat to Republican. Unlike Boyle Heights radicals, Hollywood communists joined fellow travelers in nonsectarian front organizations to pursue their politics. Few of these Jews participated directly in Jewish politics. Jewish political concerns interested them only to the extent that Jews were victims of discrimination and prejudice, a condition Jews shared with other minorities. There was no ethnic dimension to their communism. For many, communism undoubtedly represented a path out of the Jewish community into an alternative international fraternity.

In January 1934 the House Committee on Un-American Activities (HUAC) was formed. In 1937, this committee, acting under a resolution introduced by Representative Martin Dies, son of a Texas conservative, introduced legislation to suspend immigration for five years, which many felt was motivated by his own anti-Semitism and his attempts to prevent persecuted European Jews from escaping to America. Although he denied the accusations, his actions belied his words since Dies did speak frequently of restoring "Christian influence" in America, and openly met with anti-Semites, among them the head of the Nazi Bund.

Dies, not really interested in combatting Nazism, was at "war against Karl Marx, whom he believed was locked in mortal combat with Jesus Christ for the future of Western civilization. For Dies, however, the line between Marxism and Judaism seemed to be indistinct." In 1940 Dies turned his venom and the committee's attention to the Jews in Hollywood and worked fervently to tie them to the communists, including his statement that the Hollywood Anti-Nazi League was in the control of the communists. Thus began the ugly murmurings that would introduce the beginning of the notorious Hollywood "witch hunt."

After the war HUAC became active again, with one investigator from the committee quoted as saying, "You should tell your Jewish friends that the Jews in Germany stuck their necks out too far and Hitler took care of them and that the same thing will happen here unless they watch their steps." Gabler writes that was "how one investigator from HUAC, while in the presence of the committee's chief counsel, warned a Columbia University professor early in 1946. For Hollywood, the handwriting was already on the wall." Lead by another anti-Semitic politician, Mississippi Congressman John Rankin, with help from others who performed some "parliamentary shenanigans," HUAC was converted from a temporary committee into a standing committee of the House, thus setting the stage for the travesty that was to come.

Though not the committee chairman, Rankin was the voice and conscience of the group, and continued to stoke the flames of racism and hatred, pairing communism with anti-Christian ideology, accusing communists with trying to destroy Christianity and Christian principles. The paranoid rhetoric of Rankin was the same language that Nazi sympathizers and extreme right wing conservatives had been using to accuse Hollywood in the previous

Encino on the Fourth of July in the mid-1930s. The Encino Store, located at Ventura Blvd and Genesta in the San Fernando Valley was, at the time, the neighborhood "supermarket"

months. Rankin was joined by other fervid anti-Semites, like Gerald L.K. Smith, giving a thin layer of legitimacy to those previously seen as the "lunatic screed."

Things came to a boil in November 1946 when the Republicans won control of the House and Senate and they prepared to pounce on the left-wing minions and supporters of President Roosevelt's New Deal. Tensions grew, political attacks increased, subpoenas were issued and a blacklist of Hollywood talent surfaced. Ten "uncooperative witnesses" were accused of being communists and were cited for contempt. Rankin rose in the House to condemn them: "one of the names is June Havoc. We found out from the motion picture almanac that her real name is June Hovick. Another one was Danny Kaye, and we found out that his real name was David Daniel Kaminsky. Another one here is John Beal, whose real name is J. Alexander Bliedung…. Another one is Eddie Cantor, whose real name is Edward Iskowitz [sic]. There is one who calls himself Edward Robinson. His real name is Emmanuel Goldenberg. There is another one here who calls himself Melvyn Douglas, whose real name is Melvyn Hesselber." They viciously targeted celebrities with Jewish names, making the artificial but damning association between Jews and communists. And the Congress overwhelmingly passed the contempt citations thereby validating the contrived and negative association.

A meeting was quickly called bringing together the major film executives at the Waldorf Astoria in New York. Among those who attended was liberal activist Dore Schary, who had started out as a writer and, over the years, was promoted into the executive ranks. He spoke forcefully, detesting the idea of artists and performers being blacklisted for their political beliefs. Disappointed, he could see that the previous strong resolve of the studio execs was disappearing in the face of the Congressional bullying that transpired. Eric Johnston, former

Gilmore Field was home to the baseball minor league team, the Hollywood Stars. When the Los Angeles Dodgers came to town the Stars disappeared

president of the Motion Picture Association of America, organizer of the meeting, demanded that the studio heads must fire the uncooperative witnesses "if ever they wanted to earn the respect of the American people." Johnston had struck a nerve—the powerful men of Hollywood were older and wearier now, and obviously frightened, and so they caved in to the mounting pressure. Intimidated and worn down, the moguls conceded. The studios fired the dissidents until they "renounced communism under oath." Of the fifteen producers who signed and agreed to the statement vilifying the group of accused "communists," ten were Jews.

The Waldorf statement, as it came to be known, deplored "the action of the ten Hollywood men who have been cited for contempt…. Their actions have been a disservice to their employers and have impaired their usefulness to the industry." They decided to fire the ten, and then added a statement that was to cause great tragedy and pain in the future: the producers all agreed that, "they would not knowingly employ a communist or a member of any party or group which advocates the overthrow of the Government of the United States by force." The dividing line had been drawn and the strong divisions among the Jews worldwide reverberated in Los Angeles.

Despite the tensions within the Zionist ranks, "eighteen thousand turned out in October 1947 for a Hollywood Bowl rally for the freedom of Palestine," one of the largest demonstrations organized in the country in support of Israel. In the midst of the political and social chaos in America, the United Nations voted to partition Palestine into a Jewish and Arab state—the monumental vote occurring on November 29, 1947, inspiring public rejoicing in Los Angeles and other cities around the world. Although partitioned Palestine was now designated as the official homeland for the Jewish people, the days of persecution and anti-

Semitism were not yet over. "At the height of the euphoria, as the United Nations voted the future Jewish state into being, Jews in Los Angeles felt the chill of anti-communism," wrote Vorspan.

Much has been written about these dark days in American history. "Though it doesn't absolve them to say so, they [the Jewish Hollywood executives] were also in the grip of a deep and legitimate fear: the fear that somehow the delicate rapprochement they had established between themselves and this country would be destroyed, and with it their lives. 'I don't think the heads of movie companies, and the men they appointed to run the studios, had ever before thought of themselves as American citizens with inherited rights and obligations,' wrote Lillian Hellman, standing one of the typical right-wing anti-Semitic attacks on its head. 'Many of them had been born in foreign lands and inherited foreign fears. It would not have been possible in

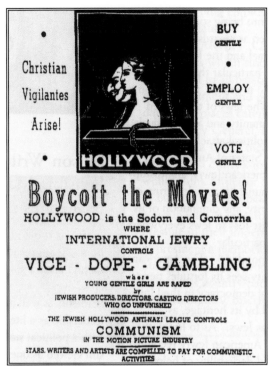

Vicious anti-Semitic poster

Russia or Poland, but it was possible here to offer the Cossacks a bowl of chicken soup.' To save themselves from the wrath of the anti-Semites, that is what they did." The ten were fired and the witch-hunt ramped up its actions. J. Edgar Hoover became involved and brought his own prejudice and the crushing weight of the FBI with him.

The Jews searched desperately for damage control. Their efforts to cooperate with Congress and the committee by appeasing Hollywood's tormentors "only demonstrated their tormentors' strength and the Jews' own weakness. Paradise was lost. It would never be regained." Thus concluded one of the ugliest chapters in America's history, dramatically played out in Hollywood, an anti-Semitic campaign that snowballed out of control, devastating and destroying many lives in its path. The first generation of powerful entrepreneurs, the Jews who had built Hollywood and the film industry, began to retire and die as an era came to an end. As Gabler described it:

> And so the empires have crumbled. The moguls' names have faded. The estates are gone and the power and the panache and the fear. But what the Hollywood Jews left behind is something powerful and mysterious. What remains is a spell, a landscape of the mind, a constellation of values, attitudes, and images, a history and a mythology that is part of our culture and our consciousness. What remains is the America of our imagination and theirs. Out of their desperation and their dreams, they gave us this America. Out of their desperation and dreams, they lost themselves.

Political and Social Reaction to Anti-Semitism and Anti-Communism

Just as anti-Semitism surfaced and threatened the Hollywood film industry—transparently obvious although thinly veiled behind vitriolic attacks against communism by the United States Congress—post war anti-Semitism was also pervasive in the rest of Southern California. Many in the Jewish community were hesitant to become involved in the political restructuring in Los Angeles following the war for fear of calling attention to themselves. Consequently, Jews were not active in local politics, although they did fill many judgeships.

When the cold war became a central issue in the late 1940s, a fresh canard expressed the old hatred. Vorspan wrote about the mood of the country in 1947 that "the most dangerous situation at the present time is the growth of the belief that communism and Judaism are synonymous." This insidious thinking began to take hold, and concern accelerated in 1950 as American intervention in Korea began generating high tensions again.

Part of the dilemma was that the term "communism" covered a multitude of statements. "Communism was defined so fantastically that anything new or 'foreign' or unwontedly intellectual could fit, and thus add another target for anti-Semitic attack by twisted minds." One of the most vulnerable areas of this increasing inquisitorial questioning was public education. Board of Education elections became bitter contests with anti-Semitic attacks on candidates routinely used as a campaign tactic. "Jewish agencies had constantly to combat vigilante proposals for 'citizen' screening of school textbooks to insure their freedom from 'subversive' content."

Out of this tense environment emerged a group of professional anti-Semites led in Los Angeles by the notorious "Christian" anti-Semite Gerald L. K. Smith, who equated "sinful" Hollywood with American Jewry. Smith's representative, Wesley Swift spoke from a platform of his "Anglo-Saxon Christian Congregation." All of these hate-mongers combined the ancient anti-Semitic myths with new ones equating Zionism with communism.

Los Angeles had its own "home-grown anti-communist," State Senator Jack Tenney. According to Deborah Dash Moore, Tenney "a right-wing Republican and anti-Semite, chaired California's Un-American Activities Committee and directed its attention to Jewish communal institutions. In 1948 he launched a bitter attack on the Soto-Michigan Jewish Community Center in Boyle Heights, charging that the center's staff, member organizations, and programs contained communists. Tenney persistently equated Jews and communists and profited politically from his accusations." Although the egregious charges had no foundation, they provoked a backlash of persecution against the Jews that culminated in loss of jobs for the adults, and harassment of the children in schools. Moore reports, "Men and women were losing their jobs…as FBI investigators hounded families accused of being communists and even children suffered taunts by their peers."

Remarkably, even the presidential election in 1952 was tainted with references to race and religion. Vorspan describes the situation, "During the bitterly controversial election, Southern California was 'flooded with rumors to the effect that Senator Nixon [candidate for vice-president] is an anti-Semite.' Anti-Semitism was intimately allied in Southern California with some of the wild-eyed anti-communism that flourished during the later presidency of Truman and the earlier years of Eisenhower. Under the embittered conditions of 1952 a hero of anti-communists, like Nixon, could easily be tarred as an anti-Semite, notwithstanding knowledge to the contrary and repudiation of the charge by official Jewish sources."

Despite this rancorous bitterly anti-Semitic backdrop, support for the new Jewish State of Israel was very favorable, both in Los Angeles and throughout America. American Jews recognized and responded to the deep psychological meaning of the State of Israel, their long awaited homeland. The feeling was that Israel's "existence and the fight to maintain itself has given Jews more self-respect and encouraged the respect for us of our non-Jewish neighbor."

Beverly Hills opened its own high school in 1927

Moore asserts "the Zionists' success coincided with the first attacks upon left-wing Jewish radicals…. The U.N. decision on partition came within a week of the Waldorf producers' conference…. These parallel, albeit unrelated, events drastically changed the style and substance of Los Angeles Jewish politics…. Jewish leaders gradually insisted that all Jews take a stand on the issues of communism and Zionism... they branded communists and anti-Zionists as deceivers…. Searching for safe ground, Jewish political energies increasingly focused upon the struggle for statehood in the Middle East. Israel became the uncontroversial core of communal concern."

The existence of the nation of Israel and cold war domestic policies in America altered in a dramatic way the Jewish communal agenda. In light of the fact that the old ethnic politics inherent in the lifestyles of the transplanted immigrants from the Northeast and Midwest did not produce a common ground, newcomers could introduce a new type of politics into Southern California. Moore explains: "The migrants contributed to a realignment of Jewish political groups in Los Angeles…and helped to wed an emerging Jewish political ideology centered on Israel to a cluster of domestic issues focused primarily on civil rights and secondarily on civil liberties. The resulting amalgam of domestic liberalism with strong support for Israel and opposition to communism had much in common with the politics of American Jews throughout the United States….Los Angeles Jews refashioned their political culture and cautiously placed a new hero, Israel, at the center of their beliefs…. Politics thus helped recently arrived Jews to participate in a Jewish community of Los Angeles even as it offered a vehicle to transform that community's relationship to the larger whole. It gave Los Angeles Jews a way to blend their allegiances as well as to define their identity in the postwar decade."

In Los Angeles, throughout the 1950s and into the 1960s Jews moved south and west, establishing an important base in the West Adams community, eventually also moving into the Fairfax area. A major migration into the San Fernando Valley helped to create today's thriving Jewish community, which is about evenly divided between the Westside and the Valley. As Jews migrated westward and south into the West Adams and Fairfax areas, they continued their social and political progressive role throughout the 1950s. They became active in the Reform wing of the Democratic Party, embodied in the California Democratic Club (CDC). Recovering from the traumatic Depression and war years, embracing the rebuilding and strengthening of a world safe for democracy in the 1940s, and coping with the political maelstrom in the early 1950s, Los Angeles was preparing itself for the next chapter in its quixotic history. Thus was the stage set for dramatic political, social, and economic upheaval as the citizens of Los Angeles along with the rest of the country, prepared to enter the turbulent and radical environment of the sybaritic Sixties.

Eddie Cantor: Hollywood Jewish Activist

by Rabbi William M. Kramer

Eddie Cantor, father of five daughters, has a "son," a baby actor who played his little boy in Cantor's film, Forty Little Mothers

Pictured here upon their arrival in Los Angeles in the early summer of 1926 are Eddie and Ida Cantor and their four children. Eddie Cantor came to California to begin his career in motion pictures with Paramount. He had already won fame in musical comedies on the stage, and was well known for his devoted fundraising efforts for Jewish sufferers in Europe following World War I, and his work for Zionism. Residing in Los Angeles, Cantor became one of the regular Hollywood stalwarts who could be depended on to aid in Jewish Welfare Fund drives

The famed stage, screen and broadcast artist Eddie Cantor (1892-1964) was a staunch Jewish community activist. In this regard, no other entertainment industry figures can be compared to him as volunteers of Mitzvah, except for Dore Schary and Monty Hall. The entertainment industry has supported Jewish life well, but these people were unique and Cantor was the model.

Cantor was born Israel Iskowitz in New York on January 31, 1892. His parents, Michael and Minnie, both died before he was two. His 62-year-old grandmother, Esther Kantrowitz (from whom his name Cantor was derived), became his sole caretaker and Cantor grew up in a home that was poor and kosher. As a child he spent his summers at Surprise Lake Camp for under-privileged children, an affiliate of the Educational Alliance on East Broadway. Later he supported it and a host of other children's activities. He once related about his camping experience that it was there that he learned, "fruit actually grew on trees and not on pushcarts."

❊ ❊ ❊

Throughout the height of Cantor's illustrious career on the stage, on the air, and on the silver screen he was first in line to help Jewish and non-Jewish causes. He gave money, provided leadership and was the headliner at a thousand benefits. This study only incidentally deals with his role as an entertainer. Cantor was always aware however, that his stardom created the opportunities for him to serve the Jewish people.

On September 16, 1952, The Guardians, the major fundraising auxiliary of the Los Angeles Jewish Home for the Aging, honored Cantor as "Citizen of the Year" at its banquet at the Hillcrest Country Club. Campaign Chairman, Max Firestein chaired the event; Mendel Silberberg, president of the Jewish Community Council, was the presenter. Silberberg said:

> Eddie, you've always been foremost in attacking any threat to America, and in warding off the problems of financial and moral crises. There has never been an American problem, whether it be the sale of bonds, the building of morale or the pumping of vitally needed blood that you have failed to tackle. These have been deadly serious problems, you've kicked them personally more than anyone we know, and you've come up smiling. We're proud of you.

※ ※ ※

In 1943, Cantor summarized his Jewish values. He said, " Are you as a Jew ready to stand up and be counted? Or will we once again sit back and let other speak for us…or against us…others will not, cannot, do it for us. We must stand up and be counted, or lie down and die." Because he was so involved with Jewish charitable work, anti-Semite Father Charles Coughlin in 1935 singled out Cantor for hatred, according to a *Time* article. It quoted Cantor from an address given to a B'nai B'rith convention in Los Angeles:

> Father Coughlin said in Detroit a few months ago that Jews have only three ene-mies to fear—Bernard Baruch, Eddie Cantor, and the motion picture industry. Father Coughlin is a great orator but I doubt that he has a sincere atom in his entire system. We Jews have nothing to fear from good Christians. We are their brothers and sisters. But I am afraid of people who pretend to be good Christians.

The well-known bigot, Reverend Gerald L.K. Smith objected to Cantor using his name in fundraising for the United Jewish (Welfare) Fund, according to Smith's paper, *The Cross and the Flag*. Smith wrote, "The Jew Eddie Cantor makes his contribution to the hate promo-tion program by using my name and the names of other Nationalists to raise money to under-write their Jewish-operated Gestapo organization." Cantor, in a letter to concerned Jews, attacked Smith and Gerald Winrod.

When Henry Ford accepted a medal from Adolph Hitler, Cantor said, "I question the Americanism of Henry Ford for accepting a citation from the biggest gangster in the world." He called Ford a damned fool and said, "I don't think he is a real American or a good Christian. The more men like Ford we have, the more we must organize and fight."

Cantor kept in touch with the unfolding Jewish tragedy in Nazi Germany. He reported in 1936 that he had a source there who told him, "When the Olympic Games are over in Germany you will see a program that will make Russia and Poland look like Sunday School picnics." He told a gathering at the ballroom of the Waldorf-Astoria in New York City that the older Jews in Germany had no chance, but one might still save the children. For his anti-Nazi activity he had:

> Organizations threaten me, threaten my family, call up the people for whom I work, and frankly, I tell you I am a little bit frightened. I am not going to stop. They are threatening me only for one reason, because I believe that the Jews must have some form of unity. We haven't got it now. I don't care if you are a depart-ment store Jew or a pushcart Jew—a West End Avenue Jew or a Canal Street

Jew—you are Jews or you are not Jews at all!

❋ ❋ ❋

In 1960, a color documentary film, *Israel Today*, was prepared in the United States and premiered on West German television. Cantor did the introduction to the featurette, the "first of its kind to be shown in Germany in 30 years…a great vehicle against intolerance and bigotry."

Cantor was a major voice for several organizations, including Bonds of Israel, Youth Aliyah and like groups in the United States and overseas. It was said of Cantor, that there was no philanthropy about which he was so enthusiastic as he was for Youth Aliyah, which sought to transfer Jewish children between the ages of 15 and 17 out of Nazi Germany to the Yishuv in Palestine.

Another Youth Aliyah event took place when Cantor visited England in 1938 and there raised over half a million dollars. In the midst of the Hitler era he was to report with sorrow that, "in the year1938…I heard of the younger school children who are beaten so severely during the recess in school that the continuance of their education is no longer possible; children…are growing up with intense hatred for their parents because their mothers and fathers were born Jews."

Eddie Cantor portrayed a bullfighter

❋ ❋ ❋

Cantor celebrated his 50th birthday in New York City with a dinner sponsored by Bonds of Israel. Nearly 2.5 million dollars were raised from the thousand people who attended the dinner. The celebration had an entry price—the purchase of at least a $1000 bond. For that day famed Henry Street in New York was renamed "Eddie Cantor Street."

❋ ❋ ❋

In 1947, Eddie Cantor starred in a five-minute dramatic film play titled, *We Must Not Forget*. It was prepared for the United Jewish Appeal for Refugees, Overseas Needs and Palestine. His friend, Paul Muni, also did a documentary at that time for the same cause. In June of 1950 Cantor was invited by Prime Minister Ben-Gurion to come to Israel. He was a dinner guest at the Prime Minister's home and he heard him say, "Cantor, I am counting on

The interior of the Temple Israel of Hollywood Rabbi Max and Ruth Nussaum Sanctuary. The building was constructed and dedicated in 1948

you to raise one-fifth of all the money that comes to us from America."

In 1954, the Zionist movement chose Cantor to sign a full-page ad in the *New York Times* addressed to the Secretary of State protesting the United States arming of Israel's Arab enemies. He said in part:

> ...Frankly I am worried as a Jew. Hitler removed millions of my co-religionists from the world. Less than two million of the remnants have found a refuge in Israel. I would not be human if I did not feel a special responsibility for that little handful that has remained.

Cantor was as active in general charities as in Jewish ones. He was available to other faiths and one time he went to Wichita, Kansas, to help the Salvation Army. Impressed by Cantor's fundraising ability, Cardinal Spellman said, "Edward, how we could use you in the Catholic Church!"

It was characteristic of Cantor that upon receiving an award, he said:

> I should like to share this award with all of you [who] have demonstrated the great human qualities of the American heart. I would like to share it with the men and women of America, Christians and Jews alike, who were willing to share their good fortune and economic blessings with those for whom even hope was fading.

❋ ❋ ❋

In 1956 Cantor received a special Academy Award for distinguished service to the motion picture industry. In Los Angeles a B'nai B'rith lodge bears his name. Temple

University gave him an honorary degree. President Lyndon B. Johnson gave Cantor the Presidential Citation in 1964. For his efforts, Cantor was much honored. Hadassah planted a 15,000-tree forest bearing his name in Palestine in 1938, calling him "Hadassah's No. 1 boy friend."

He received the United Jewish Appeal Humanitarian Award in 1947 for "outstanding humanitarian service." He had been a leader in the UJA program for the "relief, rehabilitation and resettlement." When the presentation was made by Paramount Pictures President Barney Balaban, the mogul said:

> In those trying days when the world is striving for a formula for peace and brotherhood among all men, the humanitarian work men like Eddie Cantor do is vitally important. Through his deeds, he has given expression to his convictions in a land of freedom while men and women in other parts of the world are living in the shadow of death, without homes, without food and without hope.

As president of AFTRA, the National Vaudeville Artists Association and the Jewish Theatrical Guild, Cantor wielded much influence in the entertainment world. He was also the president of the Screen Actors Guild in 1933 when he successfully got President Franklin D. Roosevelt to change some NRA rules that the actors objected to. Later, FDR asked him to lead the March of Dimes, a concept Cantor had suggested to raise money for the alleviation of infantile paralysis through the president's Warm Springs Foundation.

❄ ❄ ❄

Cantor would spare nothing for charity. There is the wonderful story about the time when famed philanthropist and art collector, Walter H. Annenberg invited him to perform for a crowd at a fundraiser. Cantor reminisced:

> I went through my routines, got some laughs, and got some money, too—a big sum, several hundred thousand dollars. I thought we were through when suddenly a voice rang out: "Hey Cantor, what'll you take for that suit?"
>
> "Make me an offer," I replied.
>
> "Five thousand dollars," the man said.
>
> "Sold," I said. " I'll just go to my room and take it off and send it back to you."
>
> "I bought it; I want it now," my customer demanded.
>
> People grabbed me and removed my suit. Then they sold my socks, my shirt, my tie and my undershirt. The audience was screaming. I looked like a plucked owl. The manager of the hotel finally took a pity and brought me a bathrobe three times my size, and I departed with a corny tag line:
>
> "Now you've seen Gypsy Rose Cantor," I said.

❄ ❄ ❄

Eddie Cantor was anxious for the world to know the importance of Judaism in his life. In 1952 he had prepared a film, a television show that would play on Kol Nidre night. Anxious that no one would think that he was making levity at a time of piety, he issued a release that made it clear that the program had been pre-recorded and that when it was on the air he would be in his temple at worship.

When you watch Eddie on the late show on television, be proud of the service that he rendered the Jewish community and the nation, and be glad that both honored him. Cantor once said that neutrality was a crime, a sin against yourself and your society. He pointed out that the word "neuter" suggested that something is sterile and he observed that you can't stay sterile and make much of life. For him it was clear that a person must pick his side and fight for it.

Eddie Cantor (right) "kibbitzes" with W.C. Fields and Fanny Brice

When Cantor died in 1964 at the age of 72, *Variety* noted his "all-faith, all-purpose charitable works." Interment was on October 12, at 3:00 p.m. at Hillside Cemetery. The funeral was private with just the immediate family present, except for his life-long friend, George Jessel. His obituary in the *London Jewish Chronicle* said that Cantor "after a career of world fame as a screen and stage comedian, devoted himself almost wholly to helping needy causes. He was impelled by suffering brought about by Nazi persecution."

A simple obituary for Cantor appeared in the national *B'nai B'rith* publication following his death in October of 1964. It read, "Eddie Cantor...who died at 72 was active in Jewish causes. Mr. Cantor, during the 1930s and 1940s, worked closely with B'nai B'rith Anti-Defamation League in fighting the pro-Nazi movement in the United States, and after his retirement in 1953 he was especially active in the UJA and Israel Bond Organization."

Cantor, the entertainer, was an international Jewish hero. No one in his industry was more forthright and forthcoming than he was for the Jewish charity. He was not movie or stage Marrano; his Jewishness was upfront.

◆

Living History: A Tribute to Rabbi Alfred Wolf

by Rabbi William M. Kramer

Rabbi Alfred Wolf's impact on the Reform Movement is powerful, pervasive and persuasive. In his own gentle way, he has made enormous contributions to Reform Jewish life in many significant directions, encompassing every phase and function of the American synagogue.

Alfred Wolf was born in Germany in 1915, and was one of a number of students whom Dr. Julian Morgenstern saved from the Nazis and helped to enroll at the Hebrew Union College. Wolf was ordained at the college in 1941.

In 1940 Alfred married Miriam Jean Office. Their home life incorporated the noblest ideals, the most enduring traditions and the most heart-warming rituals of the Jewish faith. The Wolf household was blessed with remarkable children who, reared in the glow of their parents' philosophy of Jewish living, made their own impressive contributions to education and public service.

The Wolf home has been for nearly half a century, like the synagogue, a *Mikdash Me'at* [a small sanctuary], a sacred abode, permeated with religious and personal devotion, creative Jewish art and the ideal of Jewish learning, all of which provide the indestructible foundation of Jewish survival. From there it radiated the illumination and the inspiration for Alfred Wolf's monumental innovative contributions to the enhancement of Reform Judaism and K'lal Yisrael. His formula: from the nuclear family to congregational family to the family of humankind.

Rabbi Wolf's first challenge in the rabbinate was that of circuit rider in the no-man's land of southern and eastern Alabama. He met the challenge by piloting his own plane and temple-hopping. His next chal-

Rabbi Alfred Wolf of Wilshire Boulevard Temple and Msgr. Royale Vadakin at old St. Vibiana's Cathedral. The two men were leaders in developing interfaith relations in Los Angeles for 35 years

lenge came in 1946 when he was appointed West Coast director of the Union of American Hebrew Congregations. In that capacity he distinguished himself by his remarkable organizational ability, creating a number of Reform congregations in the difficult terrain of what was still the American frontier.

In 1947 he launched the Los Angeles College of Jewish Studies for the training of religious schoolteachers and for adult education. A few years later pre-rabbinic classes of the college developed into the first Los Angeles campus of the Hebrew Union College, while the college of Jewish Studies itself developed into the Rhea Hirsch School of Education. Together with Rabbi Raphael Levine of Seattle and Rabbi Iser Freund of San Jose, he pioneered annual camping programs for Reform Jewish high school youth from Arizona to Washington. Conducted at rented quarters at Lake Tahoe and Asilomar from 1947 to 1951, they led to the development of the UAHC Camp Swig at Saratoga.

By far the most severe test of his rabbinical talent came in 1949 when Rabbi Wolf was invited to join Rabbi Edgar F. Magnin and Rabbi Maxwell Dubin as third rabbi of Wilshire Boulevard Temple, the largest Reform congregation in the West, and one of the most prominent in the world. What could young Rabbi Wolf achieve in the shadow of world-renowned Magnin, and of Dubin, the outstanding Jewish educator? What could he do that they hadn't already done?

It was here that the creative genius and the organizational brilliance of Alfred Wolf, as well as his superb statesmanship, were revealed in full measure. An excellent speaker and a

Celebrating Chanukah at Vista Del Mar in the 1950s

marvelous Jewish educator in his own right, he did not compete with his senior rabbinical colleagues in their areas of expertise, but rather supported their efforts. He functioned admirably as a rabbi and won the affection, admiration and respect of the huge temple membership by his unswerving loyalty and total immersion in his work. Yet his penetrating insight and innovative vision perceived areas of unfulfilled potential on which he proceeded to concentrate.

Rabbi Wolf introduced two programs that were new to Wilshire Boulevard Temple, which were designed to enhance the Jewish self-image of our youngsters and to strengthen the ties that bind them to the Jewish faith and its institutions. In both instances he had to overcome the powerful resistance of classical Reform, which dominated the temple, but he preserved and prevailed. The bar mitzvah ceremony was slowly returning to Reform worship. Rabbi Wolf recognized its value and introduced it at Wilshire, together with the bat mitzvah ritual and systematic Hebrew instruction, not without some struggle. He was also a pioneer in the development of the religious camping program, and his handiwork, first Camp Hess Kramer and the Gingling Hilltop Camp, remains a model facility in structure and in substance, emulated far and wide in the Reform movement to this very day.

✳ ✳ ✳

Alfred Wolf's vision inspired many congregants to realize the importance of active endeavor rather than passive membership. Accordingly he was instrumental in enlarging the scope and activity of the Temple Brotherhood. Expanding on the national sponsorship of the Jewish

Chautauqua Society, he spearheaded a concerted drive during which he and his laymen associates filled the shelves of the colleges and universities in the Southwest with vital volumes on Jewish themes. The effect was electrifying, winning friends for the Jewish people among students of all denominations in the institutions of higher learning. Rabbi Wolf himself became Adjunct Professor of Religious Studies at Loyola Marymount University, and carrying on a Magnin tradition, became a lecturer on Judaism at the University of Southern California. He co-authored, with Joseph Gaer, an important book, *Our Jewish Heritage*, and succeeded in establishing a weekend retreat program of Jewish lifelong learning for adults, set in the picturesque locale of Camp Hess Kramer.

Shortly before his 1985 retirement at age 70, he developed a plan for an exhibit center to turn the temple's broad corridors into lively, colorful teaching about Jewish holidays, the history of Los Angeles Jewry, Israel, etc. The plan was completed after his retirement and was named the Maxwell H. Dubin and Alfred Wolf Exhibit Center.

Rabbi Alfred Wolf has helped preserve the dignity and self-esteem of countless Reform Jews by providing them with an intimate study and profound appreciation of their historical heritage.

✳ ✳ ✳

Early on Rabbi Alfred Wolf joined the Board of Rabbis of Southern California, which included rabbis of all persuasions. Rabbi Magnin had been one of the organizers of the group and the first Reform rabbi to serve as its president. The office rotated among the Orthodox, Conservative and Reform. Rabbi Wolf was the second Reform rabbi to hold the presidency. When he assumed office, the Board had a negligible status in the Jewish community. He infused it with new vitality at a time of rapid growth of the Jewish community. He brought it into close association with the Los Angeles Jewish Federation and the Community Relations Committee, dominating influences on the Jewish scene. Wolf's statesmanship and the high regard in which he was held united the Board and gave it a voice in Jewish affairs, which it had not previously enjoyed, and a program of action which attracted more and more rabbis, including the reluctant Orthodox.

Rabbi Alfred Wolf, symbol of a coordinated Jewish religious leadership, elevated the stature of the Board of Rabbis of Southern California, and respect for Reform Judaism increased perceptibly.

Rabbi Wolf has initiated a number of interracial and interreligious projects and programs, as well as those designed for social amelioration. He enjoys the confidence and the high esteem of a cross-section of people in all walks of life. He has been president of the Los Angeles County Commission on Human Relations.

Of major significance is Rabbi Wolf's cooperative effort with Msgr. Royale Vadakin of the Catholic Archdiocese of Los Angeles. Together, and with lay representatives both Catholic and Jewish, they issued a joint statement on abortion, "The Respect for Life Dialogue." This was the first public pronouncement and is still the only joint official statement on this thorny subject. The two religious leaders are the moving spirits behind an ongoing discussion between priests and rabbis, leading the publication by the Church of "Liturgical Readings for the Lenten and Easter Seasons," in order to prevent an anti-Semitic interpretation of the

Celebrating the expansion of the Valley Jewish Community Center now known as Adat Ari El. Pictured above are (left to right) Isidore Familian, Sunny Familian, Herman Burke, Rosella Familian, George Familian, and Rabbi Aaron Wise

Crucifixion. Wolf and Vadakin led a flying visit to Rome, Jerusalem and Geneva by Catholic, Protestant, and Jewish religious leaders, and the two have published *A Resource Manual on Catholic-Jewish Relations.*

The dynamic duo probably made their most profound impact on the Los Angeles community by their role in founding and directing the Interreligious Council of Southern California. Starting in 1971 as a fairly traditional Catholic-Jewish-Protestant coordinating organization, the council soon became the umbrella for the official bodies of most of the major world religions represented in multicultural Los Angeles: the Roman Catholic Archdiocese, the (Protestant) Ecumenical Council, the Board of Rabbis of Southern California, and the Baja's Buddhist, Greek Orthodox, Mormon, Muslim, Sikh Dhama and Vedanta (Hindu) denominations. As the founding president Rabbi Wolf is frequently consulted by his successors and remains involved in the council's many activities in the fields of dialogue, interreligious study and social concerns.

In 1987, on the occasion of the visit of Pope John Paul II to Los Angeles, Rabbi Alfred Wolf was designated as the official Jewish spokesman among the non-Christian faiths, representing the Board of Rabbis and the entire Jewish community. And at present, as the Senior Rabbi Emeritus of Wilshire Boulevard Temple, he is the director of the Skirball Institute on American Values, of the American Jewish Committee.

Rabbi Alfred Wolf is one of the outstanding luminaries in pursuit of the interfaith ideal on a worldwide scale.

As one of the requirements for his doctor of philosophy degree at the University of Southern California, Alfred Wolf wrote an excellent dissertation on the symbolism of the tree of life. He has nurtured, with gentle strength and with loving care, the *etz haim* which sustains us.

CHAPTER EIGHT

Transformation of the Los Angeles Jewish Community: 1955-1970

Celebrating Israel's victory—the end of the Six-Day War—at a mass rally at the Hollywood Bowl, June 11, 1967

Continuing prosperity and increasing social and economic mobility contributed to the growing well-being of the Jewish community.

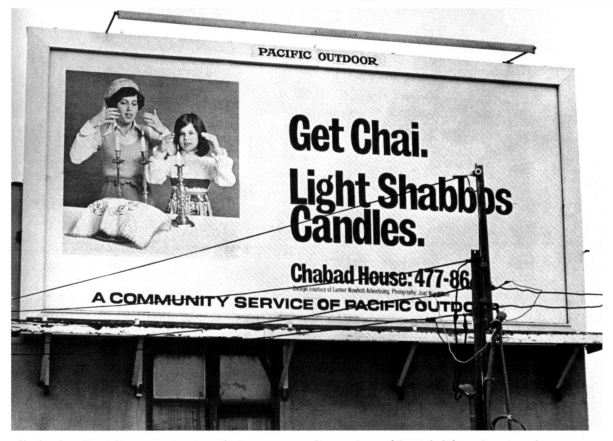

Chabad, a Hasidic organization, brings a new dimension of Jewish life to Los Angeles

Los Angeles was facing the growing pains of a mature city by the 1950s. The wide-open spaces and clean air that made it a golden city in the 19th Century were overtaken by unlimited growth and development in the middle 20th Century. The evidence of urban living was everywhere, beginning with the smog and clogged freeways, chaotic urban sprawl with the resulting overcrowded schools, and the poor and underprivileged neighborhoods overrun by minorities loosely grouped together by ethnicity.

The fear and hysteria over the loss of privacy coupled with the communist accusations that had enveloped Hollywood in the thirties and forties, culminated with the ugly chapter in America's history instigated by Senator Joseph McCarthy and other political racists. The Korean War was causing chaos in that part of the world, the spy trial of the Rosenbergs took center stage in the United States, and the communists were assuming power in China and Eastern Europe. America relinquished its dominance in the nuclear arena when the Russians created their own bomb in 1949 and children learned that their little wooden desks could serve a more frightening and unconventional function. Richard Nixon defeated Helen Gahagan Douglas (wife of actor and activist Melvyn Douglas) and won a seat in the Senate by attacking her as a liberal and trying to brand her as a communist.

Throughout the 1940s and 1950s America was overwhelmed with concerns about the growing threat of communism that was on the rise in Eastern Europe and China. Capitalizing on those concerns, U.S. Senator Joseph McCarthy made a public accusation that more than two hundred "card-carrying" communists had infiltrated the United States government. Though eventually his accusations were proven to be untrue, and he was censured by the Senate for unbecoming conduct, his zealous campaigning ushered in one of the most repressive times in 20th Century American politics.

The House Un-American Activities Committee [HUAC] had been formed in 1938 as an anti-communist organ, and during the 1950s Senator Joe McCarthy's accusations heightened the political tensions of the times. Known as "McCarthyism," the paranoid hunt for infiltrators was notoriously difficult on writers and entertainers, many of whom were labeled communist sympathizers and therefore were unable to continue working. Some had their passports taken away, while others were jailed for refusing to give the names of other alleged communists. The trials, which were well publicized, could often destroy a career with a single unsubstantiated accusation. Among those well-known artists accused of communist sympathies or called before the committee were Dashiell Hammett, Waldo Salt, Lillian Hellman, Lena Horne, Paul Robeson, Arthur Miller, Aaron Copland, Leonard Bernstein, Charlie Chaplin, and Group Theatre members Clifford Odets, Elia Kazan, and Stella Adler. In all, more than three hundred artists were blacklisted, and for many of them this meant the end of exceptional and promising careers.

During this time there were few in the press willing to stand up against McCarthy and the anti-communist machine. Among those few were comedian Mort Sahl and journalist Edward R. Murrow, whose strong criticisms of McCarthy are often cited as playing an important role in his eventual removal from power. By 1954, the fervor had died down and many actors and writers were able to return to work. Though relatively short, these proceedings remain one of the most shameful periods in modern United States history.

Another political "hot potato" in the post war era was public housing. In the early 1950s public housing came under attack by the real estate lobby, a group that was supported by the conservative *Los Angeles Times*, which branded construction of homes for the poor as a "huge socialist scheme." Los Angeles' Mayor Fletcher Bowron, a strong supporter of public housing cryptically pointed out that federal subsidies for the poor were deemed by critics as "socialistic," but ironically the same federal subsidies were not considered "socialistic" when the money was given to the business community.

"But the conservatives were on a political roll in America and in Los Angeles," wrote Gordon DeMarco, "they didn't have to answer Mayor Bowron or anybody else. The city council and the press went on a hunt

Mendel Silberberg (left), chairman of the Community Relations Committee, receives citation from Charles Brown, president of the Jewish Community Council, 1958

Protesters from 18 Jewish organizations march in front of the German Consulate in Los Angeles objecting to the German government's refusal to extend the expired deadline on the statute of limitations for Nazi war crimes, 1965

after members of the CHA [California Housing Authority] who had 'communist sympathies.' In 1952 the California State Un-American Activities Committee investigated it. '*Red Plot to Control Los Angeles Housing*,' shrieked the *Herald-Express*. The week following the investigation HUAC returned to Hollywood to burn some more witches." Bowron was defeated by conservative Congressman Norris Poulson, when Poulson ran on a platform to eliminate public housing, in a "clear victory for the McCarthyite real estate interests." Those who suffered from this bombastic political rhetoric and disruption of the housing market were the disenfranchised poor and minority groups—primarily African Americans and Hispanics. Many of these members of minority groups had fought in the war to make America safe for democracy and were now "rewarded" by being denied the only housing they could afford. As DeMarco points out, "Los Angeles would live to regret its shabby treatment of its minorities. The clock was ticking. The public housing wars brought the hands a little closer to midnight."

Los Angeles Grows With the Times and Enhances Its Image

As the uneasy time of the communism attacks and witch-hunts concluded, Los Angeles, along with the rest of America, turned its attention to recovery and the return of good times. Now the City of Angels, always the leader in keeping people entertained, looked beyond the movies and the new drive-in places to eat and do their banking, and found more frivolous pursuits to engage in. Both the Frisbee and hula-hoop were introduced, and the biggest thing to hit Southern California since the "talkie"—Disneyland—opened to Los Angeles and the world in Anaheim in 1955. "Almost instantly it became a metaphor for both good, wholesome family fun and fantasy and the sanitary unreality of a pre-packaged culture. Frontierland, Tomorrowland, and Fantasyland were all a part of the phantasmagorical image that America, and especially Los Angeles has of itself all set down in a theme park.... The American/Southern California Dream is alive and well at Disneyland. In fact, down through

A business section of Fairfax Avenue

the years, the Dream and Disneyland have almost become interchangeable terms. It seemed that when it came to the good life, Los Angeles did have more than its share."

Apparently one of the few things lacking in the Southern California paradise was a major league baseball team. This was quickly remedied in 1957 when the Brooklyn Dodgers moved their franchise west and became the Los Angeles Dodgers. The site chosen for the stadium was the Chavez Ravine, called "an impossible wilderness" because of its steep hills and other challenges in the landscape that made construction very difficult. Opening Day in 1958 took place in the Dodgers' temporary home—the Coliseum—where the team was greeted by nearly 80,000 enthusiastic fans. A few years later, in 1962, Dodger Stadium officially opened in the Chavez Ravine.

At this time citizens of Los Angeles were trying to adjust to a rapidly changing culture. The new social and political environment was moving quickly from a post war recovery to developing new standards and values led by runaway consumerism. People looked to the 1960s to return some balance to life. As DeMarco speculated, "the Sixties would be different some felt. Young and alive. There were new frontiers to be conquered by an energetic new generation. Los Angeles would turn things around, too."

A building boom began in the 1960s with a relaxation of height restrictions, enabling high-rise buildings to take a prominent place in the landscape. A surge of interest in support of the arts was also taking place. A new arts complex was built with a big fundraising drive spearheaded by Dorothy Chandler, wife of *Los Angeles Times* publisher, Norman Chandler. In December 1964 the new Music Center for the Performing Arts was dedicated, the celebration highlighting a performance by the Los Angeles Philharmonic Orchestra directed by Zubin Mehta. The completion of the complex took three additional years as they also built the Dorothy Chandler Concert Hall and two theaters that were added as part of the civic center.

In 1965 the Los Angeles County Museum opened, which included the Frances and Armand Hammer Wing that was established to accommodate traveling art exhibits.

Social Unrest Causes the City of Angels to Erupt— the Turbulent Sixties

While the upper end of the social register was collecting healthy donations from wealthy patrons, the other end of the social and economic spectrum was suffering and struggling. Tremendous unrest and dismay existed in the black sections of Los Angeles, when black workers arrived in droves in the 1940s to man the defense plants and work in the aircraft industry. The African American population increased by 800 percent, from 75,000 to nearly 600,000. The majority of the black workers lived in Watts and the area became a self-made ghetto.

By the 1960s instability and dissatisfaction had become epidemic. Unemployment was high in Los Angeles, in excess of 30 percent, as compared to 9 percent in the rest of the country. Six out of every ten families were on welfare, and the segregated schools had the highest dropout rate in the country. Disease was rampant, and the closest hospital to Watts was a two-hour bus ride. There were no fair housing practices in Southern California for blacks or Mexicans—housing was segregated by voter mandate in 1964, with Proposition 14, a despicable piece of legislation that further inflamed the despondent and angry Watts residents.

Los Angeles had attracted black residents for the same reasons that the whites came—new opportunity and economic stability. Then the 1960s arrived with the civil rights movement, emotional speeches from leaders like Martin Luther King, Jr., freedom rides and lunch counter sit-ins, fiery rhetoric from Malcolm X and the Black Muslims, and the march on Washington in 1965. Elizabeth Poe wrote in 1965, "They knew that the city slum was no longer an incubator for the middle class, but a prison. They were jobless, hopelessly alienated, and tired of waiting." Los Angeles was a tinderbox just waiting for a lighted match.

In August 1965 an incident with a white policeman and a black man arrested for drunk driving drew a tense bunch of residents together in Watts. The policeman used more force than

Nationwide coverage of the Watts Riot in Los Angeles, 1965

necessary and the black man became belligerent. A frustrated muttering crowd formed, angry about the all too familiar scene, and the situation began to get out of hand. Many were taken from among the crowd and arrested, the people turned ugly and became an unruly mob, a youth flung a soda bottle that shattered against a police car and, in an instant, the Watts Riot erupted. The fatal match had been ignited and the city began to burn.

At the end of the first day, 35 people had been injured and 50 vehicles burned or damaged. The damage quickly spread to buildings and shops, as looting, burning and violence escalated. As the situation worsened, the media entered the fray and the Watts Riot became a huge national media story. A young angry black man was quoted saying the "Negroes were fed up" and they were going after "whiteys." He threatened the shaky equilibrium, stating they would be going into the white neighborhoods like Playa Del Rey and Inglewood. According to DeMarco, "the news team loved it. They had a scoop. It was broadcast throughout the Southland that night… 'For the first time…many [whites] discovered how it felt to be hated solely because of the color of their skin. The awareness shocked and frightened them.' The white backlash would date from this night… Watts had turned into a war zone. An American version of Beirut, Lebanon. People were being killed."

A controlling and insensitive chief of police, William Parker, added fuel to the incendiary fire when he stepped in front of the microphones, assuring the people of Los Angeles that "we have them" under control. The "them and us" comments only served to further inflame the situation, as he compared the actions of the black community to the behavior of "monkeys in a zoo." While denying any charges of police misconduct and brutality, later investigations proved that this type of racial bias was systemic in the Southland. The toll of the riots was dev-

Lankershim Blvd in North Hollywood is now part of the vast network of streets lacing together the San Fernando Valley, home to a significant segment of the Los Angeles Jewish population

astating—emotionally, physically, and financially. DeMarco states that the tally numbered "34 people killed (31 by police gunfire), 1032 injured, and 3,952 arrested… 6,000 buildings were damaged or destroyed with property damage estimated at $40 million."

The Watts Riot reflected a much more massive and insidious problem in the country, with Southern California representing a microcosm of the looming national threat. Long neglected social questions were being asked and a loud demand for answers was reverberating throughout the country. The civil rights movement, college protests against the Vietnam War, divisive racism—all of these fundamental issues were forcing America to take a closer look at the cli-

The National Guard was called in to help restore order during the Watts Riot

mate in the culture. Politics was becoming more vocal and radical groups were emerging everywhere to confront the failures of the past and the unrest in the present.

In Los Angeles a similar situation was evident in the Mexican American Chicano barrio as had been witnessed in Watts. Facing nearly identical problems—high rates of immigration, rampant unemployment, failures in education, poor housing and health accommodations, along with a well documented record of police harassment—all these factors combined to make the Mexican American population as much a disenfranchised group as the African American community. The Mexican American unrest erupted in August 1970 when the Chicano Brown Berets led an anti-war march and a riot ensued leaving 3 dead, nearly 100 injured, and millions in property damages. According to an article in the *Christian Century*, "It seems clear that the police over-reacted to a minor scuffling on the edge of a crowd gathered for a peace rally and used it as a reason for charging the assembly without warning, clubbing and tear-gassing people."

Los Angeles clearly had its own problems, but they reflected the social unrest and turmoil occurring in the rest of the country from the 1960s to the mid-1970s. The golden city of dreams had become a troubled city with many of its citizens in despair. Racism, violence, runaway crime, the public viewing of the assassination of Robert Kennedy in Los Angeles, the grizzly Manson family murders—the city seemed on the verge of spiritual self-destruction.

Growth in the Jewish Community—
Expansion of Jewish Education

In the Jewish community during the post war 1940s and the transitional decade of the 1950s, the education of Jewish children underwent its own evolution, as educational leaders arrived at their objectives in ways quite different from each other. The Reform Sunday School's emphasis was based on the child's being comfortable with his Jewish religion, so that he or she would understand what it was to be part of the Jewish people and their history, drawn against the backdrop of the history of all mankind. Conservative Judaism focused on a more traditional approach, emphasizing learning Hebrew and Jewish history. Impacting the dilution of the influence of Jewish schooling was the shortage of qualified teachers and educators; salaries were low while competency standards were high. The Jewish schools were also coping with the rapid changes in population in the Jewish neighborhoods.

In 1947 the University of Judaism was established by the Jewish Theological Seminary (representing Conservative Judaism), with a Teachers Institute as its primary branch. This connected the city with a major Jewish academic center, Los Angeles's first institution for higher Jewish studies. As Vorspan explains, "With the Hebrew classics and traditionalist religion its core, the University of Judaism aimed to embrace the whole of Jewish thought and expression in its scope. It commenced a slow growth in developing a body of teachers and Judaic intelligentsia. Another institution was the College of Jewish Studies and the Hebrew Union College [HUC], California School, opened under Reform auspices in 1954. There, the principal emphasis was placed on teacher and rabbinic training. Quite special in character was the countryside Brandeis Camp Institute near Santa Susana in Simi Valley, the creation of its imaginative director Dr. Shlomo Bardin, where a rather secular, slightly Israeli Judaism was projected in dramatic, aesthetic terms."

As the Jewish community built up its educational opportunities throughout the 1950s, efforts to find a balance between Judaism and the general culture were achieving modest success, as more attention was being paid to elevating the "impoverished intellectual standards of Jewish life." Informal Jewish education—Jewish music, dance, art, Yiddish language and holiday observance—was also supplemented by activities in the Jewish community centers, which specifically directed programs to the young people and the elderly. A model for these new and expanding centers was the magnificent facility, the Westside Jewish Community Center, which opened in 1954. Satellite centers soon followed in the San Fernando Valley, Santa Monica, and the Hollywood-Los Feliz neighborhood.

Unification in the Jewish Community— Social, Political, and Economic

Los Angeles Jewry became stronger as it progressed through the post war 1940s, the fundamental changes in the 1950s developing and evolving into the revolutionary new thinking and ideas emerging in the 1960s. Continuing prosperity and increasing social and economic mobility contributed to the growing well being of the Jewish community. The merger of the Federations and Community Councils in May 1959 added another level of confidence and unity.

Expansion in Jewish population continued to draw from immigration rather than through increases in birth rates and family size. Most of the new arrivals came from other parts of the United States and Canada, with the only substantial foreign arrivals coming from Israel. Jews continued to trickle in from Cuba, Egypt and other parts of North Africa, and Romania.

Rapid progress in transportation and communication, and the convenience of jet airplanes and telephones, eased the coordination of efforts of the Los Angeles Jewish community in their interactions with New York and other major cities. Jewish neighborhoods flourished, especially in the San Fernando Valley where the Jewish population rocketed by 70 percent to around 120,000 in 1965. The other highest-ranking areas of Jewish population were in the

Hillel Hebrew Academy, one of the largest Jewish Orthodox day schools in Los Angeles, with nursery school through middle school, emphasizes the current trend in intensive formal Jewish and secular education

three areas of Beverly-Fairfax-Hollywood, Cheviot Hills and Beverlywood, and Beverly Hills, Westwood and Brentwood. Jews in Los Angeles resided in some of the most attractive areas, which reflected both their economic success and economic and social comfort. While the Jews shared in the benefits of the general economic prosperity evident in the early 1960s, the city could not escape from the growing social concerns vexing the rest of urban America.

Environmental concerns resulting from the population explosion, ever increasing auto congestion with its accompanying air pollution, lack of adequate public transportation, and the escalating racial tensions were combining into bigger and more difficult challenges. "Most menacing was the racial problem," writes Vorspan, "arising from the economic inferiority, physical isolation, and alienation from the larger society of several hundred thousand Negroes. The disastrous, nihilistic Watts riots during the summer of 1965 shocked the city and nation, but whether any far-reaching measures would be devised to improve the Negro position and prevent further outbreaks was far from certain."

The Jews in Los Angeles remained politically moderate and liberal, and avoided the conservative policies that were prevalent in Orange County, Glendale, and Pasadena, the predominantly white suburbs just south of the city. Jews noticed with a growing uneasiness the newly arising and disturbing phenomenon of anti-Semitism coming from the "New Left, which included some Negroes, Arab sympathizers, and political radicals." None of these factors deterred the Jewish community from their battle to preserve equality for all races and ethnic groups. Gradually Jewish leaders returned to politics and the state was represented by a Jewish senator, two Jewish assemblymen, and three Los Angeles City Council members.

Wilshire Boulevard Temple

With determination and attention to the needs of their community, Jewish organizations continued to run smoothly, especially since the merger of the Federation and community centers. Another important merger occurred in 1961—the two Jewish hospitals, Cedars of Lebanon and Mount Sinai, joined forces and became the Los Angeles Jewish Medical Center. A full-fledged Jewish psychiatric hospital, Gateways, became part of the medical landscape.

Continuing in the forefront of education, the University of Judaism and the West Coast branches of Yeshiva University and Hebrew Union College, consistently showed substantial increases in enrollments and an ever expanding offering of courses of study in their curriculum, including training for teachers and rabbis, thus establishing a Jewish "learned class." Programs offered in Near Eastern Studies at UCLA also contributed to the healthy growth of Jewish education.

Hollywood Fights Back Against Communism— Transition from Cinema City to Television

The enormous resources and great wealth and prestige of the movie industry exerted significant cultural influences on the Jewish community. In 1940 nearly half a million dollars was contributed to the annual United Jewish Welfare Fund by the Hollywood movie makers, representing over 50 percent of the total raised in Los Angeles.

The Hollywood "newcomers" had a huge impact on the occupations and business profiles of the Jews. As the number of professionals and those working in the service businesses increased, their numbers were inversely proportional to the decrease in retail and wholesale trade and self-employment. Although Hollywood movie people were suffering from the "black list" horrors and anti-communist witch hunts of the 1950s, the rise of television as a new medium offered Jews alternative opportunities in this popular new field of entertainment.

The influx of population in the post war era added great support to the Los Angeles Jewish community in ideas, energy, and pure numbers. They contributed their talent, time, and financial backing to schools, community centers, synagogues, hospitals and social and welfare organizations, and especially to Zionist endeavors.

Politically the Jews were a very diverse group. Deborah Dash Moore describes the political picture at the time:

> The visible, immigrant, Yiddish-speaking community centered in Boyle Heights ardently supported FDR and the New Deal. A minority leaned further left toward radicalism, both socialist and communist. Liberal and radical Zionist organizations also recruited members among Boyle Heights Jews. German-speaking refugees who arrived in the 1930s usually supported Roosevelt and the Democratic party, which they perceived as having saved them from Nazism.

Ethnic coalitions were discouraged in Los Angeles politics, mainly due to the discrimination and prejudice that would predictably be targeted against the participating minorities. Party labels like Democrat and Republican carried different meanings in Los Angeles than they did in the Northeast and Midwest. Changes in the Jewish Community Centers were brought about by ideological debates. The Zionist program, according to Moore, dominated communal and local Jewish politics. Zionists became a majority in the Los Angeles Jewish Community Council in the 1950s and marked the victory by voting for budgets favorable to aid for Israel to the detriment of local Federation social service agencies.

The trial of Julius and Ethel Rosenberg further divided the community politically in the aftermath of the anti-communist rhetoric. The Rosenbergs, two New York Jews, were convicted of spying for the Soviet Union and sentenced to death. The Los Angeles Jewish Community Council (Council) ignored the uproar over the trial and conviction, convinced that speaking out would inevitably align them with the communist faction.

Rabbi Edgar F. Magnin, Wilshire Boulevard Temple

Feisty editorialist and labor Zionist Samuel Gach recognized the dilemma inherent in the current political climate. Moore writes about the emotions of the times: "Because communists rallied so fervently to support the Rosenbergs and protest their death sentence, the Council avoided taking a stand. Gach took the risk. 'I abhor the death sentence and despise the judge [Irving Kaufman] who proclaimed it,' he wrote. Though he knew that 'our enemies, the communists, will take full advantage of the episode,' Gach excoriated the 'witches brew…stewed by the McCarthys and McCarrans' that tempted 'the nostrils of the Kaufmans and other weaklings too scared to hold out for the enduring sustenance to be gotten only in a pure democracy.' [He] explained that the communists had mistakenly interpreted his stand on the Rosenbergs as

Rabbi Jacob Kohn (1881-1968) of Sinai Temple

support for the communist cause. In fact, Gach saw a 'degrading fear' in Jewish willingness to jump in to attack anyone who was accused of being subversive, whether justified or not."

This then was the crux of the problem for the Jews—they were compelled to choose carefully how they expressed their political and ethical beliefs because of their fear of being tarred with the same damning brush that was sweeping through the radical left wing and communist factions. Council resolutions tried to articulate political views that would "distinguish the Jewish community's anti-communism from that of HUAC and the radical right." In this endeavor, the Council carefully straddled a perilous line.

Zionists continued to try to define a middle ground that would include financial assistance to Israel, as well as condemn the McCarran-Walter Act, which contained stiff anti-communist provisions and imposed narrow immigration quotas. By 1956 Zionists tried to create a formula to safeguard the middle ground stance they felt compelled to take, in a resolution "supporting civil rights and civil liberties while condemning the 'twin totalitarian evils of Communism and Fascism.'"

Each year Council resolutions sought to clarify the Jewish position and consistently linked support for Israel with anti-communism. "The two parallel events that had occurred ten years earlier—the U.N. decision on partition and the Waldorf meeting ejecting communists from the film industry—converged by 1957. From the point of view of many Los Angeles Jews, communism and anti-Semitism went hand in hand—as they often did in Eastern Europe—and support for Israel logically accompanied anti-communism."

In addition to their support for Israel, Los Angeles Jews consistently supported legislation for fair employment practices throughout the 1950s, as well as fighting against housing discrimination and quotas in universities. Early in the 1950s the first Jew was elected to the Los Angeles City Council in over fifty years. Rosalind Weiner [Wyman] was elected in the Fifth District, which included heavily Jewish Beverly-Fairfax. At twenty-two, Rosalind was the youngest person ever to sit on the City Council. She was reelected in 1957, winning over 90 percent of the vote. In that same year she introduced a pro-Israel resolution and legislation that would allow Jewish city employees to have a work holiday for Rosh Hashanah and Yom

Kippur. Another key issue that would serve to unite the Angelenos (discussed later in this chapter) would distinguish Rosalind Weiner Wyman's term in office in the late 1950s.

Meanwhile, successful advocacy of the FEPC (Fair Employment Practices Committee) brought Jews into the political mainstream once again. Moore writes, "Jews pursued their own political interests despite a lack of receptivity in Los Angeles. They found in political activism an important source of public identity and collective consciousness, one that defined what it meant to be Jewish in L.A. For migrants who had uprooted themselves…to seek opportunity under the sunny skies of California, ethnic politics provided crucial familiar landmarks in otherwise unmarked territory…. The creation of Democratic Party clubs on the Westside, in Beverly Hills, Hollywood Hills, Pacific Palisades, Santa Monica, and the San Fernando Valley secured Jewish allegiances. The clubs grounded Jewish politics in a social context and provided members with a feeling of camaraderie and a sense of common purpose." Thus a dual benefit accrued to the Jewish community—Jews developed their own religious and social organizations while simultaneously aligning with the larger mainstream community, giving Jews a way to "blend their allegiances as well as to define their identity in the post war decade."

As alluded to earlier, another key issue in the unification of Los Angeles as a city came to the forefront during the later stages of Rosalind Weiner Wyman's term of office. Wyman came out in support of the controversial matter of building a stadium to house the newly relo-

Rosalind Weiner Wyman, holding baseball cap, with Governor Edmund Brown (left) and Dodger pitchers Don Drysdale and Sandy Koufax (far right)

257

Jewish Community Building of the Jewish Federation Council, at 590 N. Vermont—headquarters for more than forty agencies and services, erected in 1951

cated baseball team, the Dodgers, who left their home city of Brooklyn for their new adopted City of Angels. Wyman's decision to support the stadium appeared to be the first "flowering of Jewish loyalties to their city of choice." She appealed for a larger vision of Los Angeles. Moore quotes Wyman, "'It was the first time this city ever unified for anything,' she reflected. 'We were so divided and dispersed. We had something that was our own.' The site, embroiled in litigation and controversy, held the promise of giving the sprawling city an identity and paving its entry into the major leagues. The deep identification of Brooklyn with the Dodgers suggested that Los Angeles, too, could achieve the same renown, the same commonality of purpose and culture…. The Dodgers would give L.A. a symbolic national presence and perhaps even the same sense of *achdut*—unity—that Jews valued so highly…. Sandy Koufax's growing fame as a pitcher…surely helped to cement the loyalties of Jewish fans." Jewish children and parents noted the occasion with pride when Koufax refused to pitch in the World Series because the day coincided with the Jewish religious holiday of Yom Kippur.

Zionism Takes Center Stage in Los Angeles

Ethnically and morally Jews were now dedicated to the support and development of Israel, and Zionism became a crucial interest for Jews in Los Angeles and the rest of the country. It was the "American way" for minorities to have a strong relationship with their original country, and for Jews their country was Israel. This same identification with their homeland led them to other expressions of Jewish identity like religious schools for the children and presaged the growing support for increasing the number of Jewish day schools.

The decade of the 1950s did not completely erase the political differences among Jews but by the 1960s the divisions had blurred enough so that a political profile of the Jewish voter manifested itself. To most analysts the new profile was considered liberal. Struggling to establish their identity and to avoid the smear campaign that attempted to paint all Jews as communist sympathizers, they sought a way to balance their Jewish heritage and beliefs with "a vision of an inclusive Americanism that was good for Jews." In politics they looked for a common ground that all could embrace, to distinguish themselves from the newly arrived immigrant who continued to pursue the familiar politics from their home country.

As Moore explained, "Jews championed a politics that defined them as a visible white minority in a volatile and rapidly growing society. A diverse group of migrants, Los Angeles Jews discovered in politics a Jewish identity to share with each other. As they established the parameters of acceptable political behavior by drawing upon the Jewish ethnic politics they had known, they defined the boundaries of their public community." Supporting such issues as equal opportunity legislation further defined the Jewish citizens and separated them as different from other white Americans. Jews had learned from their own history the benefits of standing for democratic principles and a society based on social and political equality; thus the Jewish community had a strong influence on the political climate and direction of reform in Los Angeles.

The Growth of Zionism—Israel Becomes a Hero in Hollywood

With Israel as a central focal point and rallying platform for Jews in the Southland, attention focused on support for the Jewish homeland, moral as well as financial. A special effort was directed at the Hollywood movie community, not only for the financial element but also to generate a bold stand by these talented young Americans for the survival and flourishing of the Jewish State. "A small group of Jews in the motion picture industry would do their best to help Israel by dramatizing its story and heroes for American." And so the talent of Hollywood put its formidable resources into making movies to communicate the Zionist message. Early films including Zinnemann's *The Search*, and Robert Buckner's *Sword in the Desert*, were the beginning of a series of movies that would mobilize and sustain support for Israel.

The studios in the 1960s were finally able to make these

Steve Broidy (left) first president of the merged Jewish Federation Council of Greater Los Angeles, and Walter S. Hilborn, chairman of the Merger Committee

politically themed films, since they had successfully come through defending themselves in the anti-communist days, and also due to the rapid rise of the new medium, television. With the changing direction of movie making, the independent producer became a powerful and active participant in the process. One of those prominent producers was Stanley Kramer, who wanted to tell Israel's story. Working in collaboration with the Jewish writer, Michael Blankfort, they produced and released *The Juggler* with Kirk Douglas as the male lead. The movie tells the story of a DP (displaced person), a survivor of the concentration camps, and seeks to describe the physical and psychological devastation wreaked on the Jews by the Nazis. The film's intense subject matter was highly controversial, although most agreed it served to bridge the link between survivors and bring the Jewish state into stark awareness. It shed light on the problem and fate of the hundreds of thousands of recently arrived refugees and the enormous and overwhelming adjustments facing them.

Perhaps the most powerful and influential of the films made during this time was the movie *Exodus*, based on the book of the same title by Leon Uris. Uris began researching the novel *Exodus* in 1956 in Israel, with an advance from MGM. When the Sinai War interrupted him in his work, he covered the campaign as a war correspondent. "It was a revelation to me when I was researching *Exodus* in Europe and in Israel. And the revelation was this: that we Jews are not what we have been portrayed to be. In truth, we have been fighters." Moore describes the transformation that Uris experienced: "Uris saw Jewish history made as he watched…he discovered the new Jew and proudly identified with this hero…. Uris saw his own image reflected back in the vision of the new Jew…he thought he could capture the drama in an epic novel of Israel's creation."

Exodus immediately soared to the top of the bestseller list in 1958 and its popularity spread like wildfire by word-of-mouth. So remarkable was the novel that the audience went far beyond the Jewish reader and became extremely popular with gentiles as well. "Its vision of the creation of the State of Israel influenced an entire generation of American Jews," wrote Moore.

Otto Preminger was among the American Jews who were captivated by the book, and he could envision the book as a powerful film. Preminger was a persecuted Jewish refugee forced to flee Vienna in the 1930s to escape Nazism, and came to the United States seeking new opportunities. After working his

Director Otto Preminger and author Leon Uris review script of Exodus

way up in Hollywood (and New York) he became an independent producer and purchased the screen rights to *Exodus* in May 1958. Although Uris wrote the treatment for the film, Preminger turned to another writer for the screenplay, one of the Hollywood Ten that was not Jewish, the black listed Dalton Trumbo. Preminger's decision to give Trumbo screen credit, announced before filming began, was instrumental in breaking down the demonic black list. The movie "symbolically marked the end of the painful post war era of anti-communist investigations."

The *Exodus* story was dramatic, poignant in its stark reality—based on historic events of the time that exploded in headlines throughout the country and the world. It portrayed the end of World War II leaving the surviving Jews of Europe crushed. They had

Paul Newman prepares for his leading role in Exodus

lost six million people in Hitler's crematoriums, a fact that could barely be comprehended by citizens in the world community. In the story line that was used to market the film, the situation was described as the "end of hope. But hope was not gone. The hope that burned anew is symbolized by a ship loaded with refugees moving into the harbor at Haifa. And the world watched as hundreds of thousands of the survivors of the Holocaust picked themselves up and, in defiance of blockading British warships, made their way to Palestine. There, in defiance of five Arab armies and the whole logic of history, they built a nation."

Exodus was a huge box office success, establishing itself as a landmark for American Jews. The film portrayed Jewish heroism and the struggle for freedom. Star of the film, Paul Newman, played a young Jewish resistance leader who rescues Holocaust survivors from a British detention camp on Cyprus. When the ship filled with survivors reaches Haifa, the story then chronicles the birth of the nation of Israel. Movie critic Lester Friedman wrote at the time: "The glory of the Jewish military man wipes away the shame of the Jew as victim, implying that what happened in Germany will never occur again because now, at long last, the Jew can defend himself." Moore posits, "By drawing upon the western genre familiar to Americans, *Exodus* gave Israel a persona. The movie placed the figurative white hat on Israel's head, endowing the state and its leaders with good guy status. *Exodus* spoke powerfully to American Jewish ethnic self-consciousness."

The lead character, Ari Ben Canaan (played by Paul Newman), defends the Jew's right to be different, thereby directly challenging the familiar and contrary belief of many American

Otto Preminger directs Sal Mineo during the filming of Exodus

Jews. As Moore explains, "Ari's forthright defense of the right to be different rejects the values of 'ambivalent American Jews' and identifies the new Israeli Jew with a proud assertive creed of Jewish differentness.... Los Angeles Jews imagined in Ari an Israeli hero who eschews any pandering for gentile approval...projecting an alternative to the path taken by most Los Angeles Jews seeking acceptance and integration into American society as well as recognition and respect for Jewish group survival...and [*Exodus*] assures the audience that Ari will not lose his ethnic distinctiveness."

Preminger's *Exodus* "produced an enduring image of Israel and its Jews." Israel captured the imagination of American Jews and offered a homeland of redemption. The new Jewish nation had become a central heroic figure and an important foundation for Jewish identity. This identification came to life once again in a most dramatic way during the May-June crisis in Israel in 1967.

Newspaper headlines screamed out the fear invoked by confirmed reports of the mobilization of the Egyptian and Syrian forces on the Israeli border—tanks and guns ready for invasion—fear was further fueled by the inflammatory rhetoric of Arab leaders. Still, there was no help for Israel from any Western nation. Emerging alone, just as the proverbial Hollywood hero, Israel faced the "massed military might of the entire Arab world." Moore writes, "Then, in six brilliant, tension-filled days, the Israeli military not only single-handedly fought off the Arab armies of Egypt, Syria, and Jordan, but reunited Jerusalem, recaptured the Sinai, and doubled the territory of the state. In the Six-Day War Israel miraculously lived up to its legend. Image and reality fused; Israel redeemed its promise, and heroic visions became living history."

The three movies represented a transition for American Jews from Zionist ideology to "pro-Israeli piety." The tone of Zionist politics became the rallying force for Jews worldwide to support Israel as a homeland and a refuge for Holocaust survivors. Deborah Dash Moore analyzes the transformation:

> Israel's arrival on the world scene coincided with the efforts of...Los Angeles Jews to seek roots and forge an identity for themselves. Israel beckoned to them; Israel suggested the possibility of rebirth.... Newcomers proved particularly receptive to the drama of Israel because it let them come to terms with their

Jewishness.... Through Israel they seized the opportunity of fashioning anew the substance of an American Jewish identity. Israel allowed them to reimagine home and roots in an alternative homeland.... In Los Angeles Jews projected heroic dreams onto the new state. These frontier visions—of pioneering, striking roots, building a new home, and defending it against enemies—spoke to their specific situation as newcomers as well as to their need to define themselves as American Jews in a post-Holocaust age. Israel entered their consciousness first through its commitment to rescue survivors. But Jews in...Los Angeles secured Israel's place by transforming rescue into a promise of redemption.

Los Angeles Turns a Corner and Enters a New Era— City Elects an African American Mayor

Los Angeles, along with the rest of America, went through a time of social turmoil and unrest from the mid-1960s to the mid-1970s. As the newspapers and television anchors reported on the lurid and destructive behavior of the city's inhabitants, it exploited and exacerbated the tinderbox atmosphere. DeMarco writes, "The situation was frightening, to be sure, but the electronic and print media did its best to dramatically instill fear that was far out of proportion to the actual dangers at hand...The media not only reported what was happening, but molded and shaped events that produced what might be called the 'California psychosis.' There was a psychosis that significantly affected the mood and thinking in the Golden State's great urban centers during the 1970s."

The environment was tense and thus the stage was set for a dramatic turn of events. Politically the groundwork had been laid in the 1950s for the emergence of a remarkable historic coalition that would challenge the white dominated conservative hegemony of Los

Los Angeles Mayor Tom Bradley is presented the Haym Salomon Medal by the Jewish War Veterans, 1973.

Children at Vista Del Mar have dinner and chat with their counselor, circa 1950s

Angeles. In a most unique and unpredictable scenario, Latino, African American, and Jewish leadership joined forces and formed a multiracial coalition, which grew quietly behind the scenes during the social upheaval of the 1960s. The apex of the coalition mobilized behind Councilman Tom Bradley's campaigns for city council and mayor. Bradley's coalition began in the Tenth District when a large bloc of African American and Jewish activists came together seeking minority representation and political reform. The multi-racial group of Bradley supporters built a bridge between minority aspirations and concerns of middle class whites. This extraordinary consensus of support coming from a cross section of voters resulted in Bradley defeating incumbent Mayor Sam Yorty in 1973.

Sinai Temple, one of America's leading congregations of Conservative Judaism

The historic election in 1973, in which Jewish support for Bradley helped to forge one of the nation's most unprecedented bi-racial coalitions, culminated with Bradley receiving the largest share of the white vote of any African American candidate in a major American city. Bradley took 46 percent of the white vote, with an overwhelming number of Jewish voters included and it was that support that translated into a crucial element of this victory.

With Bradley's election, Jews, African Americans, Latinos, and Asian Americans emerged from the wall of civic exclusion and rose to a central role in the governance of Los Angeles. For twenty years, the Bradley coalition dominated Los Angeles government and the civic and social role of Jews and other minority groups expanded. This powerful coalition provided key political backing for Bradley policies that most dramatically impacted minority communities: diversity in appointment of city commissioners, affirmative action in the hiring and promotion of city employees, and civilian accountability for the actions of the Los Angeles Police Department.

The city went through a time of recovery and healing in the 1970s as the painful memories and discord of the previous decade began to recede. Social injustice was confronted and

Low cost housing was available for returning World War II veterans in North Hollywood in 1947. In 1944 only 170,000 people lived in the Valley and by 1960 there were nearly one million

This early 1950s photograph illustrates typical Los Angeles traffic; in the background is the towering Los Angeles City Hall built in 1928

remedies were put into place, local leaders controlled the unrestrained urban sprawl, and the elimination of crime became a critical priority. The riots had startled the population into recognition of the plight of the minorities, especially since the various groups combined into a significant majority of the citizenry of Los Angles. As DeMarco noted, "a new cooperation was on the agenda in Los Angeles. The metropolis that was founded by a group of racially mixed *pobladores* two hundred years earlier…finds itself with a similar multi-racial population of more than three million as it heads into the 21st Century."

Los Angeles—the enticing city of hopes and dreams—was peering intently into the future as it recaptured and reinvented itself in the 1970s. The City of Angels with its multi-racial flavor, innovative vitality, a plethora of professional sports teams representing baseball, basketball, hockey, and football, its incredible history in the arts and entertainment, the national home of the film and music industry, a city that possesses an alluring climate that nurtures vegetation, easily coaxed its population into a euphoric idyllic state of believing that they lived in paradise.

As the city approached the latter decades of the 20th Century, all of its citizens looked forward eagerly to a time of social and economic stability, and a backdrop against which to create new and undreamed of technologies and opportunities in the traditional arenas which had given rise to Los Angeles becoming the entertainment mecca of the world.

The Jewish community, beginning with those first brave pioneers in 1850, had long established itself as a fundamental part of the city's history and development. That same spirit of freedom and adventure continued to inspire and motivate and propel the Jews in business, politics, social stratification and rebirth, and economic mobility. The Jewish community, as well as the rest of Los Angeles' polyglot population was entering a new era—one in which all hoped for peaceful relations between the many diverse groups, envisioning the next century and all the extraordinary progress and innovation that was to come.

The Man You Never Had To Ask:
The Allen Ziegler Story

by Rabbi William M. Kramer

Allen and Ruth Ziegler embody extraordinary commitment to family, to the Jewish community, and to living a philanthropic life based on generosity and integrity. Rabbi William Kramer wrote this article with love and respect for Allen and his wife, Ruth—an eloquent tribute to this wonderful couple and the many others they symbolically represent. The Zieglers exemplify the pioneer spirit, perseverance, and lifelong dedication that are enduring qualities of the many pioneers, philanthropists, leaders, and volunteers that have made inspiring and incredible contributions to the building and expansion of Los Angeles, in its remarkable 160-year history with the Jewish people. Volume II in this history of Jewish Los Angeles series, (presently in development), will focus on the many pioneers that are prominent throughout the city's history—those who have continued the impressive tradition demonstrated by Allen and Ruth Ziegler.

It was a long time ago, maybe three decades, when I met Allen and Ruth Ziegler. The occasion was an art show with work for sale done by the faculty of the University of Judaism.

The place was the old school in the former Hollywood Athletic Club on Sunset. The work on display was meant to be only for the "studio people" who were doing painting and sculpture in the Fine Arts program of the University of Judaism.

As a courtesy, maybe even as a joke, I was invited to participate although I was teaching art history and Jewish artistic symbology. I had been doing two-dimensional art for some years, but this was the first time that my work was exhibited for sale. Allen and Ruth bought a small mixed media collage, which I had done. I forget what they paid.

Following Allen's funeral on January 24, 1994, my bride, Dr. Betty Wagner Kramer, and I went to pay a shiva (condolence) call at their beautiful home. We were hardly in the door when Ruth

Ruth and Allen Ziegler at the Sinai Temple dinner dance, Coconut Grove, Ambassador Hotel, 1957

excused herself and almost immediately returned with "my" collage. Over the between years I saw them at various occasions and followed their family career. Whatever I have learned about them does them honor.

As *Heritage* newspaper publisher and California poet Herb Brin put it, "Allen came to prominence by way of parents who dared to homestead the rocks of North Dakota a century ago, and a baking supply company, which started as a Boyle Heights dream that incredibly came true beyond understanding." Allen's father was born in Lithuania and when he was fourteen years old, with almost no money, he managed to migrate to Baltimore. From there he worked his way to South Bend, Indiana where a sister of his lived. After South Bend, John Ziegler moved on to Chicago where he courted Eva Kurtzon, and they were married in 1902. At that time, new Jewish immigrants were attracted to homesteading and agriculture from New Jersey, west.

John and Eva set out for Antler, North Dakota near the Canadian border. There is a family tradition that knowing nothing about grain-raising (the goal), they ended up "cultivating rocks." More romantically it was said that John "rode with the Indians" and that he was at home in the saddle. Allen's evaluation of the Antler experience was that when his father applied for and got the homestead, "they gave him one of the lousiest parts of North Dakota. It was a dinky place called Antler. My father didn't know wheat from corn, barley or anything. And it was rocky as hell. The family kept its Jewish ties through a small synagogue in a nearby town." The pioneer life had its charm, but the young family left North Dakota for Chicago when babies started to come. Allen and Ziegler's brother Paul and sister Ruth, were born in Chicago. And brother Ray had been born in Grand Forks, North Dakota. Allen was born in Chicago 1915.

Once the family heard about the West Coast, Chicago no longer satisfied them. In 1922 the Zieglers headed for California. They came by way of the Santa Fe Railroad. Mother Eva prepared four or five days provisions for the train journey, which turned out to last seven days. Allen remembered stopping in Needles, for supplies. He also remembered that it was the hottest day in his life. Father John Ziegler found a small house in Boyle Heights.

Paul and Allen became students at the Congregation Talmud Torah better known as the Breed Street Shul. Paul became a Bar Mitzvah there during the tenure of Rabbi Solomon Neches. At Breed Street Shul, Allen said, "They wanted to make a cantor out of me. My voice hadn't changed yet." Actually, his studies at Breed Street were in the little building that still survives and is used despite the structural insecurity, not helped by earthquakes, of the old main sanctuary.

In 1928 Allen celebrated his bar mitzvah at Sinai Temple, but Boyle Heights was always to remain important to Allen. Some of his other memories of that East Los Angeles Jewish motherland include going to the Wabash movie theatre at Wabash and Evergreen and attending affairs for the Jewish Home for the Aging held in Lincoln Park. The décor of the Ziegler home always included a Jewish National Fund blue box *pushke*.

From his bar mitzvah onward, you couldn't quite tell where Temple Sinai left off and Allen Ziegler began. Fifty years after bar mitzvah, Allen became the honorary president of the congregation. At the very same pulpit where Allen had his Jewish manhood confirmed, Ruth and Allen's son, Larry, received the same rite.

❋ ❋ ❋

Ray [Allen's brother] had already become a minor businessman in Los Angeles. Practically on the family's arrival in 1922 Ray began vending newspapers at a stand at the corner of 9th and Hope Streets, the corner on which Wilshire Boulevard Temple was then located, of course under its corporate name of B'nai B'rith Temple. Allen's brother Ray made a connection through which he got another newsstand, which he turned over to Allen. It was located in front of the Doheny Oil Building. Allen sold the old *Los Angeles Herald*. The paper cost three cents in those days and Allen recalled that he began to make his fortune when oilman E.L. Doheny, Sr. himself would buy the three cent paper from him and give him a dime.

❋ ❋ ❋

Following normative public school training, Allen went on to Los Angeles High. There he earned a unique reputation among his fellow students. Steve Loew said that Allen

Allen Ziegler arrives home, greeted by Ruth

was more of a bookworm than one of the "guys on the town." He was studious and ambitious and as Loew said, "he was always running around in order to get his hands into everything." After high school, Allen went on to the University of Southern California (USC), which Ruth also attended. In 1937, he was graduated from USC law school and he used that education although he never practiced as an attorney.

❋ ❋ ❋

During the time that Allen was in naval service, the firm took on new opportunities presented by World War II prosperity and it began to manufacture supplies for the bakery trade. Formerly its activities had been largely limited as a wholesale house for jobbers who served retailers. More expansion and Westco began making the ingredients and not just distributing them and it developed a large product line. Allen returned to the business following his career with the Navy and he saw the firm become the largest bakery supply house on the West Coast.

The only job Allen had outside of being a newsstand operator was in the family business except for his U.S. Naval service. Following the events of Pearl Harbor, Allen joined the navy and became an officer. He was much beloved by the men with whom he served, both officers and crew. He was a morale builder during kamikaze raids. He attributed it to his work experience in the food business that he was a man who could find beer for his ship when no one else in the South Pacific could. Afterwards he returned to Westco.

Events led to Allen's heading the [Westco] firm. Rabbi Max Vorspan characterized him as CEO of a huge corporation, who personalized his business and his charities, with Ruth, like one who is running a "mama-papa" store. Among the accounts that Westco developed, were tiny donut stores in the ghettos and various barrios of Los Angeles as well as some of the super accounts such as Gelsons and Ralphs food market chains. He took great pride in his products as well as the high quality of Westco's management-employee relationships. The business spread from the Far East to the near East, from the Pacific Rim to Saudi Arabia.

Allen was a Jew who practiced the Protestant work ethic par excellence. He could be on the job as early as five o'clock in the morning typing out data for the day on a typewriter described as so old that it might have come from the 12th century, before typewriters were born! If there was anything critical that could be said about his management style it was that Allen micro-managed the business. It wasn't just "fussbudgetry," it was that he cared about each and every detail in the same way that he cared about whatever went on in the many philanthropies that he and Ruth so generously provided for.

❊ ❊ ❊

It was in 1939 that he first met Ruth Bernstein. And for reasons he tended to reflect back on as stupidity, he didn't see her again for two years. He thought that maybe he just wasn't ready for a woman of her quality. In 1941 they were married. Together again they stayed together. They belonged together. Their caring for others, their philanthropy, was an overflow from their personal devotion. About the time of Allen and Ruth's golden anniversary, he said that he regarded himself "as a very lucky person, and I have had maybe not a charmed life, but it has certainly been a pleasant one and a happy one and Ruth is the major reason for it."

How did Allen get started in his career as a philanthropist? He told the story that at one High Holy Day season he was seated next to his mother at the old Sinai Temple on New Hampshire. Pledge cards had been distributed. The kind with little turn-down tabs. Allen's mother took her card and turned down the tab that constituted a most generous pledge. Allen said he just sat there when his mother gave him a *zetz* (poke) with her right elbow, and she said, "You can give a little, too, so I did. I pushed down the lowest tab possible, which was fifty dollars and that was my first recollection of my first charitable act, at least as far as Sinai Temple is concerned." Rabbi David Lieber told the story that when the time came to build Sinai Temple and it needed money, the Zieglers looked after the finances of the congregation while postponing the building of their own home. Allen's sister Carolyn said, "A lot of people make money, but they keep it. Allen shares his and I admire that very much about him."

Allen has his own philanthropic style. Rabbi Vorspan said, "when a fundraising affair was being held, if you were looking for Allen you wouldn't see him. However, when money was being called for he would suddenly emerge from a dark corner and raise his hand and pledge the largest sum and then disappear. Allen was a man you never had to ask. He enjoyed volunteering charity and you made him feel good by accepting it.

❋ ❋ ❋

On May 20, 1985, Allen was inducted into the Society of Fellows of the University of Judaism. On that occasion, then University of Judaism President David Lieber said that although "he [Allen] prefers to stay in the background, he has shown the way to others, freely giving of himself to further our religious heritage. Time and again, he has proven himself to be an extraordinarily loyal friend who can be counted on whenever we need him." The Zieglers are known as founders of the University of Judaism and its affiliated Camp Ramah where there is a cabin, which bears the Ziegler name. At the time of his induction, it was noted that the University of Judaism had "benefited from Allen Ziegler's counsel and advice as a longtime member of the Board of Directors and its Executive Committee." He had been honored by its Patrons Society in 1960 as its first recipient of the Eternal Light Award.

Ruth and Allen Ziegler following ceremony at the City of Hope at the naming of a building in their honor

At the University of Judaism, the Sunny and Isadore Familian campus contains the Ruth and Allen Ziegler Administration Building. When the building was dedicated, the weather was perfect. The program went well although it ended in a downpour. That gave everybody an excuse to linger on the second floor entranceway drinking champagne and visiting with friends. When the time to depart came, the rain stopped and 500 people had 500 smiles as they went back to their vehicles under conditions that were as dry as the good dry wine they had been served.

❋ ❋ ❋

On March 26, 1991, the Zieglers endowed the "Ruth and Allen School of Rabbinic Studies" at the University of Judaism. Under its auspices, students are able to pursue post-baccalaureate degrees: Bachelor of Literature and Hebrew Letters or Master of Hebrew Letters. "The program is designed for those seeking careers as rabbis, educators, and scholars." Rabbi Vorspan playfully suggested that the school might bear the name A to Z University of Judaism to honor Allen through his initials.

On making the gift [endowment for University of Judaism], Allen said, "My wonderful wife of almost 50 years, Ruth, agrees with me and has always supported our contributions, especially for medical institutions and Jewish education. Our special attachment to the Rabbinic School perhaps stems from the fact that Ruth's late father, Louis Bernstein, who was ordained by Hebrew Union College, was a leading rabbi in Baltimore, Maryland and St. Joseph, Missouri."

❋ ❋ ❋

Allen was a second-generation member of Sinai Temple where his bar mitzvah was held in 1928. It was then located at Fourth and New Hampshire. When a changing demography made it necessary for the congregation to move westward, Allen was a major underwriter in the successful establishing of the congregation in its current location on Wilshire Boulevard in Westwood. The hall in the new structure was named Ziegler Hall in honor of Ziegler's parents. At the dedication of the Hall, Allen has said that one of the great memories of his life was when he and Ruth and his sisters and brothers brought their then 86-year-old mother to the dedicatory event.

The Zieglers also presented the congregation with the Kohn Memorial Chapel, the Silverman Succah, and funds for the Sinai Akiba Academy Day School. Among the offices that Ziegler held at Sinai Temple were president and, as noted, honorary life-president. Ziegler family gifting made possible the Ziegler Laser Research Laboratory for the Reestablishment of Coronary Circulation. On October 29, 1983, the hospital gave him its "Heart of Gold Award." This was an acknowledgement not only of his generosity financially, but his advice and counsel over the years.

❊ ❊ ❊

In January 1994, Allen Ziegler passed away. The entire back page of the *Heritage* chain of Jewish newspapers carried a memorial to him. The announcement was signed by the Committee of Concerned Christians Advisory Committee, which had recently been co-founded by Allen and Ben Friedman and was instituted in order to eliminate the falsehood known as "Holocaust Denial." In it Allen was described as, "one of the great Jewish leaders of the world…the man of great kindness and generosity who made our dreams of a Committee of Concerned Christians into a reality. We shall forever be indebted to him for his caring, wisdom, and inspiration…. Among the activities of the Concerned Christians, which include some of the leading clergy, is to define the Holocaust as "the continual mistreatment and slaughter of Jewish people from circa 300 of the Common Era to the Twentieth Century." The group says that it has "no reason to think the abuses will stop during the 21st Century unless organized efforts are made to end them forever." Among the items on its agenda, one is to encourage clergy to present "at least one sermon a year—every year—about the tragedy of the Holocaust and anti-Semitism so everyone will always remember that the tragic Holocaust happened."

The tribute of Herb Brin in *Heritage* said much the same. "One of the great pioneer leaders of Jewish life in the West, Allen Ziegler, 78, died this week after an extended illness." The funeral service was held at Mt. Sinai Memorial Park in Los Angeles. Hundreds were present to hear Rabbi Schranz, who, on another occasion, said that Allen was "a good person, a giving person, a righteous man. He is a *tzadik* who gives *tzedakah* [charity], and who by his example, brings other people to righteousness and *tzdakah* giving. Allen is a righteous person." Cantor Meier Finkelstein chanted the liturgy.

Wife, Ruth Ziegler, described her philanthropist husband by saying, "he'll do really anything for anyone he really cares about, or for any organization or institution that expresses values that he holds to be precious." At a birthday event for Allen, Dr. David Lieber similarly observed "Allen is that unique person who both gives out of a sense of charity, a sense of love and concern, and also a sense that this is the right thing to do. He is a man who recognizes what his responsibilities are, and a man who basically enjoys giving."

CHAPTER NINE

Los Angeles Jewish Community Emerges in Leadership: 1971 to the Present

The light of Jewish life in Los Angeles continues to glow

The most significant event with its immediate ramifications came in 1967 with the conclusion of the dramatic Six-Day War...

Three major events in the history of the Jewish community occurred in the dramatic, mega-changing 1960s—events that might be said led to a heightened sense of Jewish self-esteem and identification that emerged in the 1970s and continues into present day. These three seemingly unrelated events were: the release of the motion picture *Exodus* in 1961, sports hero Sandy Koufax declining to pitch during the 1965 World Series because the base-ball game fell on the holy day of Yom Kippur, and the stunning victory by the Israelis over the massive armies of its neighboring Arabs in the Six-Day War in the Middle East. These three events were key factors in redesigning the landscape for Jewish life, not only in Los Angeles, but also across America.

In 1961, the three-hour epic feature film, *Exodus*, renewed feelings of respect, admiration, and endearing love for the new Jewish homeland. The film compassionately portrayed the emotional and physical devastation of the Holocaust alongside the euphoria and passion of the birth of the new Jewish State of Israel. *Exodus* presented to the world the modern State of Israel, a symbol of freedom and democracy that reflects the indomitable will of Jewish people around the world to stand firm and resolute to protect their homeland in its struggle for survival. The story of the creation of this great nation, memorialized so poignantly in the film, is vital to the continuity of the generations.

LA's famous Canter's Delicatessen

Sandy Koufax sitting out the World Series game against the Minnesota Twins in order to honor the sacred holiday of Yom Kippur, reminded the Jewish people of their feelings of pride in their Jewish roots and the richness of their culture. Dovid Zaklikowski, journalist, described it this way: "October 6, 1965, the first game of the '65 World Series, the Los Angeles Dodgers versus the Minnesota Twins. It's Yom Kippur night at Metropolitan Stadium, 47,797 in attendance. Sandy Koufax, lead pitcher of the LA Dodgers, refuses to play. Koufax's refusal to pitch on Yom Kippur gained him the respect and admiration of many Jews. His courage gave many Jews the strength to not be ashamed of their Judaism."

The day after the game, Koufax had a surprise visit from a local clergyman, Rabbi Moshe Feller. Feller congratulated Koufax for not playing on Yom Kippur and for "the great assist he gave rabbis and Jewish educators the world over." Rabbi Feller also brought Sandy a pair of *tefillin* [phylacteries—small black boxes containing passages of scripture with black straps attached to them, worn by men on the head and arm at weekday morning prayers]. Koufax accepted the gift and thanked Rabbi Feller for visiting. "The Talmud says that *tefillin* is representative of all the *Mitzvot* of the Torah," Feller later explained. "So I could not think of a better way to honor a person for enhancing Jewish values, than by presenting him with a pair of *tefillin*." Noted businessman and Los Angeles Jewish community leader Lon Morton was also personally influenced by Koufax's actions: "Knowing the commitment of Sandy Koufax to his Jewish background inspired me in my professional baseball career as a Jewish pitcher."

It was a remarkable occasion in history for Jews in Los Angeles and around the world. A Jew who did not hide his Jewishness, and was willing to declare it in as public a way as Sandy Koufax did, and to sacrifice something important for his Jewish heritage—it was a deed that was viewed as heroic beyond words. More than forty years after this unprecedented and inspirational action, people remember and talk about the World Series game that became history because of the pitcher who did not play.

One of baseball's greatest pitchers, Sandy Koufax, who, playing for the Los Angeles Dodgers, refused to play on Yom Kippur *during the 1965 World Series*

The third and perhaps the most significant event and its resulting ramifications, occurred in 1967 with the conclusion of the dramatic Six-Day War—so named because it took only six days for the Jews in Israel to defeat the combined Arab armies of Egypt, Jordan, and Syria. At the war's end, Israel had gained control of the Gaza Strip, the Sinai Peninsula, the West Bank, and the Golan Heights. The political importance of the 1967 war was immense; Israel demonstrated that it was not only able, but also willing to initiate strategic strikes that could change the regional balance. Egypt and Syria learned tactical lessons, but perhaps not the strategic ones, since they launched an unprovoked attack in 1973 in another unsuccessful attempt to reclaim territory.

Rabbi William Kramer at home in Los Angeles; renowned and honored historian on Jewish life in Los Angeles, and throughout the West

A war fought and won by Israel, demonstrated to the world that Jews were not weak physically or emotionally and that they were determined to fight for their freedom and independence. In the conflict with multiple Arab nations, Israel's military troops were outnumbered 22 to 1. Jews fighting for their rights in the Holy Land would impact the perception of the world's population—a population that recalled the war time images of Jews being arrested, marched into death camps, and exterminated during the Holocaust. Jews in the post World War II era were widely perceived as a subjugated group. As a result of the admirable, heroic, and stunning victory (reminiscent of, and often compared to, the biblical story of David and Goliath) by the "people of the book," Jews worldwide remember and revere the self-respect and dignity they felt when the Israelis displayed their courageous military strength and persevering endurance in yet another chapter in their four thousand year quest for freedom.

During the 1960s, the growth of Jewish activism motivated the community to reject the *sha-shtil* [hush, be quiet] syndrome approach to sensitive Jewish-related issues. In their long history of persecution and oppression, Jews had learned to quietly remain out of sight of their tormentors as a method of survival. They adopted a self-defensive position of staying "quiet" so as to avoid being targeted. In light of the dramatic global events that took place during the 1960s, Jews were emboldened to speak up and claim their rights and privileges as citizens of the world. The Rosenberg trial in the Fifties might have been perceived and responded to very differently by the Jewish community in the post Six-Day War period of the Sixties.

What was the political, social and emotional climate in Los Angeles following the 1960s revolution? The end of the decade climaxed in apprehension and unease when people watched in horror as presidential hopeful Senator Robert Kennedy was assassinated in a Los Angeles hotel ballroom in full view of television cameras. Los Angeles citizens (along with the rest of the country) were shocked and thrown off balance by this and a series of unimaginable events that rocked the city and shook it to its core.

The emotional shake-up was soon followed by physical forces in nature that would again shock and propel Los Angeles into action. In 1971, the City of Angels experienced an earthquake in the space of sixty seconds which resulted in a half billion dollars' worth of damages including the destruction of twenty highway overpasses and a veteran's hospital. The same year, Charles Manson and three women in his homicidal "family" were sentenced to death for some of the most brutal cult killings in America's history.

Californians were frustrated, angry, disturbed, and looking for radical change—a way to regain their equilibrium and achieve balance in their environment. Stepping into this atmosphere of unrest, a new face emerged in the political arena: Ronald Reagan. He found his political foothold, not in *Death Valley* (the TV series the actor hosted), but in the entire state of

President Samuel L. Kaye signs contracts to begin construction in 1972 on the final phases of the master plan which provided more than six million dollars worth of new buildings for the Jewish Home for the Aging. Standing (from left) at the historic ceremony were past presidents H. Lew Zuckerman, Harry B. Seelig, Harry Cooper, Mischa F. Berg (who led the first phase of the building program in 1976), Sol Levine and Sol's son, Alvin, who preceded Kaye as president

Guilford and Diane Glazer with Armand Hammer and Mayor of Los Angeles Tom Bradley, who vigoroursly supported the Jewish community. Hammer was an acknowledged philanthropist

California. Lyn Nofziger, Reagan's press representative, speaking about the 1966 California gubernatorial election noted, "Ronald Reagan materialized out of thin air with no political background, no political cronies, and no political machine . . . He didn't even run his own campaign." It was clear that reaching for the stars in California was neither limited to Los Angelenos nor to the Jewish pioneers. California dreams were accessible to all Californians.

An important facet of Reagan's rise to power was the role played by a small group of wealthy conservatives known as his "kitchen cabinet." This handful of men initiated, funded, and guided Reagan's political career. Many in the group subsequently invested in renowned think tanks and nonprofit organizations promoting anti-communist, libertarian, and conservative social causes. There was one Jewish member in the "kitchen cabinet"—Theodore Cummings, a real estate developer that owned Food Giant supermarkets among other investments. In Los Angeles and the national Jewish community Cummings was respected because of his business and political associates and wealth, but he was also considered an enigma—Cummings was a Jewish Republican, a most unusual entity at the time. Cummings was a close confident of Reagan's. When Reagan was elected to the White House, installed in his new role as president he appointed Cummings as United States Ambassador to Austria in 1973. The long-time Reagan friend, although born in Austria, honored his Jewish American heritage and spoke powerfully in his role as ambassador; it was as if his family origins were "rooted" in pioneer Los Angeles.

Rabbi Susan Laemmle, Dean of Religious Life at University of Southern California, 2006

The kitchen cabinet coalesced after Reagan delivered a Republican fundraising speech at the Coconut Grove nightclub in Los Angeles in 1964, prior to his first election campaign. Five or six influential men seated in the audience asked Reagan if he would deliver the same speech on national television in support of Barry Goldwater's presidential bid if they purchased the airtime, and he agreed. The result was the famous "A Time in Choosing" speech that was broadcast over the NBC television network on October 27, 1964. Reagan biographer Bill Boyarsky has compared the effect of the "Time in Choosing" speech on rank-and-file conservatives and anti-communists, with William Jennings Bryan's 1896 "Cross of Gold" speech and the consequent impact it had on farmers and laborers. Goldwater (an Episcopalian with Jewish ancestry) had not invited Reagan to deliver the speech. The two men, rivals for the leadership of the conservative movement, were not close. In 1976 Goldwater endorsed Gerald Ford (a man regarded by Reagan with disdain) for president over the Californian.

Social change increasingly revealed a new Los Angeles in the latter decades of the 20th Century. In 1973, in a startling political upset, Tom Bradley, the first non-white mayor of Los Angeles defeated incumbent Mayor Sam Yorty. Another premonition of underlying racial issues surfaced in 1974 when the Teamsters Union and Caesar Chavez's Farm Union engaged in a bloody conflict to control the migrant farm workers. The farmers benefited from a 43 percent increase in incomes that year, but the costs were dear. Alongside these fomenting racial and labor issues, there were vast changes in transportation in Southern California that were to heavily impact the social climate in the Southland. By 1975, the Los Angeles streetcar transportation system, built almost a century earlier, was replaced by forty-four square miles of parking space. With little or no access to mass transportation, travel became predominantly via automobile, and the poor and disenfranchised suffered.

A Tale of Two Riots: 1965 and 1992

Today when Americans think about Los Angeles, some images from the past are troubling: urban riots and severe earthquakes (two of each in the past forty years), traffic congestion, smog, and unsightly urban sprawl dominated by an asphalt jungle of freeways and shopping malls. Perhaps the reality lies somewhere in between the extreme grandeur of glorious paradise and the stressful urgency of civilization—always Los Angelenos are striving to develop the beauty and culture of their city while avoiding the chaos inherent in an ever-expanding widespread metropolis.

Following the massive changes in civil rights legislation and policy in the 1960s, school busing concerns became a dominant topic in the political landscape. In 1974 an informal broad census illustrated that southwest Los Angeles' 10th District was about 50 percent black, 12 percent Asian American, 20 percent Jewish, with the remaining 12 percent a mix of minorities: Mexican American, Native American, and other Caucasian. The Board of Education began to search for alternatives in a determined effort to achieve a more equitable balance in the educational system and the placement of its students.

More than any other urban area, Los Angeles rejected the impact of Federal government policies and subsidies that promulgated suburbanization, auto dependency, and racial segregation. In the post war period, the city's business and civic elite forged a local growth coalition that promoted a combination of suburban sprawl and

Rabbi Harold Schulweis, Valley Beth Shalom (Encino), an innovator in Jewish ideas

downtown redevelopment, but unfortunately locked out the poor from the benefits of both. The resulting economic and racial disparities led to the wave of urban riots in American cities during the 1960s, which materialized first in Los Angeles. Once again the City of Angeles was in the forefront of the social evolution that was rapidly surging throughout the country. Despite the racially based riots of 1965 and 1992, Los Angeles remained America's virtual Garden of Eden—the land of sunshine, beaches, open spaces, opportunity, wealth and ambition. It was the home of Hollywood, the nation's dream factory, and it was a city to which Americans moved in order to follow their dreams.

A positive element that emerged from the Watts Riot, energized the city's liberal forces to form an alliance comprised primarily of African Americans and Jews that coalesced around Tom Bradley. Bradley was a police lieutenant with the Los Angeles Police Department (LAPD) prior to his election as the first black member of the Los Angeles City Council in 1963. He ran a strong mayoral campaign in 1969 to replace incumbent Mayor Sam Yorty. Bradley was a strong critic of the LAPD, which substantially strengthened his support in the black community. Although backed by the "liberal' alliance, Bradley narrowly lost his attempt to unseat Yorty, but was successful four years later. Bradley went on to serve as mayor for twenty years.

Bradley's early years in office might be called a "feel-good era" in Los Angeles—in effect, it was a new beginning after the radical changes brought about in the 1960s. He nearly won the white vote in the 1973 mayoral election (he carried it decisively in all four of his subsequent reelections). Never in America's history had so large a majority of the white population voted for a black candidate. Bradley—a figure of great dignity, and almost sphinx-like reserve—became a symbol of the city's racial enlightenment. Jewish support for him was extraordinarily strong.

One of the peak experiences of the Bradley era took place in 1984 when Los Angeles hosted the Summer Olympic Games. The Israeli team was welcomed to Los Angeles with many parties and receptions. The *Los Angeles Times* published a tribute to the team and to Israel, which was co-published by *Israel Today* (now *The Jewish News*), and edited by Rosalie Zalis, prominent journalist and political figure.

Dynamics of the Persian, Russian, and Israeli Communities in Los Angeles

Los Angeles is one of the most diverse cities in the world, with residents from a multitude of nations encompassing many races, religions, and cultures. Through the natural process of families and immigrant countrymen living and working together, ethnic enclaves have arisen that allowed residents to live together in communities with those of similar backgrounds and beliefs. The Russian Jews have a long history in Los Angeles and one of their current enclaves is in the Fairfax District. Their history there began many years ago.

During the 1940s and 1950s many Jews settled near Fairfax Avenue, between Wilshire Boulevard and Melrose Avenue. There were a large number of apartments in this locale, which appealed mainly to elderly Jews or those who were not as affluent. This area soon emerged as a most important Jewish residential and shopping district — it was an updated, smaller-scale version of Boyle Heights. The Fairfax area became the symbolic focal point for the Jewish community during the post war years, and retains this strong Jewish identity in present day.

In the late 1970s, West Hollywood and adjacent neighborhoods became a major destination for Jews from the Soviet Union (USSR). This pattern continued during the 1980s and 1990s; a great many elderly Russian refugees arrived in Los Angeles and found it difficult to adapt to the American economic system and learn English. Because these Jews had been strongly discouraged and persecuted in attempting to pursue their religion in the USSR, the Russian Jews that arrived in Los Angeles had little knowledge of Judaism. The City of West Hollywood is mainly defined by these Russian Jewish refugees. Although this group of West Hollywood residents encompasses multiple backgrounds: Russian ancestry, Eastern European immigrants, and Israeli immigrants—they still share similar ideals in terms of living space, generally choosing middle and upper class neighborhoods in more urban areas.

Following the 1978-79 Islamic revolution that resulted in the overthrow of the Shah in Iran, thousands of Iranian Jewish families were compelled to start new lives in other places. Some 70 to 90 percent of Iran's Jewish population—estimated at anywhere between 70,000 and 120,000—

Rabbi Paul Dubin, Executive Vice President Emeritus, Southern California Board of Rabbis, at the historic Breed Street Shul, meeting with members of the neighborhood

left the country, driven by fear of persecution under the sometimes violently anti-capitalist, anti-Zionist regime. The majority of them went to Israel, but some 50,000 to 55,000 Iranian Jews now live in the United States, mostly in Los Angeles and Long Island, New York.

Most of the Iranian refugees abandoned not only property, careers, close friendships, family graves and even elderly relatives, but also the language and familiar rhythms of daily life in the comfort of tightly knit communities that have existed in Iran—known as Persia until 1934—for over 2,500 years.

In an article written by Julia Goldman in 1999, she illustrates the collective experiences of these Persian Jews through the personal experiences of one of the Persian immigrants, Soraya Masjedi Nazarian, who fled Iran in 1979 and moved to Los Angeles. Nazarian, a governing cabinet chair of Hadassah Southern California, talked about her childhood in Tehran, and described one of her most vivid memories—her grandmother's preparations for Passover. "After Purim, we started to clean every single thing," from the closets to the dishes, she said. "Grandma used to have a big pot of boiling water" into which she put a small stone "and they would dip all the pots in there and say a special prayer."

While most Israelis came to Los Angeles between the early 1950s and the present, Harry Edelson arrived with his family in 1920. Born in 1907 in Jaffa, Israel, he graduated from Jefferson High School and entered USC. Edelson played on the university's football team. USC went on to win the National Championship on January 4, 1929. The Los Angeles Times *(October 9, 1928) described Edelson as the "hard-hitting Jewish boy who performs at inside halfback." He enjoyed a notable career as a coach for Los Angeles, Fremont, and Jefferson high schools*

Nazarian, like many Iranian-born Jews living in the United States, subsequently worked to maintain an identity she considers distinct from that of the Ashkenazi and Sephardi Jews. The first Iranian woman to sit on the executive board of her synagogue, Nazarian initiated a cultural exchange at Congregation Temple Sinai, where the rabbi estimates that one-third of the congregation is Iranian. One of those programs includes a Persian-style Passover Seder. Students learn the Iranian custom of "whipping" one another with the green tails of scallions during the singing of "Dayenu," an act meant to mimic the Egyptian slave masters.

In addition to her strong memories of Passover, Nazarian remembers a different kind of Seder. She wrote and translated from Farsi, the Persian language, the text of a Rosh Hashanah

Rabbi Yedidia Shofet, thirteenth generation Persian rabbi who is the spiritual leader of Nessah Educational and Cultural Center, Santa Monica

Seder, a singularly Iranian Jewish custom. In addition to apples and honey (for a sweet year), seven symbolic foods—pomegranates, dates, beets, zucchini, black-eyed peas and the head or tongue of a cow or sheep—are blessed and eaten, each representing an aspect of health and good fortune. Nazarian was inspired to create the English language Seder guide for the children of Iranian immigrants raised in America. "If they cannot read and write Hebrew or Persian [Farsi]," said Nazarian, "they're not going to have a Seder. This is our tradition. We have to keep all the holidays."

Another of the representative experiences of Iranian Jewish community involvement is one concerning Jimmy Delshad, who arrived in Los Angeles in advance of the large immigrant blitz. He was elected president of the Sinai Temple in Westwood, a congregation founded by Ashkenazi Jews. Later Delshad was elected to the Beverly Hills City Council and following this service assumed the position of mayor of Beverly Hills. David Nahai, a prominent Los Angeles attorney of Jewish Iranian ancestry was appointed to the Los Angeles Coastal Commission.

Beyond family bonds and social networks, Iranian Jewish Americans have established synagogues, Persian chapters of national Jewish organizations, as well as other organizations devoted to the community's needs. In Los Angeles alone, Nazarian counts anywhere between 12 and 28 Iranian Jewish groups. One group, the Center for Iranian Jewish Oral History, represents a concrete attempt to preserve and interpret the Iranian Jewish experience through an archive of hundreds of interviews, bilingual publications, documentary films, international academic conferences and programs showcasing young talent from the community.

Israelis arrived in Los Angeles in large numbers prior to and following the 1967 Six-Day War; many of them were students enrolled in the universities who then took advantage of the job opportunities that were available to them. Israelis have a very different relationship than other groups within the Jewish community in Los Angeles. Their dual loyalties are dedicated both to the Jewish State as well as their home country in which they reside and raise their families. In 2002, the U.S. State Department issued a travel warning advising American citizens against travel to Israel because of the Muslim radical intifada. At that time there were about 70,000 to 120,000 people in the Los Angeles Israeli community, and they were forced to make difficult decisions about returning to Israel to visit family and friends.

Councilman Marvin Braude (right) and Dr. Uri Herscher dedicating Skirball Center Drive and inaugurating the 405 Freeway signage, 1989

It is a common and real life situation in which Israelis in Los Angeles, whether they are new to America or second generation, find themselves living in two distinct, albeit related worlds. Jane Ulman, a reporter for the *Los Angeles Jewish Journal*, writes about Dr. Yehuda Handelsman, 2002 president of the Council of the Israeli Community (CIC), an organization founded to meet the needs of local Israelis and generate support for their concerns. In the words of Dr. Handelsman, "We're torn. On the one hand, Iraq has been a constant threat to Israel and it's time to get [those] guys out of there. On the other, most of us have seen fighting and do not relish another attack on Israel. We're worried."

CIC's more than 1000 members organize rallies and letter writing campaigns to assist Israel. The Council works closely with the Jewish Federation and the Israeli Consulate in their endeavors. Israelis contribute greatly to their homeland and take pride in their work in support of the Jewish State. Bracha Loren, a marriage and family therapist in the San Fernando Valley affirmed, "Israelis are doers; we don't sit and contemplate, we get up and do."

An example of this proactive approach was demonstrated by ten Israeli couples who founded an organization called Urgent Aid for Israel. In their first two months of operation they raised $130,000 to buy an armored ambulance for Magen David Adom, the first responders to assist in bombings and other attacks on Israel. The group raised funds for heart defibrillators for ambulances, and walkie-talkies for the settlement communities. Another organization, Volunteers for Israel, has instituted a one-week program for volunteers to fly to Israel and help on Israeli army bases and aid in the country's self-defense procedures. A small group of Israelis immigrated to Los Angeles in the early 1950s following the War of Independence. Several of them, including real estate developer Jona Goldrich, became leading philanthropists in support of community wide projects.

Los Angeles Jewish Community—City at the Center of Activism for Human Rights

Raphael J. Sonenshein in writing about activism in Los Angeles states "Jews have played a pivotal role in the struggle for human rights in Los Angeles. From the early days of Los Angeles' development as an American city, through the political struggles for minority representation and equality throughout the 20th Century, Jews have played a critical role as an unusually progressive white community in a city where liberalism had only a tenuous hold for many decades." The history of Jewish activism in support of human rights is long and well documented.

Prior to World War II the Boyle Heights area was the center of Jewish population. From this geographic base, Jews, who were the mainstay of the garment industry, were very involved in the unions representing the garment workers and gradually more and more active in the overall labor movement itself. According to Sonenshein "Jewish labor organizing was particularly noteworthy because of the avid opposition of the powers-that-be in Los Angeles, including the *Los Angeles Times* and the notorious Red Squad of the Los Angeles Police Department."

The Jewish community in Boyle Heights was working class and often militantly progressive in its politics. Deborah Dash Moore wrote that the "visible, immigrant, Yiddish-speaking community centered in Boyle Heights ardently supported FDR [President Franklin Delano Roosevelt] and the New Deal." The first minority city council member elected in the 20th Century, Edward Roybal, won the election based on the crucial support of the Jewish community in Boyle Heights.

Jews also voted overwhelmingly in support of a Fair Employment Practices Committee in the 1946 election championing the issue of equality in employment, another strong indicator of the depth of their community's anti-discrimination positions. This discrimination concern was to resurface in a more complex gambit in 1964 when the unconstitutional and outrageously unfair Proposition 14 was passed by a majority of voters in California. Proposition 14 was intended to negate the Rumford Fair Housing Act, an action that would have effectively legalized unfair housing practices in the state. The records indicate that only the Black and Jewish areas of Los Angeles voted in large numbers against Proposition 14.

In the 1950s and 1960s many Jews were migrating to the West Adams and Fairfax areas, continuing their progressive stance politically and socially. Extremely active in the Democratic Party, they elected their first Jewish officeholder in 50 years with the election of Rosalind Weiner [Wyman] to the city council in 1953 [see Chapter Eight]. According to Sonenshein, "Beginning with Edward Roybal's election to the city council in 1949 with Latino and Jewish support, biracial and multiracial coalitions grew in strength and scope through the 1960s. The apex of the coalition was the mobilization behind Councilman Tom Bradley's campaigns for city council and then for mayor."

With Bradley's election in 1973, Jews, African Americans, Latinos, and Asian Americans emerged from the wall of civil exclusion and moved into a central role in the governance of Los Angeles. The Black-Jewish coalition that supported Bradley helped that administration to survive the bitter and confrontational aspects of school busing. This coalition was especially effective in policies that most impacted minority communities: affirmative action in hiring and promotions of city employees, diversity in appointments of city commissioners, and civilian accountability for the actions of the LAPD.

Among the many individual achievements in the arena of Jewish activism, one of the leaders in the Jewish community, Phil Blazer (co-author of this book), was a key player in advancing the causes of Jewish Los Angeles. One of the many activist proceedings that Blazer would bring about placed him in a position in which he directly confronted one of the biggest oil companies in the world in 1973—Standard Oil. In a letter sent to employees and shareholders, Chairman of the Board of Standard Oil, Otto Miller, stated

Albert Smith, Mayor of Skokie, joins Phil Blazer in an emotional rally and ceremony at the Skokie synagogue. Blazer, accompanied by more than 200 activist Los Angelenos, united to take a stand protesting the Nazi march in the Chicago village. The commitment and outrage of the protesters, known as the "Skokie Skytrain," inspired the CBS movie, "Skokie" in 1978.

that the United States under the Nixon Administration had become "aligned with Israel." In his transparent and visibly anti-Semitic letter, Miller was obviously instigating an anti-Israel campaign and using the might and wealth of the giant oil company to influence public opinion.

Blazer, publisher of *The Jewish News* and host of his weekly radio show, requested that newspaper readers and radio listeners send him their torn and cut up Standard Oil credit cards. Blazer felt that this would be a dramatic and effective demonstration of opposition to the biased stand that Miller had taken. As soon as Blazer distributed the press release an immediate storm of media attention attached itself to the crusade. Terry Drinkwater, West Coast correspondent for the *CBS Evening News* anchored by Walter Cronkite, requested an immediate interview with Blazer. The interview and other media coverage prompted instant reaction. Within the week, bags of letters filled with mutilated credit cards flooded Blazer's office. Some of the more creative had even cut out Jewish stars in the middle of the card, while others simply sent in their cut-up credit cards. They were all uniformly determined to never again do business with Standard Oil.

Quick to take action in light of this enthusiastic response, Blazer took the effort a step further and decided to personally carry all the destroyed cards to the Standard Oil headquarters in San Francisco. The media loved the idea of this one man taking on an enormous oil company and were quick to point out the "David and Goliath" aspects of this unusual activity. TV crews followed Blazer into the offices of Standard Oil where Blazer was positioned to hand over the bags full of cards to Otto Miller himself. Needless to say, Miller refused to meet with Blazer and would not appear before the television cameras and instead sent his secretary to accept the cards. It was clear, however, that the point had been made and underscored— Standard Oil would be a long time recovering from both the financial repercussions and public relations fiasco that ensued.

Dr. Uri D. Herscher, Jack H. Skirball and Moshe Safdie (left to right) walking the building site of The Skirball Cultural Center, 1985

Beyond the revelation of the anti-Semitic practices of Standard Oil, however, Blazer and his supporters made a much more important and significantly impressive point. Many in the Jewish community, both in Los Angeles and around the country, had been fearful of speaking out too bluntly or being in the public eye—they were afraid that the exposure would generate too much criticism. In light of Blazer's actions and those of other activists, it became clear that within the context of the Holocaust and the Six-Day War, that the Jews in America and throughout the world were ready to stand up and defend themselves and reclaim their rights as citizens of the world.

An even more poignant experience in Blazer's activist career highlighted the newly discovered forthright courage in the collective Jewish psyche. It involved an incident that took place in the former Soviet Union (USSR) in 1973. One of the worst kept secrets in geo-political corners was the repression and persecution of Jews trying to practice their religion in the USSR. Various methods of revealing this moral and political travesty were attempted including letters to Congress, walkathons, newspaper articles, and radio editorials. While these were useful methods, some urgent action was needed to dramatically increase public and political awareness.

Blazer was notified by activists Si Frumkin and Los Angeles County Supervisor Zev Yaroslavsky that twelve Torahs had been confiscated by the KGB from the Great Synagogue in St. Petersburg (then Leningrad.) The KGB agents had ripped open the Torahs and defiled and desecrated them, including urinating on them—vile acts of such an unspeakable nature that the local Jewish community was devastated, and Jews worldwide were outraged. Blazer and several supporters went into action quickly and decided that they needed to "smuggle" a Torah into St. Petersburg. This was an extremely delicate and potentially dangerous situation since the KGB operatives and spies had infiltrated America and fomented a communist scare

Jewish Labor Committee (JLC) participates in the Annual Caesar Chavez Walk supporting the United Farm Workers. The JLC was founded in 1934 simultaneously in Los Angeles and New York

in the country. Blazer and his supporters purchased a plane ticket for Rabbi Ellis Sultanik, the man who volunteered to carry the Torah into St. Petersburg via London.

When Rabbi Sultanik appeared at the Russian embassy in London to process his visa, he was shocked when questioned by the abrasive Russian clerk. "Are you the rabbi from Los Angeles smuggling the Torah into St. Petersburg?" Fortunately the rabbi was a quick thinker and calmly replied, "What's a Torah?" After a series of other potential roadblocks, the rabbi arrived safely in St. Petersburg, and went into the synagogue where he removed the Torah from his duffle bag. Congregants gathered around him weeping with joy when they realized that the rabbi had made it through with the Torah on the day of *Simchat Torah*, the Jewish holiday that honors the Torah.

It was a day of celebration and triumph, both for the Jewish heroes in St. Petersburg, and all those who heard or read about the famous Torah. These Russian Jews had sacrificed and endured great hardship to practice their religion and to honor their culture and traditions. An entire generation of "refusniks" would not submit to the persecution of the Russian government and worked in an underground organization for years in order to maintain their Jewish identity.

Throughout the 1970s and 1980s many activists were involved in behavior that raised the level of awareness regarding Jews and their support for freedom and equality for all people, regardless of race or religion. The minority coalition that worked with Mayor Bradley for 20 years in Los Angeles was critical to the development and progressive thinking in that city as it emerged from the tumultuous Sixties.

With the end of the Bradley mayoralty in 1993, the massive coalition of minority supporters became fractured. The civil unrest of 1992 "caused many Jews to reevaluate their support for liberal citywide policies and candidates, and helped lead many Jews to support Republican Richard Riordan's candidacy for mayor in 1993, and his reelection in 1997," according to Sonenshein. Minority groups began to move into more independent positions and ethnic groups in the various communities became localized. The political changes created other changes in ideology, with Jews remaining as "insiders" during the Riordan years, while African Americans became "outsiders," with Latinos emerging as a strong special interest group at the forefront of the city's political and economic life.

Demographics in Los Angeles Identify Changes in Jewish Migration and Social Habits Entering the 21st Century

There is a vast array of neighborhoods and communities that comprise Greater Los Angeles, most of which provide a familiar environment for the many ethnic groups that inhabit Southern California. Signs in different languages mark neighborhoods by their ethnic designations: Koreatown, Little Ethiopia, Crenshaw District (African American), Little Saigon, Little India, Chinatown, and the Hispanic barrio. Glendale is considered to be largely Armenian, just as Monterey Park has a predominantly Asian population.

Since the 1940s, Jewish families have been moving to what is known as the Westside of Los Angeles or north into the San Fernando Valley. The Westside area can be defined by the

A volunteer reading to a Spanish-speaking child as part of the KOREH L.A. literacy program to teach English, coordinated by the Jewish Federation Council

Rabbi Alfred Wolf joins Elie Wiesel (left) and Ida Nudel, Soviet Jewry activist

principally white and affluent population, which geographically extends westward from La Brea or Fairfax Avenue to the Pacific Ocean. Within this area are large, single family homes in neighborhoods like Beverly Hills, Bel Air, Cheviot Hills, Brentwood and the Pacific Palisades. These new sections became attractive to Jews because they were not far from earlier settlements like Boyle Heights, and offered better housing and new job opportunities. Much of the financial strength of Westside Jews came from their involvement in the film industry, television, suburban real estate development, and savings-and-loan operations. Increasingly, Jews also began to move into the San Fernando Valley, seeking a more suburban life style.

Bruce Phillips, demographer and associate of the Hebrew Union College, analyzes the changes in living patterns of the Jews in Southern California in his 2006 paper entitled: *Faultlines: The Seven Socio-Ecologies of Jewish Los Angeles*. He notes that in the period between 1979 and 1996, the greatest growth in Jewish population was in the Valley Hills, followed by West Los Angeles and the West Valley.

Phillips states that the most widely recognized Jewish area in Los Angeles is the Fairfax and Pico-Robertson district, readily

Richard (Dick) Ziman and his father, Charlie (a Lithuanian immigrant from Chicago) honored for their philanthropy

Elliott Broidy, at his bar mitzvah, Wilshire Blvd. Temple (1970). Today, he is one of America's leading investors in Israel

identifiable by Hebrew signs for various businesses such as bakeries, delis, Israeli and kosher restaurants, bookstores and Judaica shops. Many Orthodox synagogues are located on Pico Boulevard and LaBrea (within the Fairfax area). Just to the north of the Fairfax district in West Hollywood there is a substantial Russian émigré presence.

In an analysis of the changing age demographics, Phillips concludes that Los Angeles Jewry has aged since 1979, with the percentage of the Jewish population aged 65 and older doubling from 12 percent to 23 percent. Meanwhile, at the other end of the age spectrum, the proportion of children in the Jewish population declined significantly between 1979 and 1996 from 22 percent to 15 percent. The aging of the Los Angeles Jewish population is also evident in the changing household composition, which indicates that the proportion of younger households declined from 28 percent to 16 percent. In 1979 households with children had an average of 1.7 children per family, but in 1996 this ratio had declined to 0.9 children per family.

Bruce Phillips concludes that affluent Jewish suburbs such as West Los Angeles and the Valley Hills are the "most Jewish" sections of Los Angeles. Older suburbs are typically thought of as aging in place from the "baby boomers" that settled there in the post war era. The young couples that moved there in the 1940s and 1950s and raised their children there have remained and become "empty nesters." Due to the growth of the Santa Clarita Valley suburbs, the proportion of households with children in this area has steadily increased.

The most surprising change in population distribution occurred in the Urban neighborhoods, historically the oldest and therefore expected to die out as the Jewish residents aged. However, instead of getting older, the Urban neighborhoods have experienced a familial regeneration. The proportion of households with children in the Urban area doubled, due to an increase of young families moving into the neighborhoods.

A similar rebirth is taking place in downtown Los Angeles, which is quite a challenge given that the city (and adjacent suburbs) is so spread out. Robin Pogrebin in an article published in the *Los Angeles Times* (April 25, 2006), writes "It isn't easy to create a real downtown district, vibrant and intense, in a city as sprawling and diffuse as Los Angeles, [as architect] Frank Gehry admits. But that's what he has set out to do with his design for Grand Avenue." Gehry's $750 million project, which includes the first high-rise buildings he has ever designed for the city, is the first phase of a nearly $2 billion development plan being built with several related companies, with their goal to remake Grand Avenue as a pedestrian-based gathering point and to develop a community within the downtown area.

The plan calls for a final project that will constitute nine acres, and will be built in three phases, the first to be completed by 2009. The project will ultimately include 400,000 square feet of retail space, a 275-room hotel and up to 2600 residences. The Grand Avenue project will create a new downtown upscale community as well as a new destination for the Southland's 17 million residents and 24 million annual visitors. The completion of the final design in 2014 provides for plazas and walkways that will connect the Grand Avenue neighborhood to the city's downtown cultural center, which includes the Disney Concert Hall, the Music Center, the Colburn School, and the Museum of Contemporary Art.

Residents of the city are excited and enthusiastic about the design and development of a new downtown, including many in the Jewish community who can see the advantages of the individual residential aspects as well as the commercial and professional opportunities. Clearly the City of Angels has come full circle—from the original Main Street area in 1850, made up of dusty unpaved streets and mud and straw small sheds and adobe huts, to today's redesign of downtown Los Angeles into a modern 21st Century contemporary city of steel and glass skyscrapers. Angelenos will once again celebrate its uniqueness as a city, as the dramatic redesign of the city's downtown area will transform Los Angeles into a state-of-the-art megalopolis.

What remains constant for the citizens of Los Angeles is the same pioneer spirit that the earliest Jewish settlers in the 1800s demonstrated as they began their great adventure to the enchanting coast on the western seaboard of the United States. They came with dreams and determination and a deep hunger to fulfill their desires in the golden land of opportunity and natural resources, a land of sunshine and beauty, a magical place that invited health and restored vitality. These early pioneers built new lives and new homes and began a history that developed into a city that today would rival any of the major metropolises of the world. Now,

Sherrill C. Corwin (left to right), Steve and Frances Broidy, and Theodore E. Cummings at Cedars-Sinai event

as we reflect on the magnificence of that history of the past, we eagerly look into the future and the creation of dreams of the generations to follow.

The star-struck and stargazers are still coming to Los Angeles, while the Jewish community's inventiveness, creativity and exuberant energy sparks the growth and development of the city. But what of the future of Jewish life in the city built by Harris Newmark and his contemporaries?

While there is a contingent of Americans that believe that the nation's Jews are confronting groundbreaking issues around intermarriage and communal apathy, there are strong signs emanating from Los Angeles that these opinions misunderstand the evolution

Stanley Black (left) with his father Jack, enjoys a few days in Palm Springs, a popular vacation spot of Los Angelenos

taking place. It is perhaps more accurate to speculate that Los Angeles is breaking new ground and leading the way in an exciting Jewish Renaissance.

Never has there been such an abundance of Jewish music, literature, media, teachings, technology, scientific advancement, business entrepreneurship, culture, sports and educational participation. All of these elements underscore the vitality and vibrancy of the evolution of Jewish life in Los Angeles. Clearly the spirit of the Jewish pioneers of the 1850s is thriving as we enter the new millennium and discover the mysteries of the future and explore the unknown in the 21st Century.

The 1994 Earthquake Sparks Memories of Jewish History
by Rabbi William Kramer

The following edited article, written by Jewish history expert Rabbi William Kramer, underscores the quick response of the Los Angeles Jewish community following the devastating earthquake of 1994.

Los Angeles' upside may center on sunshine, previously clean and healthy air, and the gift of sun; the major downside must be earthquakes. If we analyze the citizenry reaction to earthquake destruction, both physically and mentally, we can better comprehend what makes the community, and specifically the Jewish community, tick. We begin with the earthquake of 1855 through and including the rocker of 1994, which will bring us to the current days.

The classic history recorded in *Sixty Years in Southern California, 1853-1913*, which contains the reminiscences of Harris Newmark, is a source of the area's earthquake history. Newmark recalled the first earthquake that he experienced which occurred on July 11, 1855.

He described it:

> Almost every structure in Los Angeles was damaged, and some of the walls were left with large cracks. Near San Gabriel, the adobe in which Hugo Reid's Indian wife [died in 1889] dwelt was wrecked, notwithstanding that it had walls four feet thick, with great beams of lumber drawn from the mountains of San Bernardino. In certain spots, the ground rose; in others it fell; and with the rising and falling, down came chimneys, shelves full of saleable stock or household necessities, pictures and even parts of roofs, while water in barrels, and also in several of the [irrigation] zanjas, bubbled and splashed and overflowed. Again, on the 14th of April, the 2nd of May and the 20th of September of the following year, we were alarmed by recurring and more or less continuous shocks that, however, did little or no damage.

> It was on the morning of January 9, 1857 that another serious earthquake came to the Southland. It occurred about 8:30 in the morning and at first the tremors were light, but then the shocks increased moving from north to south.

> The quake grew in power until houses were deserted, men, women and children sought refuge in the streets, and horses and cattle broke loose in wild alarm. For perhaps two, or two and a half minutes, the temblor continued and much damage was done. Los Angeles felt the disturbance far less than many other places, although five to six shocks were noted and twenty times during the week people were frightened from their homes, at Temple's *rancho* and at Fort Tejon, great rents were opened in the earth and then closed again, piling up a heap or dune of finely powdered stone and dirt. Large trees were uprooted and hurled down the hillsides; and tumbling after them went the cattle.

Los Angeles experienced another big shocker on March 26, 1872. Newmark described it as "an earthquake of sufficient force to throw people out of bed." He told how many adults and youngsters ran out of their houses "seeking safety" wearing only their nightclothes.

Los Angeles Helps San Francisco, 1906

A chapter in Newmark's book is devoted to the San Francisco earthquake-fire of 1906. The news came to Los Angeles in the early morning of April 18, and the populace was quickly apprised. Angelenos went to the newspaper and telegraph offices for information. At the latter more than a thousand telegrams were filed though none could be sent to the Bay City.

Los Angeles began to comprehend how paralyzing to her sister cities must have been the wreck and ruin following, first, the shaking of the earth, and then the much more serious fires and explosions. Soon too, refugees from the North commenced flocking into our city; and these thousands, none with complete and few with decent attire, each pleading pathetically for assistance, told the sad tale much more frankly than could the noisy newsboy, with his flaring headlines and shrill, intermittent "Extra!"

Los Angeles reacted with great generosity both on individual and corporate basis. The local press raised funds. The Chamber of Commerce, the Board of Trade and the Merchants and Manufacturers contributed. A quarter of a million dollars was raised. Maurice H. Newmark, Harris's son, chaired a local relief committee, which on a day's notice "had assembled fourteen carloads of goods, partly donated and partly sold to the Committee at cost, to go by rail, and nine carloads to go from San Pedro by water. This train full of necessaries was the first relief of its kind that reached San Francisco; other shipments of supplies followed daily...."

Jewish Educational Sites Hit in 1994

Several major Jewish learning centers of differing academic levels and denominations were severely impacted by the Northridge quake. The University of Judaism, for example, barely survived with massive loss. A University spokesperson, Mimi Sells, announced, "It's a total mess here." And in his evaluation of the scene at the University, President Robert Wexler expressed relief that no one was injured. Then in viewing the site he lamented, "It looks as if a bomb went off."

Jewish Institutions and Centers React

A letter of January 28, 1994 from the Valley Jewish Business Leaders Association, a support group of the Jewish Home for the Aging, reported that all of the Home's facilities had been declared structurally safe. However, the facilities did lack electricity for three days and water and gas for five.

There was a great deal of mechanical and cosmetic damage. The residents and the Home's 650 employees "were rather complacent about the shaking. There was no panic and no change of routine." The residents' responses are summarized in the following testimony, "We've seen a lot of *tsuris* [trouble] in our lifetime, this is just one more." Rabbi William Gordon of the Eisenberg Village Campus of the Home conducted an ecumenical service for residents and employees shortly after the seismic event.

[Among the many facilities that were badly damaged]: Bernard Milken Community Campus, in the West San Fernando Valley, which includes a full Jewish center housing many of the Jewish community agencies; in Simi Valley, an area that was hard hit, the famed Brandeis-Bardin Institute described as "an educational retreat complex;" the Freda Mohr Center of the Jewish Family Service, which serves Jews in the Fairfax area; the Jewish Community Building on Wilshire Boulevard in Mid-Wilshire. There was damage at the various Jewish cemeteries throughout the affected area. The oldest Jewish cemetery, Home of Peace Memorial Park in East Los Angeles had over $300,000 in damage. Many of its Jewish community's 19th Century pioneers are buried there, as are a number of leading Hollywood figures. The quake toppled 438 granite and marble headstones that had been put in place between the 1920s and the 1950s.

Jewish-Rooted Hospitals and Medical Centers

The City of Hope, a medical facility famed for its research at Duarte near Los Angeles, offered its assistance, both in terms of facilities and personnel at the time of the quake. It accentuated its disaster planning to provide safety factors for patients and others at its large campus. Particularly important was the provision of "pole-less litters," which are compact stretchers that can be unfolded to provide transportation for disaster victims to take them to places of safety and centers for medical triage where their needs could be evaluated and they could be directed to special help.

Cedars-Sinai Medical Center has served the public's emergency needs over the years during loss brought about by disasters such as earthquakes, fire, and crime on the streets, rioting, and carnage on the roads. With forethought, the 1976 structure had been designed as "one of the most earthquake-safe facilities in the country." On January 17, 1994 it turned out to be a true statement. The main building "experienced some broken water pipes and fallen tiles but

Freeway damage seriously impacted transportation, 1994

remained structurally sound. Fortunately, the Emergency Room facilities were able to serve double the patient load after the 6.8 temblor. However, the Schuman Building, which antedated the new structure and was originally Mt. Sinai Hospital and the Halper Building facility had to be evacuated after sustaining considerable structural damage. An early estimate declared that Cedars-Sinai sustained $40 million in damages.

The Jewish Federation Council Helps the Community to Rebound

Soon after public utilities were reinstated, the Federation made mobilized efforts to assist the community. In a flyer that was made available at gathering places of the Jewish community, it was announced that they would be holding two "Disaster Relief Forums." The agenda was the same at both. The forums featured experts from the community at large, the Jewish community, and governmental agencies and gave pertinent guidance toward locating emergency food and financial assistance, as well as managing tax issues and insurance claims.

Joining forces with the Federation in presenting these forums were the Jewish Community Centers Association, the Jewish Vocational Service, the Bet Tzedek Legal Services, the Southern California Board of Rabbis, the Jewish Family Service of Los Angeles and the Jewish Family Service of Santa Monica.

Residential earthquake damage was severe, 1994

Getting Kosher Food to Those in Need

[It was important to get food to] those needing immediate food services…. The SOVA Kosher Food Pantry in West Los Angeles had food supplies for its area and adjacent Santa Monica. And the Hirsh Family Kosher Kitchen of the Jewish Family Service responded to an urgent call from the Red Cross of Santa Monica to provide kosher meals at its makeshift shelter…. Kosher quake relief was provided also at Young Israel of Beverly Hills. Young Israel, located near the Pico-Robertson area, where several apartment complexes became uninhabitable "became de facto, the community 'shelter' for dozens of displaced youths."

The Rabbis' Board also sent a letter to its membership regarding Passover observance. It noted that "a limited amount of money, drawn from Jewish Community Disaster Relief Funds" would be made available to assist synagogues and centers, to welcome unaffiliated Jews to Seders under their auspices. Some funds were also available for needy people seeking help at Pesach for non-earthquake reasons.

As bad as it was, the earthquake did seem to many as only a rehearsal. Los Angeles County Sheriff Sherman Block, a member of the Jewish community said, "The lesson to be learned before the Big One is stark, but real." Sheriff Block felt that the January 17 earthquake represented a charitable warning in that it was not greater and so the citizenry could learn from it how to prepare for the Big One.

CHAPTER TEN

Jewish Renaissance:
The Future of Jewish Los Angeles

The perseverance and phenomenal accomplishments of those [Jewish] pioneers exemplify the survival instincts that have defined the Jewish people since the days of Abraham and Jacob.

"Califreakinfornia" is the sassy quote on a stack of exclusive designer shirts on display in Bloomingdale's trendy boutique at 60th and Lexington in Manhattan. This unique and clever play on words graphically epitomizes the free spirited on-the-edge image that many people have about California—home of the stargazing, and dream-seeking Angelenos. While it is amusing to have fun with the images of Southern California, those who live here are very serious and practical about their day-to-day lives and the opportunities available to them and to their children.

An analysis of the Los Angeles Jewish community, predicts that it will continue to spread out geographically into Ventura, Orange and Riverside counties and well as northern Los Angeles County. The heart of Jewish life for Los Angeles, however, will find its epicenter where the 405 Freeway and the Santa Monica Mountains converge—the Westside of Los Angeles and the south and west San Fernando Valley. Although satellite areas and communities with energetic synagogue congregations and community centers are likely to develop in other suburban areas, the hub of the Jewish expansion will be on the Westside and the Valley

. The vision of Jewish historians and demographers is that the Jewish community will grow and prosper in southern California. Currently there are more than 100 synagogues in the

Los Angeles "Birthright Israel" participants reflect the desire of the Jewish Federation of Los Angeles to engage the next generation as supporters of Israel

Southland and these will increase in number as the Jewish population expands and finds new space in the suburbs and rural areas. Accompanying this expansion will be a simultaneous growth in Jewish day schools to accommodate the increase in children seeking an education within the Jewish culture. Colleges and institutions of higher education will also be developed finding new avenues to grow and partner with universities such as UCLA, USC, and the University of Judaism. The same pioneer spirit that pushed into new spaces and widened city boundaries in the early days of Los Angeles will continue to open new areas of Jewish family growth and education.

UCLA Professor David Myers comments on the subject of Jewish education: "We've seen an emptying out of the Los Angeles public school system of Jews for a variety of reasons, and one of the salutary effects of that has been (and I think it is lamentable), that the public school has lost so many Jewish students. But one of the things that has come out of that is a substantial expansion of the Jewish day schools. This, I think, relates to broader trends of American Jewish social life. A generation earlier it was not considered a virtue to go to a Jewish day school. It was a virtue to go to a public school and integrate into the Jewish mainstream."

Professor Myers continues, "[There have been] different responses to Jewish culture, now we see in the third generation there is the desire to go back and recapture the original authentic Jewish culture. I think to a certain extent we are observing this in the Jewish day school movement. We are seeing the grandchildren or great-grandchildren of the first immigrants saying 'we feel somewhat removed from Jewish tradition. We know it is valuable, and we want our children to be the beneficiaries of that chain of transmission.' One of the interesting things we are seeing in Jewish education today in Los Angeles and around the country is a reversal in that chain of transmission. Now it is the *kids* that go to the Jewish day schools who are teaching their parents Jewish literacy, knowledge, and ritual. Consequently we are seeing a considerable expansion in the growth of Jewish day schools. We have also seen an expansion in Jewish institutions of higher education. [For example], in the Hebrew Union College and the University of Judaism we have witnessed the emergence of two very substantial institutions of Jewish culture."

"It's hard for me to look at Los Angeles objectively," Rabbi Will Kramer confided, "the same way that it would be hard for me to look at my parents or my children or siblings objectively. Jewish life in Los Angeles has the same problems as the general community. We are natives and strangers like everybody else. In Los Angeles, you become a native here in about six months. And you could be a stranger all your life even if you're born here.

"It's a city perhaps built on sand, not only figuratively, but literally. The watered desert we live in. We Jews have an affinity for deserts. I think because we have spent some time in them historically. Maybe the city of Los Angeles is a perpetual Pesach. We are in the desert and we try to get out of the desert since we have a vision of the sea—the Mediterranean or the Pacific....

"The best thing about Los Angeles is that it continues to fight for its life and continues to live. The worst thing about being in Los Angeles is the same "curse" of Jewish life throughout America, which is indifference or apathy. We used to worry about Jews converting out, but it is not a problem of converting to another religion, it is indifference to all religions. This is where it is necessary for us to play a role. We must get the word out; the word must be attractive and one that will please people. We have to realize what all rabbis need to realize, that he or she is not only in the business of education but also in 'showbiz.' We must be entertaining and charming. The rabbi needs to sell the merchandise along with preparing and packaging it. Judaism without a ribbon in this town is not Judaism anymore."

Since the very beginning when Jewish immigrants came to this new land of opportunity, sunshine, and freedom, arriving from Europe, Rhodes, Israel (Palestine), the Soviet Union, Iran and other parts of the world, these "foreigners" have played a fundamental and valuable role in creating what Los Angeles is today and also what it will become in the future.

Irving Berlin

One of these Jewish immigrants, Israel Bellin, better known as Irving Berlin, came to Hollywood to create music for the movies, to put into words what this country meant to him and to all of its citizens. Despite the fact that Congress declined to accept Berlin's inspirational lyrics as the new national anthem in 1946, it was a Jewish immigrant who could best put into words the passion and meaning that freedom and opportunity represented in this great nation. Berlin's song, *God Bless America*, has become an anthem of love and respect, a sacred hymn to his beloved new country.

Irving Berlin's words echo and project the dreams of pioneers who came in the 1850s, just as the new immigrants and transplanted citizens of the world arrive today with their dreams.

But what about Los Angeles today and looking forward into the future? The Jewish Renaissance is currently underway as Jewish organizations wrestle with the rapid changes imposed on them by high-speed advancements in mass communication and the explosive movement forward in technology and computer access. The Jewish pioneers of Los Angeles, in coping with and conquering the obstacles and the hardships of their era, laid a solid foundation for the remarkable growth and innovation occurring in the City of Angels at the present time. The perseverance and phenomenal accomplishments of those pioneers exemplify the survival instincts that have defined the Jewish people since the days of Abraham and Jacob.

The history of Jewish Los Angeles, as it is being written today, continues to be filled with challenges and creativity, with hopes and dreams for future generations, and new paths to explore and conquer for the young Jewish leaders of tomorrow. The present environment provides us with another exciting and compelling chapter in the impressive adventure documenting the Jewish influence in Los Angeles. Today's activities depict yet another dimension in the evolution of a culture victoriously meeting the challenges and demonstrating the success of the modern-day pioneers in "wrestling with the angels."

The following pages present capsule descriptions of many of the Jewish organizations and their views looking forward in the development of the Jewish community. These pages were submitted by each of the organizations, all of which participated in sponsoring this project and helped to make this book possible. We, along with all of the Jewish community in Los Angeles, are grateful for the dedication and continuing passion and inspiration provided by those who contribute to the achievement of these organizations, today and in the future.

Cedars-Sinai Medical Center

Since its inception more than 100 years ago, Cedars-Sinai has evolved to become the largest nonprofit hospital in the western United States—an academic medical center that is internationally renowned for compassionate, high-quality medical care, research, education, and community service. Cedars-Sinai's mission is founded in the ethical and cultural precepts of the Judaic tradition, which inspire devotion to the art and science of healing and to the care we give our patients and staff.

In 1902, as the result of Jewish community concern about meeting the health needs of a growing Los Angeles community, Kaspare Cohn Hospital, predecessor of Cedars of Lebanon, opened on the east side of Los Angeles. In 1930 the hospital moved to Fountain Avenue, where it opened as Cedars of Lebanon Hospital.

Meanwhile, the Bikur Cholim Society opened a two-room hospice in 1918, which was the predecessor of the Mount Sinai Home for the Incurables. Over the years, it grew and eventually became Mount Sinai Hospital, located on Beverly Boulevard, future site of Cedars-Sinai Medical Center.

In 1961, following years of study, the decision was made to merge Cedars of Lebanon and Mount Sinai hospitals under the name of Cedars-Sinai Medical Center. New buildings were constructed, and the first patients were moved into Cedars-Sinai Medical Center on April 3, 1976.

Today, Cedars-Sinai consistently ranks among America's top medical centers, and for more than 18 consecutive years has been rated as Los Angeles' best hospital in an independent survey of local residents.

In addition to its high-quality patient care, medical research and education programs, Cedars-Sinai is known for its many partnerships with local organizations who work together with Cedars-Sinai to improve the health of the community.

City of Hope

City of Hope is an innovative biomedical research, treatment, and educational institution dedicated to the prevention and cure of cancer and other life threatening diseases. It was founded in 1913 by a community of Jewish garment workers as a haven for those stricken with tuberculosis. Working under the auspices of the Jewish Consumptive Relief Association of Southern California (JCRA), their intent was to create a nonsectarian refuge that would care for and be supported by people in all walks of life and of every race, religion and creed.

Originally a small, local volunteer organization, it grew into a vibrant national movement. In 1914, the group purchased land in Duarte, California, and over the years raised funds from various trade union and Jewish organizations to build a thriving campus. At their 1946 convention, the governing members voted to transform the institution from a tuberculosis sanatorium into a national medical center dedicated to fighting cancer and other diseases.

Since then, City of Hope has come to mean better health for people around the world. It established one of the first, and now largest, bone marrow transplantation programs in the nation. In 1978, recombinant DNA technology developed at City of Hope led to synthetic insulin now used by diabetics worldwide. Only five years later, a grant from Arnold and Mabel Beckman established City of Hope's Beckman Research Institute, further strengthening the research programs. The National Cancer Institute designated City of Hope as a comprehensive cancer center in 1998. The ultra-modern Helford Clinical Research Hospital, opened at City of Hope in 2005, is the latest sign of the organization's ascent.

Throughout the nearly 100 years of its history, volunteer chapters and auxiliaries have continued to support and strengthen the organization. And today, City of Hope is internationally recognized for its unique, life-saving treatments and scientific achievements. This innovation is coupled with a strong culture of compassion for all humanity—the consistent driving force behind the organization since its founding.

Hillside Memorial Park and Mortuary

A celebrity who was buried twice, two brothers who understood the importance of memorializing loved ones, and a synagogue committed to the Jewish community are all part of the tapestry of Hillside Memorial Park and Mortuary's history.

What we know as Hillside Memorial Park and Mortuary today began on May 23, 1941, when B'nai B'rith Memorial Park was incorporated by Robert and Harry Groman and Lazare F. Bernhard. Nearly a year later, the park was renamed Hillside Memorial Park. In 1957, the Park was acquired by Temple Israel of Hollywood.

Robert and Harry were the sons of Charles Groman, who in 1929 joined Louis Glasband to form Glasband-Groman-Glasband, the first licensed Jewish mortuary west of Chicago. Groman's sons worked to provide the Jewish community of Southern California with a beautiful memorial park and customized services for those who have passed on and for their loved ones and friends to visit.

After entertainer Al Jolson's death in 1950, he was buried at Beth Olam Cemetery in Hollywood. A crowd of 20,000 listened as George Jessel delivered the eulogy.

But Erle Jolson, his widow, was unhappy. The cemetery refused to allow the family to build the memorial they wanted to honor Al Jolson. Hearing this, the Gromans let her know that at Hillside, she could build such a memorial.

Eleven months later Al Jolson was honored with a second funeral and interment at an elegant domed, columned hillside memorial designed by architect Paul R. Williams, FAIA. The memorial

Memorial site of Al Jolson

rises above a 120-foot waterfall that Hillside provided, honoring Jolson's last wishes.

More than 60,000 people have been laid to rest at Hillside Memorial Park. Doctors, lawyers, entertainers, business people, scientists, athletes, politicians, parents, children and beloved family members—many internationally and nationally renowned individuals who have helped shape our community, our culture and Jewish life in Los Angeles.

Tradition tells us that to create a Jewish community, a school, a synagogue and a cemetery are needed. Hillside Memorial Park and Mortuary has created a place of beauty and serenity where the Jewish community of Los Angeles can honor those who are no longer with us.

Jewish Big Brothers Big Sisters

Jewish Big Brothers Big Sisters is Los Angeles' premier mentoring agency. Founded in 1915, our mission is to assist children without adequate resources, from disadvantaged, or single-parent homes, to achieve their full potential by providing "Excellence in Mentoring" through a myriad of programs and services, including:

- Jewish Big Brothers Big Sisters, which offers one-to-one adult mentors for boys and girls ages six to eighteen within a Jewish context, providing an additional positive adult role model where there may not be one present in the child's life.

- Camp Max Straus, founded in 1938, is a non-denominational, multi-racial, residential summer camping experience, primarily for under-served children ages seven through twelve.

- Scholarship Programs offer financial assistance to motivated and deserving former Little Brothers, Little Sisters and participants in the CMS Witherbee Wilderness program who are pursuing goals of post-secondary education.

- Sports Buddies and Arts Buddies are seasonal group mentoring programs for inner-city children, ages seven to twelve, which enable children to experience positive relationships with peers and adults through informal team sports or art instruction. Working with teen and adult volunteers, the children learn life skills necessary for self-respect, integrity, and positive peer relationships.

- School Based Mentoring is our newest program, matching High School mentors with middle school mentees.

Statistics show that the work of Jewish Big Brothers Big Sisters of Los Angeles has a significant impact on the children that participate: 52 percent less likely to skip school, 46 percent less likely to begin using drugs, 27 percent less likely to begin drinking, and 33 percent less likely to act out violently towards others.

Today, our goal is to continue enriching the lives of children by providing mentoring programs that develop self-esteem, self-respect, and relationship building skills.

Cathy Siegel Weiss, the Jewish Community Foundation's chair, and Marvin Schotland, The Foundation's president and CEO, with some of the many young visitors to the Zimmer Children's Museum. A premier U.S. Jewish children's museum, founded in 1991, it is one of numerous organizations and projects established through Foundation seed funding

The Jewish Community Foundation

The Jewish Community Foundation was established in Los Angeles in 1954 from the efforts of a small but dedicated group of Jewish leaders who, in a time of post war prosperity, had the wisdom to plan for the community's future needs. Today we are a multi-faceted institution overseeing charitable assets of more than $600 million and a far-reaching grants program. We are dedicated to enhancing the scope and effectiveness of our 1,200 plus donors' philanthropy, in both the Jewish community and beyond, as we build permanent resources for the community.

Over the years, The Foundation has seeded many innovative programs and initiatives in the community, funded capital projects of Jewish institutions, and provided relief assistance during emergencies. To meet our community's ever-evolving needs, we collaborate with a wide range of nonprofits, including the Jewish Federation and its agencies. We gave critical early support to such valued community institutions as Bet Tzedek Legal Services, Beit T'Shuvah, SOVA Kosher Food Pantry, Zimmer Children's Museum, Israel Experience Program, and StandWithUs.

The impact of our partnerships in building infrastructure for Jewish Los Angeles has been especially dramatic. We provided substantial support for the Federation Building at 6505 Wilshire Boulevard; the Bernard Milken Jewish Community Campus in West San Fernando Valley; the Valley Cities and North Valley Jewish Community Centers; Hillel Centers at college campuses in Greater L.A.; Jewish Family Service of L.A.'s Valley Storefront; the Jewish Home for the Aging's Menorah Village; and youth facilities at many Jewish summer camps.

In just the last decade (1996-2005), we also helped make possible the purchase, construction, renovation or expansion of more than 25 Jewish schools including Emek Hebrew Academy, Heschel Day School, and Valley Beth Shalom Day School; and high schools including Shalhevet, Stephen S. Wise—Milken, and Yeshivah University of Los Angeles.

The Foundation's great strength continues to be the many individuals, families, and institutions that share our commitment to the continued vitality of our community— today, tomorrow, and for generations to come.

Jewish Federation of Greater Los Angeles

For thousands of years, the Jewish people have been held together by two things: the laws and rituals set forth in the Torah and Talmud; and a way of life experienced through the *kehillah*, the community.

The notion of a communal fund came out of the Jewish experience of persecution and discrimination. This uniquely Jewish self-supporting communal infrastructure helped fulfill a Jewish mandate to help the less fortunate. Community trustees divided the funds among a plethora of welfare providers. From the burial society to the soup kitchen to the dowry fund for poor girls, a communal organization existed to fit virtually every need, allowing both recipient and donor to remain anonymous. The communal fund was the ultimate safety net for Jews who, throughout the centuries from poverty to pogroms, lived through difficult times.

In 1911, a network of Los Angeles Jewish community institutions was brought under the umbrella of the Federation of Jewish Charities. Adapted from the centuries-old Jewish communal fund, the Federation's function was to consolidate independent fundraising campaigns and coordinate community services.

Today, the Jewish Federation of Greater Los Angeles serves a Jewish population of more than 520,000, the second-largest Jewish community in North America.

The Federation identifies and funds social service, educational, and humanitarian needs locally, in Israel, and around the world. Through its network of agencies and programs, the Federation helps alleviate Jewish poverty, provides emergency relief, ensures a Jewish future, and supports the greater Los Angeles community.

Last year, the Federation enabled 3,000 Holocaust survivors to live in dignity; helped 31,000 children receive a Jewish education; fed 40,000 hungry people in our city. Abroad, the Federation helped nearly 25,000 Jews immigrate to Israel; provided life's most basic needs for 250,000 destitute elderly Jews in the former Soviet Union; and served the only hot meal of the day to 50,000 Israeli children that could not afford adequate meals.

The Federation beneficiary agencies and others are tiles in the broader mosaic that comprises the Los Angeles Jewish community. The Jewish Federation is the glue that holds together the many efforts to build a Jewish future—here in Los Angeles, and around the world.

Los Angeles Jewish Home for the Aging

The Los Angeles Jewish Home for the Aging has been caring for seniors in need for nearly a century. From humble beginnings in 1912, when a small group of caring Angelenos gave shelter and hope to five homeless Jewish men at Passover, the Home has grown to one of the country's leading providers of facilities and programs for the elderly.

Our commitment to excellence in eldercare is at the core of everything we do, applying the most advanced knowledge of senior care in innovative settings reflecting the spirit of Jewish values. Believing that days filled with companionship, joy, and purpose are both life-enhancing and life-extending, we offer seniors a vibrant, nurturing environment. Days at the Jewish Home are filled with art, music, education, daily exercises, and a myriad of social activities.

The Jewish Home continues to grow and change in response to dramatic shifts in society, the most important of which is the explosive growth of America's elderly population. With Los Angeles having the fewest number of senior-care beds per capita for the Jewish community of any major city, we are expanding our capacity and community programs to meet the growing numbers of seniors for quality care facilities and supporting services.

As a result, the Home embarked on an ambitious program to benefit the seniors of Los Angeles and is in the midst of the most dramatic expansion in our history. The first milestone, the Goldenberg-Ziman Special Care Center (pictured above), opened in 2002 and is an award-winning, state-of-the-art facility for victims of Alzheimers disease and related dementia.

The new 2006 Joyce Eisenberg-Keefer Medical Center, featuring a geriatric psychiatric unit, will increase the Home's capacity by 20 percent. This new Center will be the nation's most advanced facility promoting "healthy aging" concepts in senior living. For nearly 100 years, the Los Angeles Jewish Home for the Aging has been lifting spirits, restoring health, and making the richness of life blossom every day for our elderly. Plans continue with expansion and growth focused on assuring our community's elderly enjoy life in modern facilities representative of Los Angeles' creativity and energy and reflective of the spirit of the third largest Jewish community in the world.

Young people hold American and Israeli flags in the pre-game ceremony for Jewish Community Day held annually at Dodger Stadium, sponsored and organized by Blazer Communications

The Los Angeles Jewish News • Blazer Communications

Blazer Communications was established over forty years ago in 1965, with the creation of its Jewish-Israeli music and comedy radio program. Today, Phil Blazer continues to host his successful weekly Sunday radio program, Jewish Soul.

The Los Angeles Jewish News, a Blazer publication established in 1973, employs a news-magazine format focusing on contemporary issues, while presenting a diversity of opinions and editorials, as well as factual news reports covering national, international, and local points of interest. A national edition is published as well. *The Los Angeles Jewish News* is the city's only totally independent Jewish newspaper.

In 1977, Phil Blazer began producing and hosting his weekly Sunday television show, *Jewish Life*, airing on KSCI-TV, Channel 18, a commercial broadcast station that can be seen in every home in the greater Los Angeles area. Celebrating 30 years of providing Jewish content to loyal and enthusiastic television audiences across America, Blazer's program has the honored distinction of being the longest lasting TV program currently airing in Los Angeles, the "entertainment capital of the world."

Relying on the effective impact of a multi-level media approach, the integration of print with broadcast television and radio, allows the Blazer group to powerfully cross promote its unique brand of educational, entertaining, and current information targeting the Jewish community.

In addition to the newspaper, radio and television elements, the media organization also presents popular annual Southern California events that include Jewish Community Days at Dodger Stadium and the Los Angeles Zoo, and the International Jewish Film Festival. Blazer and his company have written and published several books important to the history and culture of the Jewish people: *Herzl, Pioneers of Israel*, and the current book, *Wrestling with the Angels: A History of Jewish Los Angeles*.

Blazer Communications is in the midst of developing its most ambitious media project to date, the establishment of a 24/7 Jewish television channel for the United States, JLTV, featuring news, sports, movies, documentaries, and educational programs.

Jimmy Delshad, Soloman Gabbay, Parviz Nazarian, Bijan Nahai, Ebrahim Simhaee (left to right)

Magbit Foundation of Greater Los Angeles

The Magbit Foundation of Greater Los Angeles (Magbit) was established in 1990 by members of the Iranian Jewish community in Los Angeles to help fellow Jews settle in Israel, and to show our appreciation and support for our Israeli brothers and sisters who live on the front lines of the fight for the survival of our Jewish homeland. In order to promote these worthwhile goals, Magbit has focused its efforts on enabling students to obtain higher education in the State of Israel.

Magbit accomplishes this goal through its innovative "interest-free loan" program for disadvantaged qualified students. This program was designed to preserve the dignity and spirit of the students, as well as to instill in them a sense of responsibility. The loan recipients repay the loans when they are financially able to do so. The loan repayments go directly to the student's university, not to Magbit, so that future generations of students may also benefit from these funds.

Through 2005, Magbit has provided more than $6 million in loans to over 6,000 students in universities throughout Israel, such as Bar-Ilan University, Ben Gurion University, Jerusalem College of Technology, Hadassah College Jerusalem, Haifa University, Technion-Israel Institute of Technology, Tel-Hai College, and Tel-Aviv University.

In addition to helping students through the "interest-free loan" program, Magbit also helps Israel through grants and other fundraising activities. Most notably, in 2002 Magbit contributed over $1 million directly to Israel's victims of terrorism.

Among other programs, each year Magbit organizes a Gala dinner to honor Israel Independence Day. The annual Gala is major source of fundraising for the foundation.

Magbit's mission is to support Israel by nurturing the Jewish State's most valuable asset—its youth.

Leonard Lawrence, general manager of Mount Sinai Memorial Parks and Mortuaries, welcomes Holocaust survivors Eva David (center) and Cyla Tennenbaum (right). David and Tennenbaum are members of Cafe Europa, a survivors' group which convenes each spring at Mount Sinai in Hollywood Hills for Yom HaShoah. In the background is Mount Sinai's Heritage Mosaic, illustrating some of the important contributors to America's Jewish history.

Mount Sinai Memorial Parks and Mortuaries

From ancient times our rabbis have taught that one of the primary duties of a Jewish community is to establish and maintain an appropriately consecrated site for memorialization and burial. The first Jewish cemetery in Los Angeles, Home of Peace, was established in 1855 and today there are 21 Jewish cemeteries dotting the landscape from East Los Angeles to Simi Valley.

Mount Sinai Memorial Park in the Hollywood Hills adjacent to Burbank, California was formally consecrated as a Jewish Memorial Park to serve the entire Jewish community, on September 16, 1953 by its founder Forest Lawn. During that ceremony, earth from Mount Zion in Israel was mixed with the earth of Mount Sinai as a symbol of the ancient heritage shared by Jewish people the world over. The Chapel-Mortuary Building was dedicated May 3, 1959, making Mount Sinai the first Jewish cemetery in Los Angeles to have its own mortuary within sacred cemetery grounds—assuring that both funeral services and burial could be provided in one place, under one management.

On March 4, 1964, Sinai Temple, the oldest Conservative congregation in the Southland, acquired ownership of the mortuary and cemetery, making it the first Jewish congregation in the United States to own and operate a cemetery together with a mortuary. On March 16, 1997, Mount Sinai dedicated a second Memorial Park in Simi Valley. This 160 acre site is the largest Jewish cemetery in the western United States, with capacity to serve the Southland's Jewish community for the next 200 years.

The rich history of Mount Sinai Memorial Parks and Mortuaries carries with it an awesome responsibility: that is, to honor life as our teachings and heritage dictate. We support a full spectrum of Jewish burial ritual and practice and offer counsel in accordance with rabbinic guidance and *Halachic* (Jewish law) practices. We support families from every culture and Jewish movement with genuine concern, in a manner that dignifies the living, at the same time as it honors and perpetuates the memory of those who have come before us.

Photograph by Timothy Hursley

The Skirball Cultural Center

The Skirball Cultural Center is an educational institution, established in Los Angeles in 1996, devoted to sustaining and celebrating Jewish heritage and American democratic ideals. The Cultural Center was founded by Rabbi Uri D. Herscher who continues to serve as President and CEO. The Center is guided by a dedicated Board of Trustees, chaired since its inception by Howard I. Friedman, Senior Partner at Loeb and Loeb and past chairman of the American Jewish Committee.

The mission of The Skirball Cultural Center is to explore the connections between four thousand years of Jewish heritage and the vitality of the American democratic ideals. We welcome and seek to inspire people of every ethnic and cultural identity. Guided by our respective memories and experiences, together we aspire to build a society in which all of us can feel at home. The center was named for philanthropists Audrey and Jack H. Skirball who exemplified the Skirball's mission statement in their own lives.

The Skirball Cultural Center, built on 15 acres of land nestled in the Santa Monica Mountains on Sepulveda Boulevard, was designed by renowned architect Moshe Safdie. The 500,000 square feet complex has been admired for its intimate scale and sensitivity to the natural environment. It includes a museum, a performing arts center, conference and lecture halls, classrooms, libraries, courtyards, gardens, an amphitheater, a museum store, and a café. In its first decade the Center welcomed nearly five million visitors, among them 500,000 schoolchildren.

The Skirball's core exhibition, drawn from its permanent collection of 30,000 objects, is entitled "Visions and Values: Jewish Life from Antiquity to America," and traces the experiences and accomplishments of Jews over four thousand years. This unique series of galleries includes multimedia installations, rare artifacts, photographs, interactive computer stations, and sound recordings that lead visitors on the journey of the Jewish people, culminating with their history in the United States. The exhibition presents a story about retaining one's own culture while adapting to life in America.

Vista Del Mar Child & Family Services

Vista Del Mar is proud of its contribution to the Jewish community and is equally proud to be recognized in this volume celebrating the history of Jewish Los Angeles. For nearly 100 years, Vista has provided a safe refuge for children and a place of hope for families. From our days as an orphanage to our current multifaceted mental health facility, we have been, and continue to be, a place to turn to when a special kind of help is needed.

Vista, like the other recognized agencies, was established because in the darkest moments for a child or family, no one else was there. We have been part of a community that has opened its heart and doors in times of someone else's personal crisis. But while people came in crisis, most left with a renewed spirit, a second chance and with hope for their future. 100 years later we are still helping children and families find solutions within an environment of safety and caring.

The names of our board members are well known in this community, recognized as people who believe in making a difference. They created a haven for the child who was at risk; provided an opportunity to become a parent through adoption; built a classroom for the child with special needs; and nurtured an environment that welcomed rather than blamed. Each of our board members feels the pain of a child in need of care, and each feels the joy of that child's success. They have given parents back the child they thought was lost, and a voice to children too young to speak. Our agency would not exist if not for the vision and generosity of our board and supporters.

Vista Del Mar stands as an example of the power of compassion, caring, and dedication. We thank the community for never turning its back when others have turned to us for help. We celebrate our role in the history of the Jewish community and look forward to our next 100 years.

Mrs. Wolf Kalisher, the first president of the Hebrew Ladies' Benevolent Society, photographed in 1870

Virginia Katz, the first secretary of the Hebrew Ladies' Benevolent Society, serving from 1870 for a term of 50 years

Edwin J. Loeb was born in Los Angeles in 1886 to Leon and Estelle Newmark Loeb. Edwin was born in the family home at 7th and Grand in what is now downtown Los Angeles. His father, Leon, was the French consular agent in Los Angeles but resigned in 1898 to protest the French attitude in the Dreyfus case. Edwin and his brother, Joseph, established the respected Los Angeles law firm Loeb and Loeb. Photograph taken in 1890

Caricature of entrepreneur, Harris Newmark, who kept a journal chronicaling his life and reminiscences of the pioneer days in Los Angeles, Sixty Years in Southern California: 1853-1913

The Concordia Club, an elite Jewish social organization, was founded in 1891. Photograph taken at their masquerade ball, 1912

ACKNOWLEDGMENTS

The authors would like to thank the following people who were interviewed for and/or supported this important and ground-breaking project.

Ilene Abramson
Donnie Adlen
Ralph Amado
Hy Arnesty
Seth Aronson
Ron Barnett
William Basch
Terry and Lionel Bell
Sue and Rick Bender
Myron Berliner
Herman Berman
Stephen Breuer
Edythe and Eli Broad
Joe Broady
Steve Broidy
Rabbi Richard Camras
Dvorah Colker
Ehud Danoch, Consul General
Michael Dawson
Jimmy Delshad
Sanford Deutsch
Dr. William Deverill
Rabbi Mark S. Diamond
Frances Dinklespiel
David Dortort
Rabbi Paul Dubin
Norman Eichberg
Hershey Eisenberg
Marshall Ezralow
Evelyn Farb
Robert Feinerman
Irving Feintech
Rabbi Harvey Fields
John Fishel
Harold Foonberg
Molly Forrest
Shelley Freeman
Mark Friedman
Dr. Michael Friedman
Si Frumkin
Sol Galper
Rabbi Robert T. Gan
Arnold Geffner
Rabbi Laura Geller
Jill Glasband

Lillian Goldman
Harvey Goldstein
Pattikay and Meyer Gottlieb
Dorothy and Ossie Goren
Sherman Grancell
John Gray
Marshall Grossman
Marilyn and Monty Hall
William Harmatz
Mike Hersch
Rabbi Eli Herscher
Rabbi Uri Herscher
Gwen and Arthur Hiller
Robert Hirsch
Harriet Hochman
Abe Hoffman
Miriam Hutler
Danny Israely
Charlotte and Ed Kamenir
Arnold Kornfield
Nathan Krems
Trana Labowe
Bob Laemmle
Greg Laemmle
Ellie and Mark Lainer
Chet and John Lappen
Edwin Lasman
Len Lawrence
Pauline Ledeen
Rabbi Stephen Leder
Dr. Elias Lefferman
Henry Leventon
John Newmark Levi, Jr.
Linda Levi
Mel Levine
Shelly Levy
Branko Lustig
Frances Mandel
Leon Morgenstern
Judge Richard Mosk
Dr. David Myers
Ezri Namvar
Steve Needleman
Harris Newmark III
Linda Newton

Lynda Oshin
Bruce Phillips
Rabbi Jacob Pressman
Tom Priselac
Rabbi Joel Rembaum
Robert Rifkind
Harriet Rochlin
Vera and Lewis Rosenberg
Marcia Rosenthal
Steven Rosmarin
Rabbi John L. Rosove
Hal Ross
Rabbi Moshe J. Rothblum
Janet and Maxwell Salter
Rose and Ed Sanders
Steve Sass
Eleanor Scharff
Dena and Irv Schechter
Barry Schiff
Marvin Schotland
Gerry Schubert
Ruth Shukin
Rabbi Harold Shulweiss
Dan Shuster
Minnie Crystal Silver
Tony Simmons
Milton Slade
Jim Small
Karl Sussman
Bradley Tabach-Bank
John Van DeKamp
Rosalind W. Wyman
Dick Volpert
Mamie and Oscar Wasserman
Janet and Henry Waxman
Jonathan Weedman
Jack Weiss
Mark Wild
Karen Wilson
Rabbi David Wolpe
Barbara and Zev Yaroslavsky
Edith Yusem
Rosalie Zalis
Rabbi Isaiah Zeldin
Bruce Zuckerman

REFERENCES

Aron, Bill. (1985). *From the Corners of the Earth.* Philadelphia: Jewish Publication Society.

Cogan, Sara G. (Ed.). (1980). *The Jews of Los Angeles: 1849-1945, Publication 3 – Western Jewish American Series.* Berkeley: Western Jewish History Center Judah L. Magnes Memorial Museum.

DeMarco, Gordon. (1988). *A Short History of Los Angeles.* San Francisco: Lexicos Publishers.

Ebershoff, David. (2003). *Pasadena.* New York: Random House Publishers.

Fogelson, Robert M. (1993). *The Fragmented Metropolis.* Berkeley: University of California.

Gabler, Neal. (1988). *An Empire of Their Own.* New York: Doubleday Publishers.

Gartner, L.P. & Vorspan, M. (1970). *History of the Jews of Los Angeles.* Philadelphia: Jewish Publication Society.

Gelfand, Mitchell Brian. (1978). *Chutzpah in El Dorado: Social Mobility of Jews in Los Angeles 1900-1920.* Pittsburgh: Carnegie-Mellon University.

Henstell, Bruce. (1980). *Los Angeles*: *An Illustrated History.* Los Angeles: Rosebud Books, Inc.

Herr, Jeffrey. (2002). *Landmark Los Angeles.* Los Angeles: Angel City Press.

Howe, I. & Libo, K. (1984). *We Lived There Too.* New York: St. Martin's/Marek.

Kahn, Ava F. (Ed.). (2002). *Jewish Life in the American West.* Los Angeles: Autry Museum of Western Heritage.

Kronzek, Lynn C. (1998). Los Angeles: *Place of Possibilities.* Carlsbad: Heritage Media Corp.

Kuehn, Gernot. (1978). *Views of Los Angeles.* Los Angeles: Portriga Publications.

Lavender, David. (1980). *Los Angeles Two Hundred.* (E. S. Blakley, Ed.). Tulsa: Continental Heritage Press, Inc.

Leadabrand, Russ. (1975). *Yesterday's California.* Miami: E.A. Seemann Publishing, Inc.

Longstreet, Stephen. (1977). *All Star Cast, An Anecdotal History of Los Angeles.* New York: Crowell

Malamut, Joseph L. (Ed.). (1926). *Southwest Jewry, Volume I.* Los Angeles: The Sunland Publishing Co., Inc.

Malamut, Joseph L. (Ed.). (1957). *Southwest Jewry, Volume I-III.* Los Angeles: Los Angeles Jewish Institutions and Their Leaders.

Massarik, F. (1953). "A Report on the Jewish Population of Los Angeles." *Jewish Federation Council of Greater Los Angeles.*

Massarik, F. (1972). "Jewish Population Trends in the Beverly-Fairfax Area: 1960/72/82." *Jewish Federation Council of Greater Los Angeles.*

Massarik, F. (1972). "Supplement to San Fernando Valley Demographic Study." *Jewish Federation Council of Greater Los Angeles.*

Meyer, Martin A. (1916). *Western Jewry.* San Francisco: Emanu-El Publishers

Moore, Deborah Dash. (1994). *To the Golden Cities: Pursuing the American Jewish Dream in Miami and L.A.* Cambridge: Harvard University Press.

Newmark, Harris. (1916). *Sixty Years in Southern California: 1853 – 1913.* New York: The Knickerbocker Press.

Phillips, Bruce. (2006). *Faultlines: The Seven Socio-Ecologies of Jewish Los Angeles.* Los Angeles : Hebrew Union College.

Pitt, Leonard. (1998). *The Decline of the Californios.* Berkeley: University of California Press Ltd.

Starr, Kevin. (1997). *The Dream Endures: California Enters the 1940s.* Oxford: Oxford University Press.

Stein, Robert. (2002). *Jewish Americans.* East Sussex: The Ivy Press Limited.

Stern, Norton B. (Ed.). Clar, R., Cohen, T., De Marco G., Kramer, W. M., Lipman, S., Meyer, R., Wilson, B.D. (1968 – Present). *Western States Jewish History, Volume I – XXXVI.* Los Angeles: Southern California Jewish Historical Society.

Wilson, Karen. (2003). *Citizens of Los Angeles: Jewish Familes and the Naissance of the Metropolis.* Hebrew Union College–Jewish Institute of Religion.

Zollo, Paul. (2002). *Hollywood Remembered.* New York: Cooper Square Press.